Security for Web Services and Service-Oriented Architectures

Elisa Bertino · Lorenzo D. Martino · Federica Paci ·
Anna C. Squicciarini

Security for
Web Services and
Service-Oriented
Architectures

 Springer

Elisa Bertino
Purdue University
CERIAS
Dept. Computer Sciences
West Lafayette IN 47906
USA
bertino@dico.unimi.it
bertino@cs.purdue.edu

Lorenzo D. Martino
Purdue University
Dept. Computer &
Information Technology (ICT)
Knoy Hall
West Lafayette IN 47907-1421
USA
lmartino@purdue.edu

Federica Paci
Università Milano-Bicocca
Dipto. Informatica e
Comunicazione
20135 Milano
Italy
paci@dico.unimi.it

Anna C. Squicciarini
Purdue University
CERIAS
Dept. Computer Sciences
West Lafayette IN 47906
USA
squiccia@cs.purdue.edu

ISBN 978-3-540-87741-7   e-ISBN 978-3-540-87742-4
DOI 10.1007/978-3-540-87742-4
Springer Heidelberg Dordrecht London New York

Library of Congress Control Number: 2009936010

ACM Computing Classification (1998): D.4.6, D.2.11, K.6.5, H.3.5

Cover design: KuenkelLopka GmbH

Printed on acid-free paper

Springer is part of Springer Science+Business Media (www.springer.com)

To my parents, Stella and Mario, for their constant encouragement. To my nephews Giordano, Jacopo, Luca, Marino and Susanna in the hope that they will follow a career in Computer Science.

E.B.

To my parents, Teresa and Antonio.

L.D.M.

To my beloved mother for her unconditional love and for her teachings that I will treasure for the rest of my life.

F.M.P.

To my parents, Grazia and Vito, for their constant support.

A.C.S.

Preface

Web services technologies are advancing fast and being extensively deployed in many different application environments. Web services based on the eXtensible Markup Language (XML), the Simple Object Access Protocol (SOAP), and related standards, and deployed in Service-Oriented Architectures (SOAs) are the key to Web-based interoperability for applications within and across organizations. Furthermore, they are making it possible to deploy applications that can be directly used by people, and thus making the Web a rich and powerful social interaction medium. The term Web 2.0 has been coined to embrace all those new collaborative applications and to indicate a new, "social" approach to generating and distributing Web content, characterized by open communication, decentralization of authority, and freedom to share and reuse.

For Web services technologies to hold their promise, it is crucial that security of services and their interactions with users be assured. Confidentiality, integrity, availability, and digital identity management are all required. People need to be assured that their interactions with services over the Web are kept confidential and the privacy of their personal information is preserved. People need to be sure that information they use for looking up and selecting services is correct and its integrity is assured. People want services to be available when needed. They also require interactions to be convenient and personalized, in addition to being private. Addressing these requirements, especially when dealing with open distributed applications, is a formidable challenge. Many of the features that make Web services an attractive approach for distributed applications result in difficult security issues. Conventional security approaches, namely those deployed for networks at the perimeter level, such as firewalls and intrusion detection systems, are not able to protect Web services and SOAs. Web services and SOAs are very dynamic in terms of their interactions and compositions and moreover they are seldom constrained to the physical boundaries of a single network. As SOA-based applications may consist of a large number of components from different security administration domains, each using different security techniques, security interoperability is a crucial issue. Data exchange applications built using Web services organized according to SOAs very often need to pass through intermediaries, and therefore trust and strong protection of transmitted contents is essential.

In the context of such trends, this book aims at providing a comprehensive guide to security for Web services and SOAs, with the twofold goal of being a reference for relevant standards and of providing an overview of recent research. As such the book covers in detail all standards that have been recently developed to address the problem of Web service security, including XML Encryption, XML Signature, WS-Security, and WS-SecureConversation. With respect to research, the book discusses in detail research efforts and proposals covering access control for simple and conversation-based Web services, advanced digital identity management techniques, and access control for Web-based workflows. The discussion on such research topics is complemented by an outline of open research issues. The book also covers relevant open research issues, such as the notion of security as a service as well as the privacy for Web services, and introduces all relevant background concerning Web services technologies and SOAs.

We trust that the contents of this book will be of interest to a diverse audience, including practitioners and application developers, researchers, and students.

Acknowledgments Part of the material presented in this book is based on research that we have carried out on topics such as security as a service, privacy-aware role-based access control (RBAC), trust negotiation systems, secure publishing techniques, and digital identity management systems. We would like to thank all our colleagues and students that have collaborated with us on those topics: Abhilasha Bhargav-Spantzel, Barbara Carminati, Alexei Czeskis, Elena Ferrari, Ninghui Li, Dan Lin, Jorge Lobo, Qun Ni, Prathima Rao, and Alberto Trombetta.

Special thanks are due to Prof. Bhavani Thuraisingham of the University of Texas at Dallas for the many discussions on security for Web services and the semantic Web and for her constant encouragement of our work.

Our research work has been made possible because of the generous support by several organizations, including IBM, the National Science Foundation, the Air Force Office for Sponsored Research, the European Union through the Sixth Framework Program, and the sponsors of CERIAS (Center for Education and Research in Information Assurance and Security). We would like to acknowledge not only the financial support, but also the research suggestions and insights of their researchers and program directors.

West Lafayette (IN),   *Elisa Bertino*
May 2008   *Lorenzo Dario Martino*
                                                               Federica Paci
                                                   Anna Cinzia Squicciarini

Contents

1

Introduction

Recent advances of Web service technology will have far-reaching effects on Internet and enterprise networks. Web services based on the eXtensible Markup Language (XML), Simple Object Access Protocol (SOAP), and related open standards, and deployed in Service Oriented Architectures (SOAs), allow data and applications to interact through dynamic and ad hoc connections. Web services technology can be implemented in a wide variety of architectures, can coexist with other technologies and software design approaches, and can be adopted in an evolutionary manner without requiring major transformations to legacy applications and databases. Despite the heterogeneity of the underlying platforms, Web services enhance interoperability and are thus able to support business applications composed by chains of Web services. Interoperability is a key promise of Web service technology and therefore notions such as Web service composition and systems such as those for workflow management are being investigated and developed. Such technology is also facilitating a second generation of Web-based communities and hosted services, such as social networking sites and wikis, which support collaboration and sharing between users. The term Web 2.0 has been coined to embrace all those new new collaborative applications and also to indicate a new "social" approach to generating and distributing Web content, characterized by open communication, decentralization of authority, and freedom to share and reuse. Web service technology is thus emerging as the technology making the Web the "place" where the majority of human and societal interactions are taking place.

1.1 Security for Web Services and Security Goals

Web services, stand-alone or composed, must provide strong security guarantees. Security is today a relevant requirement for any distributed application, and in particular for those enabled by the Web, such as e-health, e-commerce, e-learning, and social networks. Providing security guarantees in

E. Bertino et al., *Security for Web Services and Service-Oriented Architectures*,
DOI 10.1007/978-3-540-87742-4_1, © Springer-Verlag Berlin Heidelberg 2010

open dynamic environments characterized by heterogeneous platforms is however a major challenge. The very features that make Web services and SOA attractive paradigms, such as greater and ubiquitous accessibility to data and other resources, dynamic application configuration and reconfiguration through workflows, and relative autonomy, conflict with conventional security models and mechanisms. Web services and SOA security encompass several requirements that can be described along the well-known security dimensions, that is:

- *Integrity*, whereby a message[1] must remain unaltered during transmission across a possibly large number of intermediary services of different nature, such as network devices and software components.
- *Confidentiality*, whereby the contents of a message cannot be viewed while in transit, except by authorized services that need to see the message contents in order to perform routing.
- *Availability*, whereby a message is promptly delivered to the intended recipient, thus ensuring that legitimate users receive the services they are entitled to.

Moreover, each Web service must protect its own resources against unauthorized access. Addressing such requirement in turn requires suitable means for *identification*, whereby the recipient of a message identifies the sender; *authentication*, whereby the recipient of a message verifies the claimed identity of the sender; and *authorization*, whereby the recipient of the message applies access control policies to determine whether the sender has the right to use the required Web services and the protected resources.

In a Web service environment it is, however, not enough to protect the service providers; it is also important to protect the parties requiring services. Because a key component of the Web service architectures is represented by the discovery of services, it is crucial to ensure that all information used by parties for this purpose be authentic and correct. Also we need approaches by which a service provider can prove its identity to the party requiring the service in order for the latter to avoid attacks, such as phishing attacks.

The broad goal of securing Web services can thus be decomposed into three subsidiary goals:

- Providing mechanisms and tools for securing the integrity and confidentiality of messages.
- Ensuring that the service acts only on the requests that comply with the policies associated with the service.
- Ensuring that all information required by a party in order to discover and use services is correct and authentic.

Security must first of all be provided at network level because the interactions between clients and Web services as well as among Web services are carried

---

[1] Here we use the term 'message' with the broader meaning of information transmitted across different entities in a system, logically and/or physically distributed.

out by SOAP message exchanges. Network-level security addresses message integrity and confidentiality as well as the guarantee of message delivery, that is, reliability. However, network-level security is not enough. Web services themselves must be protected against unauthorized access as well as against denial of service attacks by which a malicious party makes a Web service unavailable to the authorized parties. Access control in turn requires verifying identities and identity properties of parties involved in the interaction, which thus requires the adoption of modern digital identity management technologies. Finally, techniques such as those for authentication of service directories and for trust negotiation are used to protect the integrity and confidentiality of all information required to discover and use the services.

1.2 Privacy

Privacy requirements are of high relevance today because of several factors. In particular, privacy legislation, such as, in the US, the early Federal Act of 1974 [102] and the more recent Health Insurance Portability and Accountability Act of 1996 (HIPAA) [127] and the Childrens Online Privacy Protection Act (COPPA) [80], require organizations to put in place adequate privacy-preserving techniques for the management of data concerning individuals. Compliance with such legal regulations has today become a primary motivation for investment by companies in information security technology. Consumers are also increasingly worried about privacy breaches in that these may lead to identity thefts, under which a malicious party misuses the personal data of other individuals.

It is important to note that, even though the term privacy is often used as a synonym for confidentiality, the two are quite different. Techniques for information confidentiality may be (and often are) used to implement privacy; however, assuring privacy requires additional techniques, such as mechanisms for obtaining and recording the consents of users and for enforcing obligations [203]. Supporting privacy preferences of individuals to whom the data refer to is a key issue in privacy. Because different individuals may have different requirements with respect to privacy, managing privacy preferences of a large number of users can be quite a challenge. Obligations refer to actions that must be executed before or after a data access is performed; relevant examples of obligations include requiring parental consent when collecting personally identifiable information about minors or periodically notifying customers about the intended use of their personal data. Also, confidentiality can be achieved by withholding information from access, whereas privacy may have to be enforced even after the information has been disclosed. For example, privacy may require that the information be removed from the system after a specified time interval. Also, as we mentioned, privacy is very often regulated by laws. Recent work has shown that to support several privacy regulations one may need simple condition languages governing access to the information, such as "parental consent = YES or NO" [201, 202]. Confidentiality, however, especially for commercial purposes, is regulated by policies specified by the organization owning the data. As such there could a much larger variety of policies and one may need very complex policy languages, for example, policy languages supporting spatial, temporal, and contextual conditions.

Because Web services are expected to manipulate a lot of information related to individuals and are also expected to support frequent interactions with end users, privacy is a relevant requirement for Web service technology. To date, significant research has been carried out on privacy techniques, ranging from anonymization techniques [58, 59] to fine-grained access control mechanisms specific for databases recording personally identifiable information [271], to secure multi-party computation techniques [113]. However, understanding how to apply or modify such techniques for use in Web services and SOA is an open research issue. An important challenge is represented by compliance in the presence of potentially dynamic and fragmented application environments implemented by Web services and SOA.

1.3 Goals and Scope of the Book and its Intended Audience

The aim of the book is to provide a comprehensive view of security for Web services and SOA; such a view must encompass efforts and initiatives in the area of security standards for Web services as well as recent research proposals. Standards are crucial when discussing Web service security in that a large number of standards, addressing various security aspects, have been developed and to date no comprehensive critical analysis of such standards exists. It is also important to cover research proposals in that some interesting approaches have been recently proposed addressing issues such as access control for Web services and innovative digital identity management techniques.

The book intends to serve as a reference text to a broad and diversified audience:

- Practitioners can find in the book a comprehensive, critical reference to Web service standards. The exposition includes illustrative examples as well as analysis of their critical issues.
- Researchers can find in the book a report on the latest research developments in Web service security. Chapters covering such developments include discussions on innovative research directions.
- Students at both undergraduate and graduate levels can use the book as a textbook on advanced topics in computer and system security, namely security for Web services, digital identity management, and trust negotiation techniques and systems.

The book will not cover fundamentals of computer and system security in that several textbooks already exist covering such material. The bibliographic notes at the end of this chapter provide relevant references to such textbooks. The book includes, however, an appendix compiling basic notions about access control models; this important topic is often not covered in security textbooks and yet today plays a crucial role in many innovative security solutions.

1.4 An Overview of the Book's Content

Chapter 2, Service-Oriented Architecture and Web Service Technologies: Principles, Architectures, and Standards, introduces the main concepts of SOA and the key foundations of Web services technology that are needed for the presentation in the subsequent chapters. It discusses the various notions of SOA as well as of Web services and contrasts them with existing notions such as those of distributed computing, client-service architectures, and event-oriented architectures. It also discusses the relevant architectural elements involved in the discover-find-use usage pattern of Web services, such as UDDI registries, with reference to industrial implementations such as those of Microsoft .NET (WSE Web services extension) and Java platforms. The last part of the chapter provides an overview of the most relevant standards, such as XML, SOAP, and WSDL; for some of these standards the overview will be very short since they are well known and documented (e.g., XML and SOAP).

Chapter 3, Security Threats and Countermeasures, introduces the concept of security incident life cycle and the related concepts of asset, threat, risk, vulnerability, and attack. All together, these concepts provide a comprehensive framework with respect to which the threat modeling process is performed. A threat model typically describes the capabilities an attacker is assumed to have to be able to carry an attack against a resource. Such a threat model is of paramount importance in order to correctly identify the security mechanisms needed to mitigate threats. The chapter overviews proposed threat models and the related attack classification, along with the main security mechanisms used as attack countermeasures.

Chapter 4, Standards for Web Service Security, covers mechanisms and tools that address the well-known security requirements of integrity, confidentiality, and privacy, applied both to the operations provided by Web services and to data and messages exchanged between Web services over the network. Different security mechanisms and tools have been developed and deployed over time to this end. The overall goal of a Web services security standard is to make different security infrastructures interoperable and to reduce the cost of security management. To achieve this goal, Web services security standards aim at providing a common framework, and common protocols, for the exchange of security information between Web services that, once implemented and deployed:

- can accommodate existing heterogeneous mechanisms, that is, different encryption algorithms, different access control mechanisms, and so forth;

- can be extended to address new requirements and/or exploit new available security technologies.

This chapter surveys some existing and proposed standards for Web services security. The chapter first introduces the different notions of standards that range from a public specification issued by a set of companies to a de jure standard issued by a recognized standardization body. This classification gives indications about the standardization process complexity and also about the maturity, the stability, and the level of endorsement of a standard. Then a framework for the security standards is presented. Such a framework is used to provide a conceptual classification of Web services security standards depending on the various aspects of Web services security they address, such as XML security, SOAP message security, access control, policy frameworks, and security and trust management. The chapter surveys the following standards, describing their specific purpose, their main features, and their current status:

- XML Encryption and XML Signature;
- WS-Security, WS-SecureConversation, and WS-ReliableMessaging;
- Security Assertion Markup Language (SAML);
- eXtensible Access Control Markup Language (XACML) and XACML Profile for Web-Services;
- WS-Policy, WS-PolicyAssertion, WS-Policy Attachment, and WS-Security Policy;
- XML Key Management Standard (XKMS) and WS-Trust;
- Extensible rights Markup Language (XrML).

For each standard the related section also highlights the specific security considerations and caveats that apply to it. The chapter then concludes with considerations about organizational issues that influence, or are related to, the adoption of standards. They include, among others, software manufacturers' support of standards as well as the costs and potential risks incurred by the users, such as the learning curve of standards and the risk of being locked into proprietary implementation of standards not fully interoperable with other manufactures' implementations.

Chapter 5, Digital Identity Management and Trust Negotiation, addresses how to securely manage digital identities, that is, the digital representation of the information known about individuals and organizations, and how to use such information when conducting interactions over the Web. The secure management of this information is crucial for interactions within any distributed system and thus is crucial for SOA. This chapter covers all relevant notions related to identity management and then discusses how this information can be used by a party when negotiating with a service provider for using a service. The chapter first provides an overview of the main concepts related to digital identity management with a focus on recent federated approaches, namely Shibboleth system, Liberty-Alliance initiative, WS-Federation, and Microsoft Infocard. The chapter then discusses issues related to identity management in the context of grid computing systems in that these systems represent a significant application context for SOA and digital identity management. The chapter then introduces the trust negotiation paradigm, its main concepts, and its protocols, and also discusses its possible applications in the context of federated identity management systems. Finally, to show the advantages of the digital identity management and trust negotiation approaches, the chapter discusses a federated attribute management and trust negotiation solution, which provides a truly distributed approach to the management of user identities and user attributes with negotiation capabilities.

Chapter 6, Access Control for Web Services, covers an important topic that has not been much investigated for Web services, even though it has been widely investigated in the context of a large variety of systems, such as database systems and operating systems. The chapter focuses on some recent research proposals, by first categorizing them according to access control granularity. Then, two approaches are described in detail. The first approach supports a negotiation-based attribute-based access control to Web services with fine access granularity. The second approach is tailored to access control for conversation-based Web services and composite services. In this approach, a Web service is not considered as a set of independent operations and therefore access control must take such dependencies into account. During a Web service's invocation, a client interacts with the service, performing a sequence of operations in a particular order called conversation.

Chapter 7, Secure Publishing Techniques, focuses on security issues for third-party publishing techniques and their application to the integrity of UDDI registries. These techniques are today receiving growing attention, because of their scalability and to their ability to manage a large number of subjects and data objects. The chapter first describes the most well-known technique developed to assure integrity of data structures, namely the Merkle Hash Tree. Then it discusses a method, based on Merkle Hash Trees, which does not require the party managing the UDDI to be trusted. Besides giving all the details of the proposed solution, the chapter discusses its benefit with respect to standard digital signature techniques.

Chapter 8, Security for Workflow and Business Processing, focuses on an important component that makes it possible to build and manage complex applications. In a Web-based environment, business processes or workflows can be built by combining Web services through the use of a process specification language. Such languages basically allow one to specify which tasks have to be executed and the order in which those tasks should be executed. One such language is WS-BPEL, which provides a syntax for specifying business processes based on Web services. A problem of particular relevance for security is the development of access control techniques supporting the specification and enforcement of authorizations stating which users can execute which tasks within a workflow, while also enforcing constraints such as separation of duty on the execution of those tasks. This chapter first introduces the main approaches to access control for workflow systems, followed by a brief introduction to WS-BPEL. The chapter then presents an authorization model for WS-BPEL that supports the specification of both authorization information, necessary to state if a role or a user is allowed to execute the activities composing the processes, and authorization constraints, placing restrictions on roles and on users who can perform the activities in the business process.

Chapter 9, Emerging Research Trends, discusses other security aspects and trends that have not been covered in previous chapters. The topics covered here include the notion of "security as a service" as well semantic Web security and privacy issues for Web services. Then it discusses open research directions.

Bibliographic Notes

Computer security is an extensively investigated topic which is also widely covered in university courses both at undergraduate and graduate levels. Several books covering security are thus available, some of which are general textbooks suitable for a broad and comprehensive introduction to computer security [47, 225, 115], whereas others focus on specialized topics, such as cryptographic foundations [219], network security [242, 107], security testing [292], and database and applications security [259]. A useful reference is represented by the Internet Security Dictionary, which provides comprehensive coverage of Internet security terms [220]. Several books address Web services security and related standards from the software architects' and developers' points of view. Web service security in the context of .NET is covered in [133]; security for Web services in the Java (J2EE) environment is covered in [155] and [244]. The latter also covers identity management standards and technologies and presents several design best practices. A detailed presentation of most of the standards related to Web services security is contained in [208].

2

Web Service Technologies, Principles, Architectures, and Standards

The development and the adoption of Web services can, to a large extent, traced back to the same driving factors that have led to the development of the Service-oriented approach and Service- Oriented Architecture (SOA). From an ICT point of view, the main vision has been to exploit methods, tools and techniques enabling businesses to build complex and flexible business processes. In order to achieve this vision, ICT supported business processes should be able to adapt to the changing needs of business in a setting characterized by the globalization of the markets, mergers and acquisitions, cross-organization and even cross-boundary operations, and the extension of the business boundaries due to the pervasiveness of the Internet. At the same time, ICT should reduce implementation and ownership costs, achieve better IT utilization and return on investment, by maximizing the reuse of existing application systems and their integration. Integration of ICT systems at a large scale raises several issues. When different business organizations merge or need to interoperate, there is not a common data, business or process model. Participating business organizations still retain at least a relative degree of autonomy. Moreover, different business ICT systems are implemented using a multitude of technologies and platforms. Finally, the business should be properly decoupled from the ICT layers, so as the changes and the evolution of the ICT layers do not hamper the business.

SOA and Web services are not a radically new architecture or technology. They can be considered, to a large extent, the point of convergence of the evolution of several ICT technologies, such as communication and distributed systems technologies, integration technologies for enterprise applications, to mention just two of them, intertwined with an increasing adoption of standards.

E. Bertino et al., *Security for Web Services and Service-Oriented Architectures*,
DOI 10.1007/978-3-540-87742-4_2, © Springer-Verlag Berlin Heidelberg 2010

2.1 SOA and Web Services Principles

The term SOA is used in an increasing number of contexts and technology implementations with different and sometimes conflicting understanding of meanings. Web service definitions too may vary, ranging from from very generic and all-inclusive ones to very specific and restrictive ones. We assume here the definition of Web service given by the World Wide Web consortium (W3C)[24]:

> "A Web service is a software system identified by a URI [RFC 2396], whose public interfaces and bindings are defined and described using XML. Its definition can be discovered by other software systems. These systems may then interact with the Web service in a manner prescribed by its definition, using XML based messages conveyed by Internet protocols"

The service-oriented approach, SOA architectures, and Web services are centered on the central role of the service concept, both at the business level and at the technological level, and share the same inspiring principles. At the business level a service can be viewed as a repeatable business task, such as opening a new account or checking a customer credit in retail banking, or reserving a visit in a health care facility. At the technical level, the service concept in SOA refers to a software artifact, and it conveys a set of different meanings. First of all, a service offers functionality to the real world, and it encapsulates reusable business functions. Second, a service has a owner, which can be a person or an organization, which has the responsibility for the service. Third, a service is realized by an agent, also called service provider and used by other agents, also called service requesters or clients. Fourth, clients interact with a service through messages and according to the specifications of the service and the rules defined by the service provider. Fifth, the specification of the service and the rules for its use constitute the contract. To invoke a service, clients do not need any other information about the internal structure of the service, such implementation language or database.

The different facets of the service concept are reflected on a set of commonly agreed principles about SOA, namely:

- A service is a logical representation of a repeatable real-world business activity and it has a specific outcome.
- A service enables to access its capabilities using a prescribed interface.
- The business context and the services themselves have a description.
- A service is a kind of "black box" to consumers of the service, in that its implementation is hidden from the service consumer.
- The implementation of a service is environment-specific, and it may depend on the business context (i.e. business goal, rules, policies).
- In order for consumers, including other services, to interact with services, the description of each service, including the terms of information exchange

has to be made publicly accessible. The service interface description can be seen as a formal contract between the service and its clients.

- Eventual consumers of a service may be unknown to the service provider.
- A service may be composed of other services.
- A service is autonomous, in that it has control over the business logic that implement. Hence, a service is managed independently of other services, within the ownership boundary of the service provider's organization.
- Services are loosely coupled. Loose coupling refers to an approach where interfaces can be developed with minimal mutual assumptions between the sending and the receiving parties, thus reducing the risk that a change in an application/module will force a change in another application/module.

SOA and Web services share the principles mentioned above. While SOA is purposely technology neutral, the Web service definition highlights the central role of specific Web technologies, namely: the Uniform Resource Identifier, and the Internet protocols, which provide, respectively, uniform identification and communication mechanisms; and XML, which is used to define and describe the application interface as well as to encode the messages exchanged between the Web service and its clients.

Of the principles described above, service autonomy, loose coupling, and the need for a formal contract can be considered the core ones.

At the business level, each organization is autonomous in exerting an independent control over its own services, that is, defining, configuring, and operating them. The autonomy of the business requires some degree of a corresponding autonomy in the Web services implementing the business services. This means that i) a Web service should own its data; ii) different Web services should not share their internal state information nor have a common data store; iii) the communications between the services should be explicit and according to their published contract (interface). Service autonomy at the business level requires loose coupling at the technical level. This way the dependencies between consumers and the service are limited to consumers' conformance to the service contract.

The separation between the service interface and its implementation allows services to interact without needing a common shared execution environment. Hence SOA and Web services differ from previous approaches to distributed applications which explicitly assumed a common type space, execution model, and procedure/object reference model. Moreover, the separation of the service interface from its implementation leads to more flexible binding of services. Traditional procedural, component, and object models bind components together through references (pointers) or names. In procedural or object-oriented systems, a caller typically finds a server based on the types it exports or a shared namespace. SOA and Web services support more dynamic discovery of service instances that provide the interface, semantics and service assurances that the requestor expects.

The implementation details being private to a service, the message-oriented interface that every service exposes insulates service clients from the implementation choices made by a particular service developer. This opacity is critical to service autonomy, since it allows service providers to freely choose programming models and languages, host environments, and to substitute one service implementation for another.

All aspects of a service that allow a potential service consumer to understand and evaluate its capabilities should be described. The service capabilities may consist of the service functions and technical requirements, related constraints and policies, and mechanisms for access and response. All these aspects contribute to the definition of the services' formal contract, which is shared between the users and the service itself. All the descriptions above need to be in a form (or be transformable into a form) in which their syntax and semantics are widely accessible and understandable.

Accordingly, SOA and Web services are based on the publish-discovery-bind paradigm, where:

- Service providers publish the availability of their services.
- Service brokers register and categorize published services and provide search services.
- Service requesters use broker services to find a needed service and then employ that service.

Service descriptions in a standard machine-readable format (such as XML) are associated with each service. These service descriptions are key to all three roles in that they provide the information needed to categorize, choose, and invoke an e-business service. It has to be emphasized that the focus of SOA is different from that of service-based architectures which focus instead on service-to-service message protocols, or on the details of how the various servers communicate rather than on the description of what they say to each other. Within a single corporate system, where the entire system is under the control of one group of stakeholders, a service-based approach can be used to break and re-organize rigid legacy systems into collaborating services that provide improvements in flexibility and maintainability. However, service-based techniques alone do not scale beyond the span of control of the single corporate environment that defines and manages the semantic definitions of the services. The service-oriented view adds service's functionality descriptions to the service-based approach. In a service-oriented view, the interoperability problem can be partitioned into two subproblems, namely, the definition of standard mechanisms for describing service interfaces and the identification of commonly agreed, standard protocol(s) that can be used to invoke a particular interface. Service-oriented interfaces provides for consistent resource access across multiple heterogeneous platforms with local or remote location transparency, and enables mapping of multiple logical resource instances onto the same physical resource.

2.2 Web Services Architecture

To facilitate the creation and assembly of interoperable Web services, the Web Services Architecture Working Group at W3C devised the need of defining a standard reference architecture for Web services [48]. Such architecture is a conceptual one, and it aims at identifying the minimal common character-istics of the global Web services network required to ensure interoperability between Web services. In other words, it defines a model, and does not describe or prescribe the specific functions that should support the model or how these functions could be grouped in specific software modules. The W3C reference architecture revolves around four models. The Message Oriented model fo-cuses on the structure of messages, the relationship between message senders and receivers, and how messages are transmitted. The Service Oriented Model (SOM) is based on the concepts of services being realized by an agent and used by another one, and services being mediated by means of the messages exchanged between requester and provider agents. The Resource model intro-duces the Web concept of a resource, that is, the concept of uniform resource identification (URI), and the separation of resource identification from re-source representation. The Policy Model focuses mainly on constraints on the behavior of agents and services, but it extends to encompass resources such as XML documents describing the services.

2.3 Web Services Technologies and Standards

As shown in Figure 2.1, the technological foundations of Web services largely rely upon technologies implementing core standards for the World Wide Web. The World Wide Web's technological foundations are basically those allowing for the identification of resources (Universal Resource Identifier, URI, [29, 32]) , the representation of their state, and the standard protocols that support the interaction between agents and resources in the Web space, such as Hypertext Transfer Protocol (HTTP). XML-based standards and technologies include the eXtensible Markup Language itself [54], XML Schema [258], SOAP [120], Web Services Description Language (WSDL) [67], and Universal Description, Discovery, and Integration (UDDI)[72].

As pointed out by Berners-Lee [29], the URI, a compact string of charac-ters used to identify or name a resource, is the most fundamental specification of Web architecture. The URI specification transforms the Web into a uniform space, making the properties of naming and addressing schemes independent

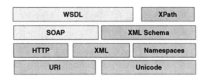

Fig. 2.1. Web services technological foundation

from the language using them.

Hypertext Transfer Protocol (HTTP) is a general, stateless communication protocol for the transfer of information on the World Wide Web. One of the most relevant feature of HTTP is its extensibility. An extension mechanism explicitly and unambiguously identifies the capabilities of implementations. Extensibility is a key requirement to provide interoperability, since interoperability in turn requires backward compatibility with software implementations of previous versions of the protocol.

XML [54], a W3C endorsed standard for document markup, is the "lingua franca" for the Web. XML can be traced back to SGML, the Standard Generalized Markup Language [112, 114]. XML is a *metamarkup language* designed for the creation of languages. Simply stated, XML does not constrain its users to a fixed set of tags and elements; rather it is inherently extensible, allowing developers to define new languages able to convey the semantics needed by specific applications (called also XML applications) as they need them. At the same time, the XML specification defines a strict grammar for XML documents, which allows one to build XML parsers that can read any XML document. Through the namespace mechanism, it is possible to extend XML by mixing multiple vocabularies in a same document, yet managing the names "meaning" in an unambiguous way [31], without incurring problems of name collision and detection. The XML namespaces specification [53] defines the constructs which allow a single XML document to contain XML elements and attributes (markup vocabulary) defined and used by multiple software modules.

The rules regarding the structure of an XML document, that is, the elements and attributes that can be part of an XML document and where they can appear, can be documented in a *schema* . XML document instances can be validated against the schema. A schema can be roughly equated with a type definition in a programming language, and the XML document adhering to the schema with an instance of a type. Several different schema languages with different levels of expressivity have been proposed: RELAX [223, 68], TREX [69], TREX, and SOX [86]. The most broadly supported schema language for XML is the Document Type Definition (DTD) which is also the only one defined by XML specification. Due to the syntax limitation of DTD, W3C defined the W3C XML Schema Language [258], and published as a W3C recommendation in May 2001. It is worth noting that,due to the declarative nature of schema languages, there are always some constraints that cannot be expressed. This requires adding code to the program which reads and interprets the XML document.

2.3.1 SOAP

Web services interactions, that is the requests sent by requesters to Web services and the responses sent by the Web service, are based on the Simple Object Access Protocol (SOAP) [120, 121, 187]. SOAP defines a standardized XML-based framework for exchanging structured and typed information between services. The specification (submitted to W3C in 2000) was designed to unify proprietary Remote procedure Call (RPC) communication, basically by serializing into XML the parameter data transmitted between components, transporting, and finally deserializing them back at the destination component. SOAP is fundamentally a stateless, one-way message exchange paradigm that enables applications to create more complex interaction patterns (e.g., request-response, request-multiple responses, etc.) by combining one-way exchanges with features provided by an underlying protocol and/or application-specific information. At its core, a SOAP message has a very simple structure: an XML element with two children elements, one containing the header and the other the body. The header contents and body elements are also represented in XML. The header is an optional element that allows the sender to transmit "control" information. Headers may be inspected, inserted, deleted, or forwarded by SOAP nodes encountered along a SOAP message path. SOAP also provides a full description of the rules that a SOAP node receiving a SOAP message must follow. Such rules are called SOAP Processing Model . The SOAP Processing Model defines how a SOAP node must process a *single* SOAP message. Moreover, the SOAP Processing Model assumes that: a SOAP message originates at an initial SOAP sender node and is sent to an ultimate SOAP receiver via zero or more SOAP intermediaries; a SOAP node does not maintain any state information; a SOAP node does not maintain any correlation between SOAP messages. The behavior of a SOAP node is determined in accordance with the *env:mustUnderstand* attribute of the SOAP header elements. If the attribute, env:mustUnderstand, has a value "true", the SOAP node must process the SOAP header block according to the specification of that block, or else generate a SOAP fault. Understanding a SOAP header means that the node must be prepared to do whatever is described in the specification of that block. The definition of a SOAP message structure is independent of the underlying transport protocol that will be used to transmit the SOAP message. SOAP messages may be exchanged using a variety of protocols, including other application layer protocols such as HTTP and Simple Mail Transfer Protocol (SMTP). The SOAP *binding* construct specifies how a SOAP message can be passed from one SOAP node to another using an underlying protocol. In practice, a SOAP binding specifies how to serialize the

SOAP envelope so that it can be reconstructed by the SOAP receiver without loss of information. The only binding formally defined and in active use today is HTTP. Moreover, the so-called SOAP binding *feature* allows one to specify other features which might be needed by the application, such as the ability to correlate a request with a response, or the need to use an encrypted transmission, or the need to use a reliable channel. Some features can be provided natively by the underlying protocol, such as a request-response correlation in HTTP, or can be represented and implemented by one or more SOAP header blocks. When using SOAP, a SOAP processor (or SOAP engine) is needed on the requester side and on the Web service side to construct and decode SOAP messages. SOAP provides for Remote Procedure Call (RPC) style interactions, similar to remote function calls, and document-style communication, with message contents based exclusively on XML Schema definitions. Invocation results may be optionally returned in the response message, or a Fault may be raised, which is roughly equivalent to exceptions in traditional programming languages. It is worth noting that the use of SOAP is not mandated or implied by the W3C Web service definition and that SOAP protocol management certainly adds complexity . A Web service could be implemented by a program, for example a Java servlet, that listens for XML-encoded messages sent over HTTP, without using SOAP. Such a program could then route those messages to a message processor component and then return the results to the requestor. However, using SOAP to invoke a Web service API provides for passing complex types across the network, better error handling, and for automating much of the marshalling and unmarshalling of method parameters and return values. As for security aspects, the SOAP protocol only defines the communication framework, and it does not address any provision for securing the message exchanges. SOAP messages must thus either be sent over secure channels, or secured by using the protection mechanisms described in chapter 4.

2.3.2 Web Services Description Language (WSDL)

The Web Services Description Language Version 2.0 [67] allows one to describe the Web service interface, starting with the messages that are exchanged between the requester and provider agents. The messages are described abstractly and then bound to a concrete network protocol and message format. Web service definitions can be mapped to any implementation language, platform, object model, or messaging system. As shown in Figure 2.2, WSDL separates the description of the abstract functionality offered by a service, called abstract interface, from its implementation details, namely, how the client and the Web service exchange messages; how the service is implemented (Java, .NET); and where the service is offered.

Basically, an interface groups together a set of abstract operations. In turn, each operation is defined as a sequence of input and output messages. A so-called message exchange pattern can be associated to one or more messages. A

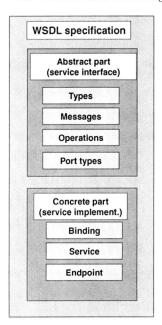

Fig. 2.2. WSDL abstract and concrete parts

message exchange pattern identifies the sequence and cardinality of messages sent and/or received by the service, as well as who they are logically sent to and/or received from. At the abstract level, WSDL defines a service as a collection of network endpoints or ports . The abstract definition of endpoints and messages is separated from their concrete network deployments or data format bindings. Such a separation allows one to reuse the abstract definitions of messages and port types that represent collections of operations. The concrete protocol and data format specifications for a particular port type constitute a binding. A port is defined by associating a network address with a binding. A collection of ports defines a service.

The concrete part of WSDL provides for the implementation details, namely:

- A binding (see Figure 2.3) specifies transport and wire format details for one or more interfaces.
- An endpoint associates a network address with a binding.
- A service groups together endpoints that implement a common interface. The service element assigns a name to the service, associates it with the abstract interface and describes where to access the service.

```
<binding name="reservationSOAPBinding"
        interface="tns:reservationInterface"
        type="http://www.w3.org/ns/wsdl/soap"
        wsoap:protocol="http://www.w3.org/2003/05/soap/bindings/HTTP/">
    <operation ref="tns:opCheckAvailability"
        wsoap:mep="http://www.w3.org/2003/05/soap/mep/soap-response"/>
</binding>

<service name="reservationService"
        interface="tns:reservationInterface">
        <endpoint name="reservationEndpoint"
        binding="tns:reservationSOAPBinding"
        address ="http://greath.example.com/2004/reservation"/>
</service>
```

Fig. 2.3. An example of WSDL binding

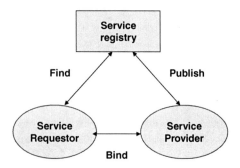

Fig. 2.4. Registries in the discover-find-use pattern

2.3.3 Service Discovery: Universal Description, Discovery and Integration (UDDI)

Service discovery (see Figure 2.4) is the process by which service users can find service providers and the description of the Web services they provide.

The discovery process encompasses two description levels, supporting two related but distinct processes:

- The first is the description of the business itself. This description is useful to prospective business client in order to limit the scope of their search to specific industries and/or market sectors.
- The second encompasses the technical description (i.e., the WSDL description) of the Web services) provided by the business previously identified.

UDDI [139, 72] was mainly conceived to provide standardized descriptions of a business and of the Web services it provides for recording them in some catalog (registry) . Such a catalog can be queried by client to easily find the services they need. UDDI defines a set of standard services supporting the description and discovery of (1) businesses, organizations, and other Web services providers; (2) the Web services they make available; and (3) the technical interfaces which are used to access those services. UDDI is based on a common set of industry standards, including HTTP, XML, XML Schema, and SOAP. UDDI, at its most basics, is a registry containing data and metadata about Web services, including services' location and information on how to invoke registered Web services. A UDDI registry allows one to classify and catalog such information so that Web services can be discovered (and consumed).

An UDDI registry supports the discovery-find-use pattern where (see Figure 2.5:

1. Businesses populate the registry with the descriptions of the services they support;
2. Standard bodies and software companies populate the registry with descriptions of different types of services
3. Customers, business applications, and search engines can query the registry to discover services at other companies. The information obtained by a registry can be used by a business to facilitate the interaction with a service and/or to dynamically compose a complex service out of a number of simpler services.

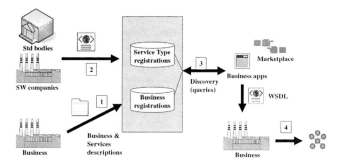

Fig. 2.5. Registries in the discover-find-use pattern

UDDI Registry data are organized in White pages, Yellow pages, Green pages, and Service Type registrations. White pages, like a phone book, contain the name of the business, a textual description of the business, the contact information (names, fax numbers, phone numbers, web sites URLs), and a list of business identifiers in accordance with known identification schema such as

Data Universal Numbering System (DUNS) [95, 281] and Thomas [72, Section 5.2.5].

The Yellow pages contain a set of business categories organized along three standard taxonomies , namely Industry, according to the North American Industry Classification System (NAICS) [205] industry codes; Product/Services, according to the Universal Standard Product and Service Classification (UN/SPSC) by ECMA [262]; and Geographic Location, according to ISO 3166 [141] for country and region codes. Taxonomies are implemented as name-value pairs so that a taxonomy identifier can be "attached" or referenced by the business White Pages.

Through the Green pages, a business provides the data needed to conduct electronic transactions with it, that is, the description of its business processes, its services, and how to bind them. The description is provided at an abstract level, which is independent of the programming language, platform, and implementation.

A Service Type Registration contains the information needed by a programmer in order to use the service. It also contains the service publisher identifier and the identifier of the Service Type Registration itself, which is used by the Web sites that implement the service as a signature.

Figure 2.6 shows the entities comprising the UDDI model and their relationships. Business and service providers (called publishers in UDDI) are represented by the top-level businessEntity entity. The businessEntity entity conveys descriptive information about a Business that provides Web services, such as the business name, the contact information , and about the services it offers. Each businessEntity entity can contain one or more businessService entities. Each businessService entity describes a family of Web services provided by the business. Such an entity provides no technical information about the service; it only contains descriptive information such as service names and classification information that are useful to describe the purpose of each Web service that it groups. A bindingTemplate entity provides the technical information needed by applications to bind and interact with the Web service being described, namely the access point of the Web service or a reference to it. The Technical Models (tModels) entity references the technical description of the Web service, such as its WSDL description and possibly other documents that describe the interface and the behavior of the Web service. tModels are used in UDDI to represent metadata about transport and protocol definitions such as HTTP and SMTP, namespaces, and categorization information. Moreover, they provide an extensibility mechanism: if a Business needs some concept which does not already exists in UDDI, it can introduce it by creating a tModel containing the URL of the relevant document.

Finally, the publisherAssertion entity is used to specify relationships among multiple businesses described by different businessEntity entities. For example, a corporate enterprise may have multiple related subsidiaries and each of them may have registered as a businessEntity in the UDDI. UDDI de-

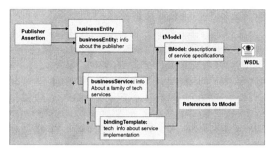

Fig. 2.6. UDDI model entities

fines standard register interfaces that allow a business provider: i) to describe the Business entity main characteristics, according to the UDDI model (i.e., the information contained in the White Pages); and ii) to abstractly describe the behavior of the Web service that implements the service. Such a description is expressed trough the tModel entity provided by UDDI. It is worth noting that the tModel itself does not contain the Web service description, but it refers to an XML document containing it.

UDDI functionalities are made available to programs through sets of predefined APIs: the Publisher API set, the Inquiry API set, the Port Type API (in UDDI V3.0), and the Bindings API (in UDDI V3.0).

The Publisher APIs allow a publisher:

- to register a new (or to update existing) businessEntity, businessService, tModel, and bindingTemplate.
- to delete existing businessEntity, businessService, tModel, and bindingTemplate.
- to obtain a list of business and tModels managed by a given publisher.
- to create, add, delete, and query publishers' assertions.

The Inquiry API set allows one to locate and obtain details on entries in a UDDI registry. The Inquiry API set provides three forms of queries, which allow a user to browse, drill down, and use the information found in the registry for the specific Web service being invoked.

2.3.4 Considerations

UDDI registries and services can be used in various scenarios. UDDI services, deployed in a software manufacturing environment, aid the software design process by storing, categorizing and making searchable the information related to already developed Web services and their access points. UDDI services can be used at run-time by applications needing to discover new and alternate sources of information based on selected criteria.

2.4 Web Services Infrastructure

Middleware plays a central role in Web services development, deployment, and operations. Broadly speaking, middleware consists of the software services that lie between the operating system and the applications on each host of a distributed information system. The ultimate goal of middleware is to shield application developers from the complexity of heterogeneous distributed environments, and to support applications' interoperability in distributed heterogeneous environments.

The notion of middleware originally encompassed database systems, telecommunications software, transaction monitors, and messaging-and-queuing software. It evolved to provide an enhanced support for Enterprise Application Integration (EAI) through functionalities such as i) support for synchronous and asynchronous transport protocols; ii) routing capabilities both as addressability and content-based routing; iii) protocol translation, data transformation and translation; iv) complex event processing capabilities: event interpretation, correlation, pattern matching, publish/subscribe; v) management capabilities including: monitoring, audit, logging, metering, vi) Quality of Service (QoS) capabilities: security (encryption and digital signing), reliable delivery, transactions; vii) process orchestration capabilities and business process definition.

Middleware supporting Web services includes Web servers, XML processors, and SOAP processors. A Web server is the software responsible for accepting HTTP requests from clients, and serving them HTTP responses. An XML processor is a software module used to read XML documents and provide access to their content and structure. A SOAP processor processes a SOAP message according to the formal set of conventions defined by SOAP. It is responsible for enforcing the rules that govern the exchange of SOAP messages and it accesses the services provided by the underlying protocols through SOAP bindings. A SOAP processor is responsible for invoking local SOAP Handlers and for providing the services of the SOAP layer to those SOAP handlers. A SOAP processor aids both clients of Web services and their providers to accomplish their task without having to worry about the intricacies of SOAP message handling. As far as the client is concerned, it invokes an operation in a similar way a remote procedure call is invoked. The Web service provider needs to implement only the logic required by the business problem it solves. The client's SOAP processor converts the method invocation into a SOAP message. This message is transmitted through a transport, such as HTTP or SMTP, to the service provider's SOAP processor, which parses the message into a method invocation. The service provider then executes the appropriate application logic and gives the result to its SOAP processor, which parses the information into a SOAP response message. The message is transmitted through a transport to the client. Finally, the client's SOAP processor parses the response message into a result object that it returns to the invoking entity.

Middleware supporting Web services is a distributed infrastructure and it can be implemented either as a gateway that handles traffic for multiple Web services or as agents co-resident on systems running a given Web service. The presence of such infrastructure is often transparent to a given Web Service and to any software invoking a service provided by it. Typically, the infrastructure addresses key areas such as security, system management and service virtualization.

Bibliographic notes

The reader interested in an in depth comparison of the features of schema languages can read the paper by Lee and Chu [160]. The book of Graham et alii [118] introduces the basic concepts, technologies and standards of Web services and also provides in depth "how to" information for Java developers. The book by Alonso et alii [9] provides a critical analysis of what Web services are and what is their foreseable future. The book by Kumar [155] is intended for Java developers interested to the security aspects, including the use of Web services security standards. The book by O'Neill et al. [208] contains a thouroghly analysis of Web services security standards.

Web Services Threats, Vulnerabilities, and Countermeasures

Securing a Web service requires us to protect, as far as possible, all of its basic components, shown in Figure 3.1, and their interactions along with the Web service life cycle, from the design to the operational phase. This is a complex and difficult task, due to the vulnerabilities which each software component may have, the large number of attacks that can eventually exploit the vulnerabilities of a specific component, and to the interactions between the components themselves. It requires us to combine and enhance methods, tools, and techniques for computers, networks, distributed systems, and application security and adopt an engineered security process. Such an engineered process consists of detailed plans and designs for security features and controls that support the delivery of solutions satisfying not only functional requirements, but also preventing misuse and malicious behavior. Core practices of an engineered security process are security planning, security requirements analysis, the design of a security architecture, secure coding, security testing, and security operations and maintenance. Each core practice encompasses specific methods and tools, or even specific methodologies.

Threat modeling is a methodology used to ensure that a software component's security is duly analyzed and taken into account at design time. Threat modeling is not a new concept, nor it is peculiar to Web services. At its most basic, threat modeling assumes that a software component might be subject to malicious attacks or inadvertent misuse and that these attacks may lead to loss or compromise of some valuable asset. At the same time, malicious attacks or inadvertent misuse arise by use of software components' vulnerabilities. Hence, it is necessary to identify in a principled way the software component vulnerabilities, which can derive from wrong design choices, from implementation errors or from the lack of appropriate control, the ways in which such vulnerabilities could be exploited by a malicious attacker and finally the suitable countermeasures. W3C also postulated the need of developing a threat model specifically targeting Web services and suggested that such a threat model should be an integral part of a Web services security framework. It is worth noting that, as we will see in Chapter 4, Web service

E. Bertino et al., *Security for Web Services and Service-Oriented Architectures*, DOI 10.1007/978-3-540-87742-4_3, © Springer-Verlag Berlin Heidelberg 2010

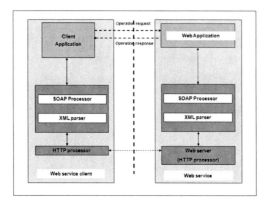

Fig. 3.1. Web service basic components

security standard specifications also recommend that standard specification implementors perform a thoroughly threat analysis.

Threat modeling, however, has suffered a lack of commonly agreed concepts and of a standardized language to define, categorize, and describe threats and vulnerabilities. For this reason, this chapter starts by introducing firstly the concepts of threat, vulnerability, attack and incident. Then the chapter shortly describes the main phases of threat modeling as applied to Web application development life cycle. Then the chapter presents the proposed categorizations and the available catalogs of vulnerabilities and attacks. Such catalogs can be used and useful not only during the design phase of a software component, but also during the operation phase of a Web service. Finally the chapter addresses how to rate vulnerabilities and how the underlying vulnerabilities metrics have to be tailored to the specific phase of the software component life cycle.

3.1 Threats and Vulnerabilities Concept Definition

Before analyzing in more depth the threats and vulnerabilities of Web services, it is worth to survey some relevant definitions of the basic concepts:

- *Threat* - According to the Glossary of Key Information Security Terms of NIST [149] [186], a threat is defined as: "Any circumstance or event with the potential to adversely impact organizational operations (including mission, functions, image, or reputation), organizational assets, or individuals through an information system via unauthorized access, destruction, disclosure, modification of information, and/or denial of service. Also, the potential for a threat-source to successfully exploit a particular information system vulnerability."

- *Vulnerability* - A vulnerability can be defined as a "Weakness in an information system, system security procedures, internal controls, or implementation that could be exploited or triggered by a threat source."[199] [225]. A vulnerability is also commonly defined as a flaw in a software component that can be exploited by an adversary, giving raise to a threat. The former definition is more general, since it considers not only software components vulnerabilities but also equally relevant organizational aspects. MITRE [75] makes a further distinction between a *vulnerability* and an *exposure*. The former is a software mistake that can be *directly* used by a hacker to gain access to a system or network, while the latter is a configuration issue or a software mistake that does not allow an attacker to directly compromise a system or a resource, but that could be used as a primary point of entry of a successful attack, and that violates a reasonable security policy.
- *Attack* - An attack, referred to also as *intrusion* or *exploit*, can be defined as an assault to a system that derives from an intentional use of a vulnerability.
- *Attack cost* - The cost of an attack can be defined as a measure of the effort to be expended by the attacker, expressed in terms of her expertise, resources and motivation.
- *Incident* - An incident is the result of a successful attack.
- *Countermeasure* - A countermeasure can be thought as any organizational action or tool able to mitigate a risk deriving from one or more attack classes intended to exploit one or more classes of vulnerabilities.

Sofware components vulnerabilities can be broadly classified as:

1. *Software defects*. They can be further refined in:
   - *Design flaws* , that is, design decisions made at the design time that create an inherently insecure system. An example of architectural level error for session-based systems, leading to a vulnerability, is the generation of easily guessable session identifiers (i.e. using a counter and not a random number).
   - *Coding errors* , that can be traced back to the lack of appropriate controls in the code that may lead to a variety of errors including for example buffer overflows or race conditions.
2. *Configuration errors* . They are becoming the major source of vulnerabilities. This is not surprising, since software components are more and more driven by configurations which are becoming quite complex to manage. Configuration errors can be further classified in:
   - *Unnecessary (or dangerous) services*. Since it is usually easier to install a software component with its default configuration, systems are often configured to bring up services and allow connections that are not strictly required.
   - *Access control misconfiguration*. Complex systems might have elaborate access control policies based on groups and/or roles and per-

missions. Properly configuring reference monitors, that is, the engines enforcing access control decisions and enforcement, is a complex and error-prone task.

3.2 Threat Modeling

Threat modeling is a methodology to identify, assess and document the threats, attacks, vulnerabilities, and countermeasures in the context of a software component life cycle. The overall goals of threat modeling are to reduce security risks during design, development and operations and to help making trade-offs in key engineering decisions. Threat modeling was initially proposed by Microsoft [248] and has become an integral part of Microsoft's Trustworthy Computing Security Development Life cycle (SDL) [169] process illustrated in Figure 3.2. In a Web service setting, threat modeling might be applied to any software component of the Web service stack, from the HTTP processor to the Web application. While the components that constitute the infrastrucure of a Web service, such as the HTTP processor, the XML parser, the SOAP processor, etc., benefit from being developed by large organizations which can afford the costs of security, Web applications are mostly developed as a custom component. Web applications are one of the weakest components of the Web service stack, since development teams often operate under tight time and/or resource constraints that may also include the lack of security trained personnel. The situations is worsened when security functions, such as authorization, are implemented by the Web application itself.

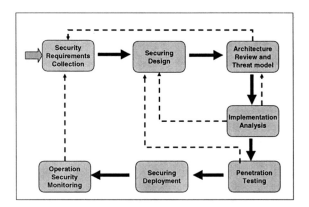

Fig. 3.2. Security development lifecycle

However, applying threat modeling to Web application requires to provide a structured framework for the security analysis. A first step in this direction is to organize threats and vulnerabilities in a set of categories, corresponding to security or security related functions . Such functions could be directly implemented by the application, or could be implemented by the infrastructure and used by the application. Depending on the application security requirements, vulnerability categories can be used during the application design phase to check which specific security functions must be implemented. At the same time, vulnerability categories can provide indications about the threats that could result from the exploitation of one or more vulnerabilities deriving from having decided to not implement one or more security functions. An example of a possible vulnerability categories framework is the one proposed by Microsoft, described in Table 3.1 below, excerpted from [176].

Application Vulnerability Category	Description (controls and/or protection techniques that the application should use)
Input validation	Controls that the application should perform on its input: lexical, syntactical and type checks; input integrity; input origin (does it come from a valid user?)
Authentication	Entity authentication checks: does the application properly authenticate the sender of the input data; does the application authenticate the users?
Authorization	Does the application verify that the requesting users can legitimately access/use the resource they are requesting?
Configuration Management	Does the application run with the least needed privileges? Does the application connect to the proper database? If the application uses its own configuration data, are they stored and accessed in a secure way?
Sensitive Data	If the application manages sensitive data, does the application use suitable techniques to protect confidentiality and integrity of data in transit and of data at rest?
Session Management	Does the application manage sessions? If so, are sessions properly protected?
Cryptography	Does the application properly use cryptography to protect data and messages confidentiality and integrity?
Exception management	Does the application fail securely? Does the application properly manage error information reported to the user to avoid information leakage?
Auditing and Logging	Does the application keep a record of who did what?

Table 3.1. Application Vulnerabilities Categories

Threat modeling is an iterative process that starts during the early phase of the design of the application and continues throughout the application life cycle. The iterative nature of the threat modeling process stems from the difficulty of identifying all possible threats in a single pass and from the need to accommodate changes to the application over its lifetime.

Building a threat model involves the following steps , that will be shortly described afterward:

1. Identify the valuable assets.
2. Define the security objectives.
3. Create an architecture overview of the Web application (or of the software component at hand).
4. Create a security profile of the Web application (or of the software component at hand).
5. Identify threats and vulnerabilities.
6. Document threats and vulnerabilities.
7. Rate the threats.

The final output of threat modeling is a threat model document. A threat model document consist of a definition of the architecture of the application and of a list of threats for the application scenario. A threat model document supports the various members of the project team in assessing the security architecture of the system, and provides a basis for a penetration test plan and for the code review activity.

The threat model constitutes the input for the identification and the evaluation of the suitable countermeasures, where the evaluation can encompass not only the countermeasures' technical aspects but also their cost/benefit ratio.

Identifying the assets

The goal of this step is to identify the assets that must be protected from attacks. It is worth noting that such assets could be resources directly managed by the Web application, resources that could be someway indirectly accessed through the application, as well assets related to the business, such as the company reputation, which do not have a direct electronic embodiment.

Defining the security objectives

Security objectives are strictly related with the the definition of the level of confidentiality, integrity and availability required for the valuable information assets and for the information systems managing them. Defining security objectives, in turn, requires to categorize the relevant information types and information systems. As for this aspect, the U.S. Federal Information Processing Standard 199 - Standards for Security Categorization of Federal Information and Information Systems - [243] identifies three security categories, confidentiality, integrity and availability, respectively. Security objectives derive from the estimate of the impact of a security breach, that is, a confidentiality, integrity and availability breach, on the valuable information assets.

Creating an architecture overview

The main goal of this step is to identify and document the functions of the application, its architecture, its physical deployment configuration and the subsystems that it uses.

Create a security profile of the Web application

In this step a security profile for the application is created, according to the chosen vulnerability categorization as, for example, the previuosly described one used by Microsoft. At its most basics, the Web application security profile identifies and documents the design and implementation approaches chosen for each of the security or security related functions that can be used to prevent or mitigate a given vulnerability category and for the other areas where applications are most susceptible to vulnerabilities. The security profile also identifies applications' entry points, trust boundaries, data flow, and privileged code, as shown in Fig. 3.3.

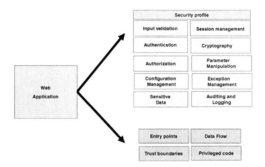

Fig. 3.3. Decomposition and security profile

Crucial activities in this phase are the identification of the Web application entry and exit points, which broadly represent the applications' perimeter, and, for each of them, the level of trust associated with the external software entities which the input originates from or the applications' output is directed to. An entry points is a location where data or control is transferred between the application being modeled and another subsystem. Trust level is basically related to wheter the external subsystem is authenticated or not and to the privileges it has. Trust levels are needed to identify data flows that are potentially malicious, and thus need to be more thoroughly validated by the application.

Identify the threats

In this step, the security or security related functions implemented or used by
the application are analyzed in order to discover possible threats. According
to Microsoft guidelines, this activity should ideally be carried out by a team
consisting of application architects, security professionals, developers, testers,
and system administrators. The main output of this step is a threat profile,
which identifies the likely paths of attack. Attacks can be also analyzed, and
categorized, with respect to the objectives an attack may intend to achieve. For
example, Microsoft describes these objectives by using the STRIDE (Spoofing,
Tampering, Repudiation, Information Disclosure, Denial of Service, Elevation
of privilege) categories [248]. Table 3.2, reproduced from [177] describes the
meaning of each threat category.

Threat Category	Threat Definition
Spoofing	The illegal access and use of a user's identitification or authentication information, such as the user's username and password.
Tampering (also called integrity threats)	An unauthorized modification of data. Examples include making unauthorized changes to persistent data, such as that held in a database, or altering data as it flows between two computers over an open network, such as the Internet.
Repudiation	The ability of users (legitimate or otherwise) to deny that they performed specific actions or transactions. An example is a user performing an illegal operation in a system that can't trace the prohibited operations.
Information disclosure	The unwanted exposure of private data.
Denial of service	The process of making a system or application unavailable.
Elevation of privilege	It occurs when a user with limited privileges assumes the identity of a privileged user to gain privileged access to an application and thereby he/she has the ability to compromise or destroy an entire system.

Table 3.2. STRIDE Categories

For each threat category STRIDE provides guidelines as to the appropriate
countermeasures to adopt in order to reduce the risk. Most common known
threats can also be grouped based on the component which may be subject to

the threat, that is, the network, the host, and the application. Such categorized threat lists can provide a more focused framework to conduct the security analysis. Table 3.3, reproduced from [177], reports the threat list to be initially considered for the application.

Vulnerability Category	Threats
Input validation	Buffer overflow; cross-site scripting; SQL injection; canonicalization
Authentication	Network eavesdropping; brute force attacks; dictionary attacks; cookie replay; credential theft
Authorization	Elevation of privilege; disclosure of confidential data; data tampering; luring attacks
Configuration management	Unauthorized access to administration interfaces; unauthorized access to configuration stores; retrieval of clear text configuration data; lack of individual accountability; overprivileged process and service accounts
Sensitive data	Access sensitive data in storage; network eavesdropping; data tampering
Session management	Session hijacking; session replay; man in the middle
Cryptography	Poor key generation or key management; weak or custom encryption
Parameter manipulation	Query string manipulation; form field manipulation; cookie manipulation; HTTP header manipulation
Exception management	Information disclosure; denial of service
Auditing and logging	User denies performing an operation; attacker exploits an application without trace; attacker covers his or her tracks

Table 3.3. Application Vulnerability Categories

Categorized lists of known threats include common well known threats. For each category, in order to identify other possible threats, other techniques based on *attack trees* and *attack patterns* can be used. *Attack trees* [233, 234] represent the possible paths followed by an attack as trees. The root node of such a tree is the global goal of an attacker. Children of a node are refinements of this goal, and leafs represent goals that can no longer be refined. Attack trees provide a formal methodology for analyzing the security of systems and subsystems, to capture and reuse expertise about security, and to respond to changes in security requirements. Attack trees can become complex, especially when dealing with specific attacks. A full attack tree may contain hundreds or thousands of different paths all leading to completion of the attack. Although the creation of an attack tree may require substantial security expertise and practice, attack trees, once organized in a library, can provide a reusable knowledge base and so contribute to an engineered approach to security.

Attack patterns are a mechanism to capture and communicate the attackers perspective. They describe common methods for exploiting software that can occur in a variety of different contexts, and apply the problem-solution paradigm of design patterns [111]. An attack pattern is based on the analysis of observed attack exploitations, and usually contains the following information:

- Pattern name and classification;
- Attack prerequisites;
- Attack Description;
- Targeted vulnerabilities or weaknesses;
- Method of attack;
- Attacker goal;
- Attacker skill level required;
- Resources required;
- Blocking solutions;
- Context description.

To promote the standardization of attack pattern description and their use in the secure software development, attack patterns are being enumerated and classified by the Common Attack Pattern Enumeration and Classification (CAPEC) [63] initiative sponsored by the Department of Homeland Security (DHS) and led by Cigital.

Altogether, the information provided by attack trees and attack patterns about the methods of attacks, the required attacker skill level, and the resources needed to conduct the attack represent one of the perspectives to be taken into account when rating threats and vulnerabilities.

Rating threats

The final step of threat modeling is rating discovered threats based on the risk they pose to the identified valuable assets, whose confidentiality, integrity, and availability should be assured. Rating threats is not a simple task, because it depends on multiple factors, such as the set of existing known vulnerabilities, the estimate of the likelihood of attacks, the estimate of the potential impact of an attack against valuable assets, to mention just a few. In principle, each perspective requires to define possibly multiple metrics. As to Microsoft guidelines, they suggest to evaluate the risk as the product of the probability of the threat occurrence and the damage potential, which is an estimate of the adverse effect of a threat occurrence on the valuable assets. Section 3.4, Threats and Vulnerability Metrics, elaborates further this topic.

Countermeasures

Countermeasures are the controls and techniques to adopt in order to mitigate or prevent the exploitation of known and/or unknown vulnerabilities of a specific software component. Countermeasures could encompass both organizational processes and technical tools. The adoption of a secure software development methodology or security design guidelines is an example of an organizational countermeasure. As for the identification of countermeasures in the threat modeling process, the security profile of the Web application provides the input to identify the countermeasures to adopt against the identified vulnerabilities and threats.

Microsoft guidelines define an initial list of countermeasures for each threat category described by STRIDE, or for each vulnerability category of the categorized threat lists, respectively. Countermeasures mainly take the form of security guidelines the application or the security subsystem should comply to (for example, the authentication subsystem should not transmit the password over the network). Countermeasures are further specialized depending on the specific system component under analysis, namely the network, the host or the application. The analysis of application level countermeasures is driven by the Application Vulnerability Categories in Table 3.3.

As far as Web applications are concerned, we already observed that a vulnerability category can be viewed as security or security-related functions directly implemented by the application or used by the application and provided by the (security) infrastructure. In an ideal world, authentication, access control, auditing and logging, cryptographic key generation and management should be implemented as functions or services of a security infrastructure provided as an integral part of the middleware. In such ideal scenario the application should take care of implementing by itself only the security controls and countermeasures strictly dependent from the the application semantics which can not be fully implemented by the infrastructure, such as application input validation, application configuration management, exception management.

It is worth noting, however, that even though the security functions provided by the middleware are becoming more and more reach and complete, providing a general purpose, customizable authorization mechanism as a security infrastructure service is still an open issue. As a consequence, Web applications continue to implement by themeselves authorization functions, relying upon authorization mechanisms provided by the Operating System or by the DBMS, such as RBAC-based authorization mechanisms.

Countermeasures, both organizational and technical ones, can be also classified according to when they are used during the Web application life cycle, namely:

- Development-time countermeasures. Examples of technical tools that can be used in the development phase are code analyzers, penetration test tools and vulnerability scanners. The first obviously requires the availability of the source code of the application or of the software component at hand, while the last can also be used for applications and or software components acquired from third parties, and for which the source code is not available.

- Deployment-time countermeasures. These countermeasures encompass the activities and the related supporting tools that allow to ascertain the correct configuration of the Web application and of the diverse software components of the Web service stack.
- Run-time countermeasures. Vulnerability analysis tools, including intrusion detection and prevention systems (IDS/IPS) and file integrity checkers are examples of tools in this category.

3.3 Vulnerability Categorizations and Catalogs

This section discusses the various sources of information about security and Web vulnerabilities, attacks, and the underlying vulnerability categorizations. Vulnerability categorizations and related catalogs are part of the ongoing effort to develop and establish a standardized approach to identify Web security issues. Vulnerability catalogs provide a knowledge base useful for security training purposes, as well as useful input to the threat modeling process during the design and the development phase of a Web service. On the other hand, information about new attacks, related newly discovered vulnerabilities and available hotfixes and security patches provides information vital for maintaining the security level of the production systems.

US-CERT Vulnerability Notes

The United States Computer Emergency Readiness Team (US-CERT) is a partnership established in 2003 between the Department of Homeland Security and the public and private sectors. US-CERT publishes information on a wide variety of vulnerabilities. Descriptions of these vulnerabilities are available in a searchable database, and are published as US-CERT Vulnerability Notes [266]. The US-CERT Vulnerability Notes Database contains two types of documents: Vulnerability Notes, which describe vulnerabilities independent of a particular vendor, and Vendor Information documents, which provide information about a specific vendor's solution to a problem. Vulnerability notes include technical descriptions of the vulnerability, its impact, the solutions and workarounds, and lists of affected vendors. The Vulnerability Notes Database can be browsed or can be searched by several key fields. Database queries can be customized to obtain specific information, such as the ten most recently updated vulnerabilities or the twenty vulnerabilities with the highest severity metric. In addition to the Vulnerability Notes, US-CERT publishes the Cyber Security Bulletins , which summarize security issues and new vulnerabilities and provide actions to help mitigate risks, and the Technical Cyber Security Alerts, intended to timely informing about current security issues, vulnerabilities, and exploits.

MITRE Common Vulnerabilities and Exposures (CVE)

Information about software components vulnerabilities and attacks grew over time and it accumulated in a variety of databases. The lack of a uniform terminology among such databases made it difficult to determine if different databases referred to the same problem. In addition, different tools of different vendors used different metrics to state the number of vulnerabilities or exposures they detected, so that there was no standardized basis for evaluation among the tools. To overcome these problems, MITRE launched in 1999 the Common Vulnerabilities and Exposures (CVE) project [74]. CVE provides a dictionary and a standard, unique name of all publicly known information security vulnerabilities (or exposures, as they are termed by CVE). Each CVE Identifier includes: CVE Identifier number (i.e., "CVE-1999-0067"); indication of "entry" or "candidate" status; a brief description of the security vulnerability or exposure; any pertinent references (i.e., vulnerability reports and advisories or OVAL-ID[1]).

MITRE Common Weakness Enumeration (CWE)^{TM}-

The Common Weakness Enumeration [76] is an initiative lead by MITRE Corp. and sponsored by the National Cyber Security Division of the U.S. Department of Homeland Security. Main goal of CWE is to provide a formal, standard list of common security weaknesses, targeted to developers and security practitioners. CWE aims to support and improve code security assessment and also to accelerate the use and utility of software assurance capabilities for organizations in reviewing the software systems they acquire or develop. CWE is based in part on the CVE identifiers of the CVE List. Associated to the dictionary, the Open Vulnerability and Assessment Language (OVAL^{TM}) [211] provides a standard for describing vulnerability and configuration issues on computer systems using community-developed XML schemas and definitions. OVAL is a collection of XML schemas for representing system information, expressing specific machine states (vulnerability, configuration, patch state, etc.), and reporting the results of a security assessment. By standardizing the transfer of this information across the different security tools and services, OVAL aims to ease the integration of security applications and help organizations in developing security checks for highly-customized networks and applications. An example of the use of OVAL for describing a vulnerablity can be found in [19]. Moreover, efforts are ongoing to provide a set of OVAL-based services in a SOA architecture [158].

National Vulnerability Database (NVD)

NVD Version 2.0 [200] is the U.S. government repository of standards based vulnerability management data represented using the Security Content Automation Protocol (SCAP). This repository is aimed at the automation of

---

[1] Open Vulnerability and Assessment Language - (see CWE below) -

vulnerability management, security measurement, and compliance. NVD includes databases of security checklists, security related software flaws, misconfigurations, product names, and impact metrics. At the time of this book writing, NVD contains: 26886 CVE Vulnerabilities; 114 Checklists; 91 US-CERT Alerts; 1997 US-CERT Vulnerability Notes; 2966 OVAL Queries; and 12458 Vulnerable Products.

NVD provides a Vulnerability Search Engine which allows one to search vulnerabilities by product or vendor name, by CVE standard vulnerability name and by a query expressed in the OVAL language. The Security Content Automation Protocol (SCAP) is a method for using specific standards to enable automated vulnerability management, measurement, and policy compliance evaluation. SCAP is part of the Information Security Automation Program (ISAP) [250], a U.S. government multi-agency initiative to enable automation and standardization of technical security operations.

SecurityFocus Vulnerability Database and BugTraq mail list

The SecurityFocus Vulnerability Database [236] provides a vulnerability database that can be searched by vendor, product and product version or by CVE identifier. General information is associated with each vulnerability including the BugTraq Identifier, the vulnerability class, the vulnerability publication and update dates, and the versions of the product that present the vulnerability. BugTraq [56] is an electronic mailing list, moderated since 1995, dedicated to the discussion about vulnerabilities, vendor security-related announcements, methods of exploitation, and vulnerability remediation. Bugtraq adopted a policy of publishing vulnerabilities regardless of vendor response, as part of the movement towards a full vulnerability disclosure.

Open Source Vulnerability Database - (OVSDB)

The Open Source Vulnerability Database is an independent and open source database created to provide technical information on security vulnerabilities. The database is available for download, can be cross-referenced by other databases, and is available for integration into security products such as vulnerability scanners and intrusion detection and prevention systems. Vulnerabilities listed in OSDVB can be referenced by their OSVDB ID, which is a unique number assigned by OSVDB. OSVDB also maintains mappings to other sources of vulnerabilities information, including Common Vulnerabilities and Exposures (CVE). CVE identifiers can be used for searching OSVDB entries. In order to provide the most comprehensive and timely information, vulnerabilities are entered in the OVSDB even if they are only posted to public mail lists and are not yet verified as true vulnerabilities. In order to distinguish the "status" of a vulnerability, OSVDB maintains the following classification:

- Verified. The existence of the vulnerability has been verified to exist by a OSVDB "datamanglers", which are OSVDB users that have contributed to the content of the database and are responsible for updating vulnerability entries to ensure accurate and complete information , or acknowledged by the vendor.

- Myth/Fake. The vulnerability appears to be non-existent, a non-issue, or disproved by others.
- Best Practice. The entry details a vulnerability that is considered a best practice issue.
- Concern. The issue may be a concern, but it is not directly exploitable for privilege escalation. It may lead to a more serious impact.

Each OSVDB vulnerability entry also contains a high-level description in textual form, aimed at helping system administrators in understanding it; a technical description providing a concise summary of technical details; manual testing notes describing how to test for the vulnerability, for example, how to check the presence of files, configuration options, and a test URL; a solution description, that is, information about an available fix.

The Web Application Security Threat Classification

The Web Application Security Consortium [273] created the Web Security Threat Classification [274]. It aims at clarifying and organizing the threats to the security of a Web site, and at developing and promoting an industry standard terminology for describing these issues. Specifically, this classification aims at identifying all known Web application security attacks, describing them in an organized way, and at agreeing on attack class nomenclature. An attack class groups the different attack techniques that can be used against security functions or against resources by exploiting a known security vulnerability. The top-level attack classes are: authentication; authorization; client-side attacks; command execution; information disclosure; logical attacks.

Open Web Applications Security Project

The Open Web Applications Security Project (OWASP)[255] maintains a commonly recognized classification of the most critical Web application vulnerabilities, Top Ten Most Critical Web Application Security Vulnerabilities (Top 10) [269], which represents a broad consensus about the most critical Web application security flaws and vulnerabilities. OWASP Top 10 Web Application Vulnerabilities for 2007 [215] are derived by the MITRE Vulnerability Type Distributions in CVE [77], and reorganized by OWASP to identify the Top 10 *web application security issues*. Top 10 focuses only on vulnerabilities and protection recommendations for the three most prevalent Web application frameworks: Java EE, ASP.NET, and PHP.

Software vendor's security bulletins and advisories

Users' searchable information about vulnerabilities and related hotfixes and patches is maintained by major software vendors and open software organizations. This information is usually accessible through the specific product support link at the product Web site. For example, Mozilla Security Center [192] provides the Mozilla Foundation Security Advisories [190] for all products and a list of the known security vulnerabilities [191] that affect particular versions of Mozilla products, together with instructions on what users can do to protect themselves. This page lists security vulnerabilities with direct impact on users, that have been fixed prior to the most recent release. Technical discussions of security-related bugs are maintained at the Bugzilla site [57]. As another example, Microsoft Security Bulletins [183] provide the following information for each vulnerability:

- an executive summary which shortly describes the vulnerability.
- the vulnerability qualitative rating (important, etc.).
- the recommendation as to the installation of the related security update.
- the known issues about the security update itself (which refer to a Microsoft Knowledge Base article).
- the affected software and the CVE vulnerability number (see later).
- the maximum security impact and the aggregate severity rating.

The section Update Information of the vulnerability entry in the Bulletin provides guidelines on how detect and deploy Microsoft tools that can identify the Microsoft software needing to install the security update (security patch) related to the vulnerability. The Microsoft Security Bulletins are searchable by Product/Technology and Service Pack, Update Severity Ratings and Bulletin Release Date.

Enterprise Vulnerability Description Language

Proposed by the OASIS Web Application Security TC, the Enterprise Vulnerability Description Language (EVDL) [99] is also based on OWASP classification. However, it proposes a more detailed breakdown of the major vulnerabilities. EVDL was conceived to become a comprehensive application security markup language whose primary goal is to facilitate communication about specific application security vulnerabilities, techniques for discovering those vulnerabilities, and measures to protect against those vulnerabilities.

3.4 Threat and Vulnerabilities Metrics

Once vulnerabilities are identified and classified, there is the need to determine their severity and hence, indirectly, the security (or the insecurity!) of the specific system at hand. Rating vulnerabilities, that is, defining a vulnerability metrics, is a difficult task. The severity of a given vulnerability depends upon several factors. These factors are related to the amount of resources needed by a potential attacker, including the skill that the attacker should have, and hence to the attack cost, and to the estimated extent of the damage to the organization's valuable assets in case of an exploitation of the vulnerability.

The latter factor highlights also the difficulty in building a metrics that can be applied in different organizational settings, since assets may vary from organization to organization and the same asset might have a different value for different organizations. Moreover, when dealing with known vulnerabilities, different vendors may adopt different methods for rating software vulnerabilities in their bulletins or advisories; the same situation also arises for different vulnerability databases. The consequence is that IT system and application managers, who are in charge of managing large and heterogeneous systems, lack consistent indications to prioritize the vulnerability to be addressed. In this section we give an overview of different proposals and efforts aimed at the development of a set of possibly standardized and commonly agreed upon vulnerability metrics.

Microsoft Security Response Center Security Bulletin Severity Rating System

The Microsoft Severity Rating [184] adopts a qualitative metric. Vulnerabilities are classified into four categories, namely:

- Critical. A vulnerability whose exploitation could allow the propagation of an Internet worm without user action.
- Important. A vulnerability whose exploitation could result in compromise of the confidentiality, integrity, or availability of user data, or of the integrity or availability of processing resources.
- Moderate. Exploitability is mitigated to a significant degree by factors such as default configuration, auditing, or difficulty of exploitation.
- Low. A vulnerability whose exploitation is extremely difficult, or whose impact is minimal.

US-CERT Vulnerability Metric

US-CERT[267] uses a quantitative metric and scores the severity of a vulnerability by assigning to it a number between 0 and 180. This number results from several factors reported by the users, including:

- the degree of diffusion of information or knowledge about the vulnerability.
- whether incidents reported to US-CERT were caused by the exploitation of the vulnerability.
- the risk to the Internet infrastructure deriving from the vulnerability.
- the number of systems on the Internet at risk because of the vulnerability.
- the impact of exploiting the vulnerability.
- whether the vulnerability can be easily exploited.
- the preconditions required to exploit the vulnerability.

As described on the US-CERT Web page, the factors above are attributed with approximate values that may differ significantly from one site to another, and hence users are suggested not to rely solely upon this metric for prioritizing vulnerabilities. However, the factors above are used by US-CERT for separating the very serious vulnerabilities from the large number of less severe vulnerabilities described in its database. Typically, vulnerabilities with a metric greater than 40 are candidates for US-CERT Technical Alerts. The factors above described are not all equally weighted, and the resulting score is not linear (a vulnerability with a metric of 40 is not twice as severe as one with a metric of 20).

Common Vulnerability Scoring System

The Common Vulnerability Scoring System (CVSS) [178] aims at providing an open framework for measuring the impact of IT vulnerabilities. CVSS is based on a quantitative model in order to ensure repeatable and consistent measurement of the vulnerabilities' impact. Two common uses of CVSS are prioritization of vulnerability remediation activities and the calculation of the severity of vulnerabilities discovered on a given system. CVSS is composed of three metrics groups: base, temporal, and environmental, each consisting of a set of metrics. The base metrics group represents characteristics of a vulnerability that are constant over time and user environments. This group includes six metrics. The first one, the access vector metric, reflects the type of access (local/adjacent; network/network) which the attacker has to use in order to exploit the vulnerability. The second one, the access complexity metric, measures the complexity of the attack required to exploit the vulnerability once an attacker has gained access to the target system. The third one, the authentication metric, measures the number of times an attacker must authenticate to a target before exploiting a vulnerability. The fourth one, the confidentiality impact metric, measures the impact on confidentiality of a successfully exploited vulnerability. The fifth one, the integrity impact metric, measures the impact to integrity of a successfully exploited vulnerability. The sixth one, the availability impact metric, measures the impact to availability of a successfully exploited vulnerability.

The temporal metrics group tries to capture the threat deriving from the time-changing characteristics of a vulnerability. This metrics group encompasses three metrics, the exploitability, the remediation level, and the report confidence metrics, respectively. The first one measures the current state of exploit techniques or code availability, which may range from the exploit being only theoretically possible, to the existence of publicly available details about how to build code that performs the exploitation. The second one allows one to take into account the existence of temporary fixes (workarounds or hot-fixes) or of official patches or upgrades. The third one measures the degree of confidence in the existence of the vulnerability and the credibility of the known technical details. The metrics above are optional and do not concur to the calculation of the overall score.

The environmental metric group captures the characteristics of a vulnerability that are relevant and unique to a particular user environment. These metrics are optional and do not concur to the calculation of the overall score.

This group is composed by the Collateral Damage Potential, the Target Distribution, and the Security Requirement metrics. The Collateral Damage Potential metric measures the potential for loss of life or physical assets through damage or theft of property or equipment and possibly the economic loss of productivity or revenue. The Target Distribution metric measures the percentage of systems that could be affected by the vulnerability. The Security Requirements metric allows one to re-weight the base security metrics (confidentiality, integrity, availability), by taking into account the relevance of the corresponding security requirement for the affected IT asset to a users organization.

The metrics described above require the involvement of different stakeholders and organizations' roles in the different phases of the application or system life cycle. Generally, the base and temporal metrics should be specified by vulnerability bulletin analysts, security product vendors, or application vendors because they typically have better information about the characteristics of a vulnerability than users. The environmental metrics, however, should be specified by users because they can more properly assess the potential impact of a vulnerability within their own environment.

SANS Critical Vulnerabiliy Analysis Scale

SANS Critical Vulnerability Analysis Scale Ratings [230] ranks vulnerabilities using several key factors and varying degrees of weight, as reported by the users, such as:

- the diffusion of the affected product.
- whether the vulnerability affected a server or client system.
- whether the vulnerability is related to default configurations/installations.
- the IT assets affected (e.g. databases, e-commerce servers).
- the network infrastructure affected (DNS, routers, firewalls).
- the public availability of exploit code.
- the difficulty in exploiting the vulnerability.

Depending on the above factors, vulnerabilities are ranked as critical, high, moderate, or low. Critical vulnerabilities typically affect default installations of very widely deployed software, and result in root compromise of servers or infrastructure devices. Moreover, the information required for exploiting them (such as example exploit code) is widely available to attackers. Further, exploitation is usually straightforward, in the sense that the attacker does not need any special authentication credentials, or knowledge about individual victims, and does not need to social engineer a target user into performing any special functions. High vulnerabilities are typically those that have the potential to become critical, but have one or a few mitigating factors that make exploitation less attractive to attackers. For example, vulnerabilities that have many critical characteristics but are difficult to exploit, that do not result in elevated privileges, or that have a minimally sized victim pool are usually rated high. Note that high vulnerabilities where the mitigating factor arises from a lack of technical exploit details will become critical if these details are later made available. Moderate vulnerabilities are those where the scales are slightly tipped in favor of the potential victim. Denial of service vulnerabilities are typically rated moderate, since they do not result in compromise of a target. Exploits that require an attacker to reside on the same local network as a victim, only affect nonstandard configurations or custom applications, require the attacker to social engineer individual victims, or where exploitation only provides very limited access are likely to be rated moderate. Low ranked vulnerabilities have little impact on an organization's infrastructure. These types of vulnerabilities usually require local or physical system access or may often result in client side privacy or denial of service issues and information leakage of organizational structure, system configuration and versions, or network topology. Alternatively, a low ranking may be applied when there is not enough information to fully assess the implications of a vulnerability. For example, vendors often imply that exploitation of a buffer overflow will only result in a denial of service.

Bibliographic notes

The book of Ross Anderson [15, 16] is recommended for the reader interested in security engineering. The book highlights how a good understanding of the potential threats to a system and the adoption of suitable organizational and technological protective measures are key factors in building dependable distributed systems. The concepts and goals for threat modeling methodology, as well a treatment as how to use it, are presented in the book of Swiderski and Snyder [248]. Attack trees are discussed in depth in Chapter 21 of the Schneier's book [234].

4

Standards for Web Services Security

Over time, different languages, mechanisms, and tools have been developed on different software and hardware platforms for specifying and implementing a variety of security mechanisms, such as encryption and access control. In a Web service setting, security mechanisms protect the confidentiality and integrity of the so-called information in transit, that is, the data and messages exchanged between a client and a Web service, and of the so-called information at rest, that is, the information stored in a Web host. Furthermore, protection of the information must not only consider simple two-way client-server interactions, but also extend to more complex interactions, as in the case of business processes implemented through multiple Web services. The need for providing end-to-end security through distributed and heterogeneous security mechanisms called for the development of standards for Web services security, with the ultimate goal of making interoperable different implementations of the same security functions.

Web service security standards were developed as part of a comprehensive framework [235], in accordance with the following underpinning criteria:

- Web services security standards have to be independent of specific underlying technologies.
- Web services security standards have to be composable.
- Web services standards have to be organized in layers, so that standards at an upper level could use and extend standards at a lower level.
- Web services standards have to be extensible, to deal with new requirements and technologies.

This chapter surveys some existing and proposed standards for Web services security. The chapter introduces first the various notions of standard, and provides an overview of different standardization bodies and organizations. Then it discusses the original Web services security standards originally foreseen by the IBM and Microsoft framework [235]. For each standard the related section describes its purpose, its main features, and and the specific

E. Bertino et al., *Security for Web Services and Service-Oriented Architectures*,
DOI 10.1007/978-3-540-87742-4_4, © Springer-Verlag Berlin Heidelberg 2010

security considerations and caveats that apply to it. We do not delve into the details needed by a developer when using the standard, or, more precisely, the software that implements the standard. Readers needing such a level of detail are referred to the books and articles reported in the bibliographic notes. The standards are presented bottom-up, starting with standards closer to the communication layer of the Internet stack and then moving up to the application layer:

- 'near the wire' standards. We discuss Secure Socket Layer (SSL) and Transport Layer Security (TLS), which provide a basic level of security at the communication level.
- XML Encryption and XML Signature. They are the most fundamental standards that specify how to represent encrypted and signed XML data.
- WS-Security. It specifies how to represent encrypted and signed parts of a single SOAP message.
- WS-SecureConversation and WS-Reliability. The former specifies how to represent information related to the exchange of multiple secured SOAP messages, while the latter is focused on message delivery guarantee.
- Security Assertion Markup Language (SAML). SAML is an XML-based framework for exchanging security information in the more general form of security-related assertions about subjects.
- WS-Policy, WS-PolicyAssertion, WS-Policy Attachment, and WS-Security Policy. The first standard provides a general framework for expressing different kinds of security policies. The second standard specifies generic security assertions. The last two standards specify the protection requirements for SOAP messages and how to represent them at SOAP message level.
- eXtensible Access Control Markup Language (XACML) and XACML Profile for Web services. These standards provide a model and a language to express access control policies that can be applied to Web services as well as to other resources.
- Extensible rights Markup Language (XrML). This standard addresses how to express and enforce access control and information dissemination policies.
- XML Key Management Standard (XKMS) and WS-Trust. The former specifies standard services interfaces and protocols for the management of cryptographic keys. The latter specifies services interfaces and protocols for the management of so-called security tokens.

The chapter does not address identity management standards, namely WS-Federation, Liberty Alliance, and Shibboleth. They are fully described in Chapter 5.

It is worth noting that standards are *specifications*. They provide not only normative indications about the *structure* for representing security information but also normative indications about *how* an implementation of the standard should behave. Not surprisingly, standard specifications can be very complex. Such a complexity might lead to non-interoperable implementations of the same standard specification. Thus, the need emerged of a further standardization effort in order to provide specific guidelines to guarantee, as far as possible, the interoperability of different implementations of a given standard. At the end of the overview of the above standards, the chapter discusses the standardization activities carried out by the Web Services Interoperability organization (WS-I) [256] and the standards issued by it in order to mitigate or solve this problem. The chapter concludes with considerations about technical, operational, and organizational issues related to Web service security standards and their adoption.

4.1 The Concept of Standard

According to the Internet Engineering Task Force (IETF) [11] a standard

"describes a specification of a protocol, system behaviour or procedure that has a unique identifier"

where the IETF has agreed that

"if you want to do this thing, this is the description of how to do it."

The concept of standard however, also encompasses different notions, which take into account the nature of the entity that defines a standard, as well as the acceptance and use of a standard regardless of the nature of the emitting entity. Accordingly, a standard is usually categorized as follows:

1. *De facto standard*: a technology that is used by a vast majority of the users of a function. Such function may for example be provided in a product from a single supplier that dominates the market; or it may be a patented technology that is used in a range of products under license. A *de facto* standard may be endorsed by a standardization initiative, and eventually become a consortium recommendation, or a *de jure* standard. The relevant characteristics are that it is widely used, meets the needs for functionality, and supports interoperability.
2. *De jure standard*: a standard defined by an entity with a legal status in international or national law such the International Organization for Standardization (ISO), national standards bodies (e.g. the BSI British Standards in the UK, the American National Standards Institute, ANSI, in the US), or continental standards (e.g., European standards). Standards developed by these organizations are relevant in specific business or application areas, such as healthcare and safety-related areas, business quality measures and long-term IT areas.
3. *Consortium recommendation*: a technology agreed upon and recommended by a group of companies in order to fulfill some functionality. Such consortia may vary in size from groups of a few large manufacturers (e.g., Microsoft, IBM and BEA) to much larger groups or organizations such as

	W3C	OASIS	WS-I
Established	1994	1993 as the SGML Open, 1998 as OASIS	2002
Overall goal	To promote Web evolution by providing fundamental standards	To promote online trade and commerce by providing specialized Web services standards	To foster interoperability using Web services standads
Main security standards issued	XML Encryption; XML Signature	XACML; WS-Security; WS-SecurityPolicy	Basic Interoperability Profile; Basic Security Profile

Table 4.1. Standards organizations

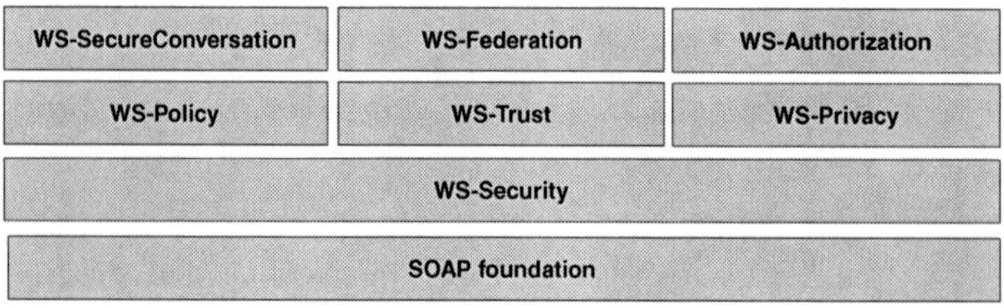

Fig. 4.1. Web services security standards framework

the Organization for the Advancement of Structured Information Standards (OASIS), the World Wide Web Consortium (W3C), and the IETF.

The definition of a standard and its issuance by a standardization body or by a consortium is a long-lasting process, subject to formalized organizational procedures. For example, W3C takes six months to establish a working group on a technology, and then 18 months to three years to agree on a recommendation, which is only released if there are working interoperable implementations of all functions in the technology, and enough of the members of W3C support it. Table 4.1 lists the main standardization bodies relevant to Web services.

4.2 Web Services Security Standards Framework

The first structured framework for Web services security standards was proposed in April 2002 by Microsoft and IBM in the white paper "Security in a Web Services World: A Proposed Architecture and Roadmap" [235]. As shown in Figure 4.1, the Web Services Security (WSS) framework encompassed different specifications, each of them addressing specific aspects of security.

According to this framework, WS-Security was intended to provide a message security model and the specification of mechanisms to attach signature and encryption headers to SOAP messages. WS-Policy was intended to describe (1) the security policies, such as required security tokens and supported encryption algorithms, as well as more general policies adopted by a Web service; and (2) the mechanisms by which trusted SOAP message exchanges could be built. WS-Trust was intended to define the model for establishing both direct and brokered trust relationships, including third parties and intermediaries, through the creation of security token issuance services. WS-Privacy would have to define a model for embedding a privacy language into WS-Policy and for associating privacy claims with a message in WS-Security.

On top of such standards, further follow-on specifications were envisaged. WS-SecureConversation was introduced with the goal of extending the single message security provided by WS-Security to a conversation consisting of multiple message exchanges, whereas WS-Federation was introduced with the goal of describing how to manage and broker trust relationships in a heterogeneous federated environment. Finally, the goal of WS-Authorization was to provide support for the specification of authorization policies and for managing authorization data.

It is worth noting that the specifications for WS-Authorization and WS-Privacy developed differently from the other standards of the roadmap. In particular, WS-Authorization was replaced by the specification of XACML (see section 4.3.7), whereas WS-Privacy does not seem to have received the same level of effort; rather it was addressed by manufacturer proposals such as the IBM Enterprise Privacy Authorization Language (EPAL) [221].

4.3 An Overview of Current Standards

4.3.1 "Near the wire" security standards

Secure Socket Layer (SSL) and Transport Layer Security (TLS)
The well known SSL [110] and TLS [93] are the de facto standards used to ensure transport level security for Web applications. SSL was originally developed by Netscape in 1996 and it served as the basis for IETF RFC 2246 Transport Layer Security (TLS) standard.

SSL/TLS is a protocol layer located between a reliable connection-oriented network layer protocol (e.g., TCP) and the application protocol layer (e.g., HTTP) as shown in Figure 4.2.

SSL/TLS enables point-to-point secure sessions by providing server authentication to the client, optional client authentication to the server, data message authentication, data confidentiality, and data integrity. With respect to SSL, TLS incorporates an optional session caching scheme to reduce the number of connections that need to be established from scratch. Such optimization is intended to reduce the computational load introduced by cryptographic operations, in particular those using public keys. SSL/TLS provides for:

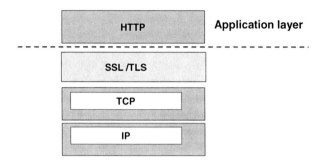

Fig. 4.2. SSL and TLS on the Internet stack

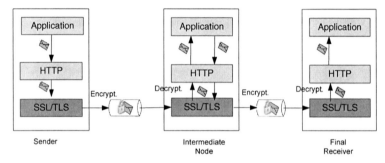

Fig. 4.3. Transport layer only encryption

- confidentiality, by the use of symmetric cryptography for data encryption (e.g., DES, RC4);
- data integrity, by the use of a Message Authentication Code (MAC) generated through a secure hash function (MD5);
- authentication, by the use of certificates and public keys.

While SSL/TLS is fairly secure for point-to-point communications, SSL/TLS alone cannot provide the end-to-end communication protection that is needed in a Web services setting. Actually, in such a setting a message transmitted by a client, such as browser or an application, might be routed (and processed) by a number of intermediary applications or services before reaching its final recipient. SSL/TLS protects the message contents only while they are being transmitted between pairwise endpoints. The message, once it is processed by SSL/TLS at a receiving end, is delivered decrypted to the application layer, as illustrated by Figure 4.3. An intermediary application or service might then, inadvertently or maliciously, examine or even modify the message before transmitting it again to the next recipient.

The other inadequacy of SSL/TLS is that it does not allow one to selectively encrypt parts of the data (payload) to be transmitted.

4.3.2 XML Data Security

XML is the language of choice for representing data payload exchanged among Web services. Securing XML data, that is, protecting their integrity and confidentiality as well as their authenticity, is a key requirement. Integrity and confidentiality are achieved by using encryption mechanisms, while authenticity is achieved by using digital signatures. XML encryption [96] and XML Signature [97] standards specify how to represent and how to convey encrypted data and digital signature in an XML document in a standard way.

XML Encryption

XML Encryption specification [96], which is a W3C Recommendation, is the cornerstone of the Web services Security Framework. It defines a standard model for encrypting both binary and textual data, as well as the means for communicating the information needed by recipients to decrypt the contents of received messages. While SSL/TLS provides confidentiality at the transport layer only, XML Encryption (see Figure 4.4) provides confidentiality at the application layer and thus assures end-to-end confidentiality of messages traversing multiple Web services.

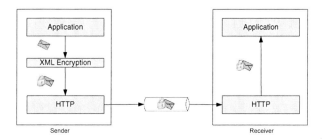

Fig. 4.4. XML encryption

Basically, the XML Encryption specification describes how to use XML to represent a digitally encrypted Web resource (including XML data). It separates encryption information from encrypted data, specifies how to represent information about the encryption key and the encryption algorithm, and supports referencing mechanisms for addressing encryption information from encrypted data sections and viceversa.

However, it is well known that encryption does not guarantee by itself the integrity of the encrypted data. If integrity is required, then signatures (represented according to the XML Signature standard) must be used. The combination of digital signatures and encryption over a common XML element may introduce security vulnerabilities. In particular, encrypting digitally signed data while leaving the digital signature in clear may make possible plaintext guessing attacks. Such a vulnerability can be mitigated by using secure hashes and the nonces [1] in the text being processed. Moreover, denial of service attacks are possible because of the recursive processing of XML Encryption. For example, the following scenario is possible: EncryptedKey A requires EncryptedKey B to be decrypted, which itself requires EncryptedKey A. An attacker might also submit an EncryptedData element for decryption that references network resources that are very large or continually redirected. Consequently, XML Encryption implementations should be able to restrict arbitrary recursion and the total amount of processing and networking resources a request can consume.

XML Signature

XML Signature [97] is a specification produced jointly by W3C and IETF. XML Signature specifies how to represent a digital signature as an XML element and how to create and verify this XML element. Like XML Encryption, it applies to both XML and non-XML data. The signed data items can be entire XML documents, XML elements, or files containing any type of digital data items. XML Signature allows one to sign multiple data with a single signature. It is worth noting that before the issuance of XML Signature, it was already possible to digitally sign an XML document, using the PKCS#7 Signature [147]. However PKCS#7 did not allow one to selectively sign parts of an XML document, or to represent the signature in a standardized XML format. As for the placement of the signature, XML-Signature allows different "packaging" strategies, namely enveloping signature, enveloped signature, and detached signature. When using an enveloping XML signature, the signed data is contained within the XML signature structure itself. An enveloped XML signature is contained within the signed document itself. A detached signature is separate from the signed entity. The signed entity is referenced to by a URI and can be, in principle, any digital content, as shown in Figure 4.5. When processing a detached signature, if the URI cannot be dereferenced, then the signature breaks. Hence, a detached signature could be used for guaranteeing the integrity of online resources.

An XML signature, when it is used alone, assures data integrity. When linked to the signer's identity, it provides for non-repudiation of data content, and may provide for the authentication of the signer.

The XML Signature standard does not address how encryption keys are associated with individuals or institutions, nor the meaning of the data being referenced and signed. Thus, XML Signature by itself is not sufficient to address all application security or trust concerns, particularly with respect to using signed XML (or other data formats) as a basis of human-to-human communication and agreement.

---

[1] The term nonce stands for number used once. A nonce is often a random or pseudo random number issued in an authentication protocol to ensure that old messages cannot be reused in replay attacks.

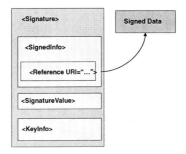

Fig. 4.5. Detached XML signature

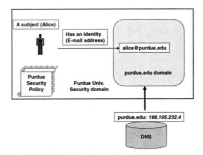

Fig. 4.6. SAML subject identity

4.3.3 Security Assertions Markup Language (SAML)

Security assertions are one basic building block of standards related to the security of SOAP messages, as well as of standards related to security policies, access control, and federated identity management. The Security Assertion Markup Language (SAML) V2.0 [222], which is an OASIS standard specification approved on 15 March 2005, was conceived as a framework for the exchange of security-related information, expressed as assertions, between trusting parties.

In SAML, security information is expressed as *assertions* about subjects, where a subject is an entity (either human or computer) that has an identity in some security domain. A typical example of a subject is a person, identified by his or her email address in a particular Internet DNS domain (see Figure 4.6).

Assertions can convey information about the attributes of subjects, about authentications previously performed by subjects, and possibly about authorization decisions as to whether subjects are allowed to access certain resources. SAML supports three kinds of assertions: attribute, authentication, and authorization decision assertions. An attribute assertion states that the subject S is associated with a set of attributes A_i with values B_i (for example, subject Alice is associated with attribute "University" with value "Purdue"). An authentication assertion states that the subject S was authenticated by means M at a certain time. It is issued by the party that successfully authenticated the subject. An example of SAML authentication assertion, stating that "Alice was originally authenticated using a password mechanism at 2006-04-02T19:05:17", is shown in Figure 4.7. An authorization decision assertion states which actions the subject S is entitled to execute on a resource R (for example, that a user has been authorized to use a given service).

```
<saml:Assertion
xmlns:saml="urn:oasis:names:tc:SAML:1.0:assertion"
        MajorVersion="1" MinorVersion="1"
        AssertionID="biuEZCGxcGiF4gIkL5PNltwU7duY1az"
        Issuer="www.it-authority.org"
        IssueInstant="2006-04-02T19:05:37">
        <saml:Conditions
            NotBefore="2006-04-02T19:00:37"
            NotOnOrAfter="2006-04-02T19:10:37"/>
    <saml:AuthenticationStatement
        AuthenticationMethod="urn:oasis:names:tc:SAML:1.0:am:password"
        AuthenticationInstant="2006-04-02T19:05:17">
        <saml:Subject>
            <saml:NameIdentifier
                NameQualifier= www.it-authority.org
                Format="http://www.customformat.com/">
                uid=alice
            </saml:NameIdentifier>
            <saml:SubjectConfirmation>
                <saml:ConfirmationMethod>
                urn:oasis:names:tc:SAML:1.0:cm:artifact-01
                </saml:ConfirmationMethod>
            </saml:SubjectConfirmation>
        </saml:Subject>
    </saml:AuthenticationStatement>
</saml:Assertion>
```

Fig. 4.7. An example of an SAML assertion

A single SAML assertion might contain several assertion statements about authentication, authorization, and attributes. Assertions are issued by SAML authorities, namely authentication authorities, attribute authorities, or policy decision points. SAML can be used to make assertions about credentials; however, it does not provide mechanisms to check or revoke credentials. This means that the party accepting a SAML assertion as true is trusting the SAML authority that issued the assertion. A service provider may need also to have detailed information about the type and strength of authentication used by an identity provider when it authenticated the user; to carry this information, SAML provides the *authentication context*, which is conveyed in (or referenced by) an assertion's authentication statement. The framework defined by SAML is intended to support many real-world business scenarios, from those in which the client is a browser to more complex ones where multiple Web services are involved. In particular, SAML supports the following scenarios:

Web single sign-on (SSO), where a user authenticates to one Web site and then, without additional authentication, is able to access resources at another site. SAML enables Web SSO through the communication of an authentication assertion from the first site to the second one, which, if confident of the origin of the assertion, can decide to allow the user to log in as if he had authenticated directly.

Attribute-based authorization. In this scenario, which is similar to the Web SSO one, one Web site communicates identity information about a subject to another Web site in support of some transaction. However, the identity information needed by the receiving Web site may refer to some characteristic of the subject (such as a person's role in a B2B scenario) rather than, or in addition to, information about when and how the subject was authenticated. The attribute-based authorization model is used when the subject's particular identity either is not important or should not be shared (for privacy reasons), or is insufficient on its own.

Securing SOAP messages. SAML assertions can be used within SOAP messages in order to carry security and identity information between actors in Web service transactions. The SAML Token Profile of the OASIS WS-Security TC specifies how SAML assertions should be used for this purpose. The Liberty Alliance's Identity Web Service Framework (ID-WSF) also uses SAML assertions as the base security tokens for enabling secure and privacy respecting access to Web services.

The SAML threat model [131] identifies the assumptions, the scope, and the security techniques to adopt when deploying SAML-based solutions, by considering the concerns arising during communications in the request-response protocol, or during the use of SAML by a receiving party. The SAML threat model makes the following assumptions:

- The endpoints involved in a SAML transaction are uncompromised, but the attacker has complete control over the communications channel.
- It is possible for a valid participant in an SAML transaction to use the information maliciously in another transaction.
- SAML allows one to make authentication and authorization statements, but does not specify how authentications are executed or how authorizations are established. The consequence is that the security of a system based on assertions as inputs depends on the security of the system used to generate those assertions. When determining what issuers to trust, particularly in cases where the assertions will be used as inputs to authentication or authorization decisions, the risk of security compromises arising from the consumption of false but validly issued assertions is a major one.

Trust policies between asserting and relying parties should always be written to include significant consideration of liability, and implementations must provide an audit trail.

- An assertion, once issued, is out of the control of the issuer. This fact has a number of consequences. For example, the issuer has no control over how long the assertion will persist in the systems of the consumer; nor does the issuer have control over the parties with whom the consumer will share the assertion information. These concerns add to the concerns about a malicious attacker who can see the contents of assertions that pass unencrypted over the wire.
- SAML protocol is prone to Denial of Service (DOS) attacks. This risk can be averted by requiring client authentication at a lower level, by requiring signed requests from a client, or by restricting the ability to issue SAML requests to a limited number of known parties.

4.3.4 SOAP Message Security

In a Web service setting, SOAP messages constitute the communication unit whose integrity and confidentiality must be protected. SOAP messages might be subject to various types of attacks, such as:

- the message could be modified or read by an attacker.
- an attacker could send to a Web service well-formed messages that lack appropriate security claims to warrant processing.
- an attacker could alter a message sent to the Web service but the attacker might preserve the message's well formedness, causing the service to process the request and to respond to the client for an incorrect request.

Moreover, SOAP messages can traverse multiple applications, that is, one or more SOAP intermediaries, and multiple trust domains within and between business entities, e.g. companies, divisions, and business units, as shown in Figure 4.8. Hence, there is the need to provide an end-to-end protection over multiple hops to assure SOAP message integrity and confidentiality, as well as to verify the requester's identity. These goals can be achieved by using XML encryption and XML signatures. However, it is necessary to standardize the representation of the additional security information within SOAP messages themselves, so that the software component processing them, that is, the SOAP processor, can properly manage the security information.

WS-Security

WS-Security [197] can be considered as a de facto standard for securing SOAP messages in the Web. Work on WS-Security began in 2001. WS-Security was then approved as an OASIS standard in June 2002. WS-Security specifies extensions to SOAP that allow one to selectively encrypt or sign parts of SOAP messages, such as encrypting different parts of a SOAP message for different

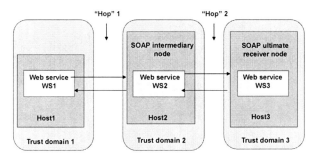

Fig. 4.8. WS-Security: multi-hop message path

recipients. This is achieved by leveraging the XML Encryption standard to protect the messages' confidentiality, and the XML Signature standard to protect message integrity. WS-Security applies to a single SOAP message. In order to secure exchanges composed of multiple SOAP messages, further extensions to it were defined in the WS-SecureConversation standard [277].

WS-Security supports multiple security token formats, multiple trust domains, multiple signature formats, and multiple encryption technologies. A security token represents a collection of declarations (also called claims) made by an entity about some its own properties which are relevant for security purposes. Examples of such properties are a name, an identity, a key, a privilege, and a capability. These security-related pieces of information can be conveyed by X.509 certificates, Kerberos tickets and authenticators, mobile device security tokens from SIM cards, username, SAML assertions and so forth.

A security token can also be signed, that is, "endorsed" or certified, by a specific third-party authority different from the entity the assertion (or claim) refers to. An example is an X.509 certificate or a Kerberos ticket. A signed security token is basically used as a means to authenticate the claim made by the entity. The token formats and the semantics for using them are defined in the associated profile documents. The SOAP extensions introduced by WS-Security take the form of a SOAP Header elements (wsse, ws security elements) which carry security-related data, as illustrated in Figure 4.9.

WS-Security specifies a general-purpose mechanism for referencing and/or including so-called security tokens within SOAP messages.

WS-Security is neutral with respect to the type of security token used. Various security token formats have been specified for use with WS-Security, including username/password, SAML assertions [62], XrML/REL tokens [280], X.509 certificates [279], and Kerberos tickets [278]. For security tokens that are not encoded in XML, such as X.509 certificates and Kerberos tickets, WS-Security provides a mechanism for encoding binary security tokens. Due to the variety of supported security token formats, WS-Security is enough flexible to accommodate specific purposes and specific security architectures. Moreover, it can be extended with profiles to support new security tokens.

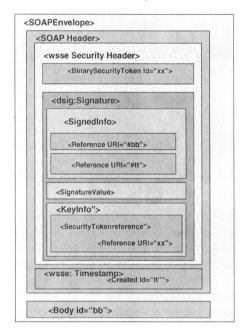

Fig. 4.9. WS-Security: wsse elements layout

Message integrity is provided by using XML Signature in conjunction with security tokens, which may contain or imply key data. WS-Security supports multiple signatures, potentially by multiple parties, and it can be extended to support additional signature formats. The signatures may reference, that is, point to, a security token. WS-Security assures message confidentiality by encrypting portions of the SOAP message according to XML Encryption standard in conjunction with security tokens. The encryption mechanisms are designed to support additional encryption technologies, processes, and operations by multiple parties. The encryption may also reference a security token.

However, it is worth noting that WS-Security in itself defines a protocol, and, as such, any implementation of it is vulnerable to a wide range of attacks. The WS-Security specification provides a non-exhaustive list of security concerns, such as replay attacks, man-in-the middle attacks, token substitution attacks and so forth, that are to be considered in a more complete security analysis of the protocol.

WS-SecureConversations

To complete a meaningful transaction, a client and a Web service often need to exchange multiple SOAP messages. Thus, it is important to secure not only a single SOAP message at time, but also multiple SOAP messages. WS-SecureConversation [277] is an OASIS standard which basically allows the two communicating parties to establish and manage a session at the SOAP message level. WS-Conversation defines extensions, based on WS-Security and WS-Trust [196], aimed at providing such secure communication across multiple messages, and in particular, the authentication of multiple messages. These extensions are based on the establishment and sharing of a so-called security context between the communicating parties and on the derivation of keys from the established security contexts. A security context is shared among the communicating parties for the lifetime of a communication session. A security context is represented by a security context token, which basically conveys a secret or a key. This secret might be used for signing and/or encrypting SOAP messages, but the specification recommends the use of derived keys for signing and encrypting messages associated only with the security context.

SOAP messages belonging to the same message exchange can reference the same security context token. Such an approach achieves a more efficient exchange of keys or of new key information, thereby increasing the overall performance and security of the subsequent exchanges. A security context needs to be created and shared by the communicating parties before being used. WS-SecureConversation defines three different strategies for establishing a security context among the parties of a secure communication:

- The context initiator can request an Security Token Service (STS), as defined by WS-Trust, to create a security context token.
- A security context token can be created by one of the communicating parties and propagated within a message; it should be noted that this scenario requires that parties trust each other to share a secret key.
- A security context token can be created when needed through a negotiation between the participants. This scenario applies when the message exchange participants need to negotiate and agree on the contents of the security context token, such as the shared secret.

WS-Reliability

Guaranteeing the integrity and confidentiality of the SOAP messages does not prevent them from being lost, duplicated, or reordered. When an application-level messaging protocol, such as SOAP, must also guarantee some level of reliability in addition to security, HTTP is not sufficient.

Delivery guarantee is assured by several middleware components implementing the "store & forward" paradigm, such as Microsoft Message Queuing (MSMQ) [182], IBM Messaging and Queuing (WebSphere, MQ) [136], and Sun Java System Message Queue[246].

WS-Reliability [143] defines a messaging protocol to manage the reliable delivery of messages between exactly two parties, a source and a destination, referred to as the Reliable Messaging (RM) Source and RM Destination, respectively, despite failures affecting a software component, an entire system, or the network. WS-Reliability does not make any assumption about the implementation of the messaging processor service: such a component could be

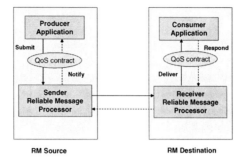

Fig. 4.10. WS-Reliability

an application, a queuing or logging system, a database, a SOAP node, or the
next handler in the message processing chain. For this aspect, WS-Reliability
addresses the interoperability of heterogeneous reliable messaging middleware.
WS-Reliability defines both a "wire" protocol, that is, specific message headers and specific message choreographies between the sending application and
the receiving application, and a protocol to be used between the application and the underlying message processor service (i.e., the reliable messaging
middleware), as shown in Figure 4.10. The latter implements a Quality of
Service (QoS) contract between the application and the underlying messaging
processor service.

Such a QoS contract consists of four operations (Submit, Deliver, Respond,
and Notify) and encompasses four basic delivery assurances:

- The AtMostOnce assurance guarantees that messages will be delivered at
  most once without duplication or an error will be raised at at least one
  endpoint. It is possible that some messages in a sequence may not be
  delivered.
- The AtLeastOnce assurance guarantees that every message sent will be
  delivered or an error will be raised at at least one endpoint. Some messages
  may be delivered more than once.
- The ExactlyOnce assurance guarantees that every message sent will be
  delivered without duplication or an error will be raised at at least one
  endpoint.
- The InOrder assurance guarantees that messages will be delivered in the
  order in which they were sent. Such a delivery assurance may be combined with any of the above delivery assurances. It does not provide any
  assurance about message duplications or omissions.

4.3.5 Key and Trust Management standards

Public keys are the basic building block for signatures and digital certificates. Public key management encompasses their creation, their safe storage,
their distribution, their use, and their cancellation. Public keys either can be

created by a software package running on the platform of the customer application and then registered to a Public Key Infrastructure (PKI) Certification Authority (CA), or the customer application may request a CA participating to a PKI infrastructure to issue them. When a party uses a public key, it needs to ascertain its validity, that is, it needs to verify that the public key has not expired or has been revoked. Public keys can be issued by different CAs too, and a given party might have more than one public key associated with it. However, the current PKIs, based on proprietary toolkits, makes the interactions between the client applications and the PKI costly and difficult. Furthermore, client applications have to implement by themselves the costly operations of signature validation, chain validation, and revocation checking. Hence, there is the need to simplify the task of the relying parties when using public keys, as well as to allow different CAs', or even different PKIs, to interoperate among them. Furthermore, public keys can be represented in XML, and are the basis of XML Encryption and XML Signature. The issues described above led to the definition of a standard for XML Key Management.

Moreover, while WS-Security defines the basic mechanisms for providing secure messaging, a SOAP message protected by WS-Security presents three possible issues with regard to security tokens: i) security token format incompatibility; ii) namespace differences; iii) the trustworthiness of the security token. To overcome the above issues, there was the need to define standard extensions to WS-Security in order to provide methods for issuing, renewing, and validating security tokens, and to establish and assess the presence of, and broker, trust relationships. These requirements led to the development of the WS-Trust standard.

XML Key Management Standard (XKMS)

XML Key Management Standard (XKMS) [106] is a W3C note, made available by the W3C for discussion only, that defines standard Web-based interfaces and protocols for registering and distributing public keys. A key objective of XKMS is to relieve the applications from the complexity and syntax of the underlying Public Key Infrastructure (PKI) used to establish trust relationships. The XKMS specification defines the interfaces to two services: the XML Key Information Service (X-KISS). , and the XML Key Registration Service (X-KRSS) .

As shown in Figure 4.11, an X-KISS service provides the client two functions, which can be implemented by the X-KISS service itself or by an underlying PKI. For encryption purposes, the *locate* function allows a sender not knowing the key bound to a recipient to obtain it. For example, if Alice wants to send an encrypted email to Bob but does not know his encryption key, Alice can use DNS to locate the XKMS service that provides a locate service for keys bound to the domain of Bob (say example.com), and then send an XKMS locate request to the discovered XKMS service for a key bound to bob@example.com. The X-KISS service, however, does not make any assertion concerning the validity of the binding between the data and the key. Alice

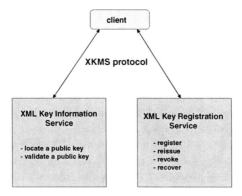

Fig. 4.11. XKMS services

has to verify that the certificate obtained meets its trust criteria by validating the certificate to a trusted root. The locate function also allows a recipient of a signed document, who does not know the key used for the signature, to obtain it.

As for the validation of a key, the information provided by the signer may be insufficient for the receiver to perform the cryptographic verification and decide whether to trust the signing key, or the information may not be in a format the receiver can use. The *validate* function allows the client to obtain from the X-KISS service an assertion specifying the status, that is, the validity, of the binding between the public key and other data, for example a name or a set of extended attributes. Furthermore, the X-KISS service represents that all the data elements are bound to the same public key.

X-KRSS defines a protocol for registration and subsequent management of public key information. The X-KRSS service specification supports the following operations:

- Register. Information is bound to a public key pair through a key binding. The bound information may include a name, an identifier, or extended attributes defined by the implementation.
- Reissue. A previously registered key binding is reissued.
- Revoke. A previously registered key binding is revoked.
- Recover. The private key associated with a key binding is recovered.

XKMS evolved further into XKMS 2.0 [125].

As described in [130], a simple client should be able to make use of sophisticated key management functionality, without being concerned with the details of the infrastructure required to support the public key management. Moreover, XML-based applications should be provided a public key management support that is consistent with the public key management requirements of XML Encryption [96], XML Signature [97], and with the Security Assertion Markup Language standards [222].

WS-Trust

The WS-Trust 1.3 Specification [196] is an OASIS standard. It defines extensions to WS-Security that provide a framework for requesting and issuing security tokens, for assessing the presence of trust relationships, and for brokering trust relationships.

In WS-Trust, trust relationships are conveyed by security tokens. A security token represents a collection of claims, where a claim is a statement made about a client, service or other resource (e.g., name, identity, key, group, privilege, capability). In particular, a signed security token is a security token that is cryptographically endorsed by a specific authority (e.g., an X.509 certificate or a Kerberos ticket). In WS-Trust, security tokens are issued by a so-called Security Token Service (STS). The STS issues assertions based on evidence that it trusts, to whoever trusts it or to specific recipients. An STS can be implemented by a Kerberos Key Distribution Center (KDC) or by a public key infrastructure. In such cases, the issuing authority is the STS.

WS-Trust assumes a Web service security model in which:

- A Web service can require that an incoming message proves a set of claims such as name, key, permission, and capability.
- A Web service can indicate its required claims and related information in its policy according to the WS-Policy and WS-PolicyAttachment specifications.
- A Web service is equipped with a trust engine that:
  – verifies that the claims in the token are sufficient to comply with the policy and that the message conforms to the policy.
  – verifies that the attributes of the claimant are proved by the signatures. In brokered trust models, the signature may not verify the identity of the claimant. It may instead verify the identity of the intermediary, who may simply assert the identity of the claimant.
  – verifies that the issuers of the security tokens, including all related and issuing security tokens, are trusted to issue the claims they have made. The trust engine may need to externally verify or broker tokens, that is, to send tokens to a STS in order to exchange them for other security tokens that it can use directly in its evaluation.

An STS service provides several functions to the clients. It allows a client to request the issuance of a new security token, or a set of security tokens. The requester can optionally specify the type of the requested security token, the desired valid time range of the security token, as well as the scope the security token is required for, such as, for example, the services to which it applies. The STS allows a client to renew an already issued security token and to cancel a previously issued security token when the token is no longer needed. A security token can be canceled also by an STS initiative. Finally, an STS allows a client to validate a security token. The validation's result may consist in a status, a new token, or both.

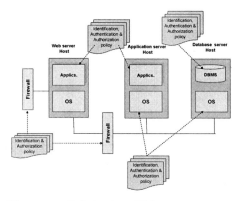

Fig. 4.12. Policies in a Web service setting

4.3.6 Standards for Policy Specification

The policy concept encompasses several different meanings, from guiding principles and procedures, to management policies represented according to the Event-Condition-Action paradigm, to authorization policies. According to the IETF [2], a policy can be defined as:

"A definite goal, course or method of action to guide and determine present and future decisions."

Moreover, a policy [2]:

"can be represented at different levels of abstraction, ranging from business goals to device-specific configuration parameters. Translation between different levels of abstraction may require information other than policy, such as network and host parameter configuration and capabilities. Various documents and implementations may specify explicit levels of abstraction."

Figure 4.12, which represents a usual three-tier configuration for a Web service in a Demilitarized Zone (DMZ), shows the variety of policies that govern a Web service setting, from firewall policies, usually conveyed by configurations, to access control policies at the operating system and database system level, to policies which control the invocation of operations provided by a Web application.

In a Web service setting, policies have to express requirements of different types related to different aspects of a Web service such as message security, access control to the service's resources, quality of protection, quality of service, and so forth. By representing and exposing policies in a standard, commonly understood way, a Web service provider can specify the conditions under which its Web services can be used, and the potential Web service clients can decide whether to use the services or not.

Web Services Policy Framework (WS-Policy)

The Web Services Policy Framework (WS-Policy) standard provides an extensible model and a single grammar that allows Web services to describe their policies. The WS-Policy standard was conceived to provide a general model, suitable for expressing all types of domain-specific policy models, from transport-level security, to resource usage policy, QoS characteristics, and end-to-end business-process-level policy. At the core of the model is the concept of *policy assertion*, which specifies a behavior, that is, a requirement or a capability, of a policy subject. The semantics of the assertions is domain-specific (e.g., security, transactions). The approach adopted by WS-Policy is to define domain-specific assertions in separate specifications. Policy assertions can be defined in public specifications, like WS-SecurityPolicy [195] and WS-PolicyAssertion [276], or by the entity owning the Web service. The assertions of the first type are called standard assertions and they potentially can be understood by any client. As an example of standard domain-specific assertions, protection requirements for SOAP messages, that is, confidentiality and integrity requirements, are defined as protection assertions in the WS-SecurityPolicy standard specification [195]. A WS-SecurityPolicy integrity assertion specifies which parts of a SOAP message, i.e. headers, body, and/or specific elements, must be signed. It is worth noting that this assertion can be satisfied by using SOAP Message Security mechanisms, that is, by using WS-Security, or by using other mechanisms out of the scope of SOAP message security, for example, by sending the message over a secure transport protocol like HTTPS. The subject which the policy applies to is a Message Policy subject (a SOAP message) and the WS-PolicyAttachment standard [1] specifies to which WSDL entity or UDDI entity the policy applies to. Policy assertions can be combined in policy alternatives, and at the highest level, a policy is a collection of policy alternatives.

To convey policy in an interoperable form, WS-Policy adopts a normal form schema shown in Figure 4.13. In this schema, which basically expresses a policy as an (exclusive) ORed set of ANDed sets of statements, * indicates zero or more occurrences of an item, while [ ] indicates that the contained items must be treated as a group.

```
<wsp:Policy ... >
 <wsp:ExactlyOne>
    [<wsp:All> [<Assertion ...> ... </Assertion> ]* </wsp:All> ]*
 </wsp:ExactlyOne>
</wsp:Policy>
```

Fig. 4.13. Normal form schema of a policy according to WS-Policy

An example of a policy that adheres to the WS-Policy specification is illustrated in Figure 4.14. This example, taken from the WS-Policy specification, shows two policy alternatives, each composed by a single policy assertion. The policy has to be interpreted as follows: if the first alternative is selected, only the Kerberos token type is supported; conversely, if the second alternative is selected, only the X.509 token type is supported.

```
<wsp:Policy xml:base=http://dico.unimi.it wsu:Id=MyPolicy>
<wsp:ExactlyOne>
<wsp:All>
<wsse:SecurityToken>
<wsse:TokenType>wsse:Kerberosv5TGT</wsse:TokenType>
/wsse:SecurityToken>
</wsp:All>
<wsp:All>
<wsse:SecurityToken>
<wsse:TokenType>wsse:X509v3</wsse:TokenType>
</wsse:SecurityToken>
</wsp:All>
</wsp:ExactlyOne>
</wsp:Policy>
```

Fig. 4.14. An example of a policy

WS-Policy does not provide any explicit language for representing the rules used by a Web service provider to evaluate a request against its own policies. However, WS-Policy defines the conditions under which a requester can satisfy, respectively, the Web service's policy assertions, policy alternatives, and finally the whole policy, namely:

- a policy assertion is supported by a requester if and only if the requester satisfies the requirement (or accommodates the capability) corresponding to the assertion.
- a policy alternative is supported by a requester if and only if the requester supports all the assertions in the alternative.
- a policy is supported by a requester if and only if the requester supports at least one of the alternatives in the policy.

The Policy Framework is supplemented by three other standards. The first one, WS-PolicyAssertions [276] , specifies the structure of a few generic policy assertions. The second one, WS-Policy Attachment [1] , defines how to associate a policy with a Web service, either by directly embedding it in the WSDL definition or by indirectly associating it through UDDI. By attaching policies to WSDL or UDDI, the service provider makes them publicly available to the potential clients of the Web service when they try to discover services they are potentially interested in. WS-PolicyAttachment also defines how to associate implementation-specific policies with all or part of a WSDL portType when exposed from a specific implementation. The third one, WS-SecurityPolicy

[195] , specifies a set of standard security policy assertions corresponding to SOAP message protection requirements, that is, message integrity assertion, message confidentiality assertion, and message security token assertion. A WS-Security policy exposed through WSDL or UDDI, allows requesters to determine if WS-Security is optional or mandatory for a given Web service. If it is mandatory, the requesters can determine the security token type the Web service understands or prefers. Requesters can also determine whether they need to sign the messages and which parts to sign. Finally, requesters can determine whether to encrypt the message and, if so, what algorithm to use.

4.3.7 Access Control Policy Standards

In a Web service setting, there is the need to define, deploy, and maintain several *access control policies* (see also Appendix A) so that the access to a given resource, be it a database, a Web service, or a Web service operation, is granted to entitled users. In addition, there is the need to protect digital information at rest, which constitutes one of the most valuable asset of an enterprise. The two aspects mentioned above constitute the scope of "traditional" access control policies. However, the explosion of digital information within business organizations called not only for protecting it against mishandling and malicious use, but also for controlling its dissemination to proper recipients, internally or externally to the enterprise boundary, by defining, deploying and enforcing suitable *information flow policies.*

In this section we briefly discuss two standards, eXtensible Access Control Mark-up Language (XACML), and eXtensible Right Markup Language (XrML), which address, respectively, access control and information flow policies.

eXtensible Access Control Markup Language (XACML)

Access control policies are complex and they must be enforced at many points. In a distributed environment, such as a Web service setting, implementing access control policies by configuring them at every point makes policy changes expensive and unreliable. Moreover, access control policies are often expressed through different and proprietary languages, preventing one to share them among different applications. XACML [188] was conceived to solve these issues, by providing a single, standard language to define access control policies. XACML version 2.0 was approved as an OASIS standard in February of 2005, along with six profiles of XACML: SAML 2.0, XML Digital Signature, Privacy Policy, Hierarchical Resource, Multiple Resource, and Core and Hierarchical Role-Based Access Control (RBAC). XACML was conceived as one component of a distributed and interoperable authorization framework, with the following underlying rationale:

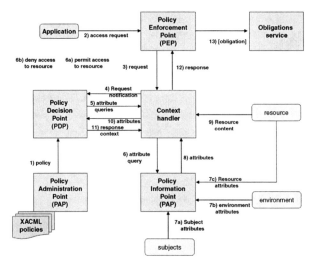

Fig. 4.15. XACML data flow model

- first, access control policies do not have to be embedded or tightly linked to the system they govern.
- second, XACML policies can be applied to different heterogeneous resources such as XML documents, relational databases, application servers, and Web services, and at different granularity levels.
- third, XACML policies should be able to take into account specific characteristics of the environment determined at runtime, such as the system load of the host running a Web service.
- fourth, a standard policy exchange format should be defined that allows different resource managers, such as Web services, to exchange or share authorization policies, as well as to deploy the same policy in heterogeneous systems. If different organizations use internally native policy languages, the standard policy exchange format can be translated into the native policy language.

It is worth noting that XACML includes also a non-normative data flow model ([188], Section 3.1, Data flow model) that describes the logical agents involved in the processing of an access request. This model, represented in Figure 4.15, can be considered as an evolution of the ISO 10181-3 model [140]. However, ISO 10181-3 defines an architecture for access control, but not a language. In ISO 10181-3 terms, XACML specifies an Access Control Decision Function (ADF), and defines its interactions with an Access Control Enforcement Point (AEF).

As shown in figure 4.15, the XACML Context Handler insulates the application from the canonical representation for the inputs and outputs used by the PDP. In practice, it is up to the Context Handler to translate application access requests from their original format to the canonical format above. At its core, XACML defines the syntax for a policy language, the semantics for processing those policies, and a request-response protocol between the PEP and the PDP.

The basic building block of a XACML policy is a rule. The main components of a rule are:

- a *target*. It defines the set of requests to which the rule is intended to apply, in the form of a logical expression on attributes in the request. The target, in turn, is a triple <subject, action, object>, which is the usual conceptual representation of an access control policy.
- an *effect*. It indicates the rule writer's intended consequence of a "True" evaluation for the rule. Two values are allowed: "Permit" and "Deny";
- an optional *condition*. It is a boolean expression that refines the applicability of the rule beyond the predicates implied by its target.

By representing the target as an XML-based logical expression, the rule or policy can be equated with a rule of a logic-based language of the form $p(x)$ -> Permit/Deny.

Multiple rules can be encapsulated in a policy, and multiple policies can be contained in a PolicySet . This choice stems from the fact that a single policy might consist of any number of decentralized, distributed rules, each managed by a different organizational group, and that multiple policies might need to be taken into account, each of them expressing the access control requirements of a particular stakeholder. As an example of multiple policies, in a personal privacy application the owner of the personal information may specify certain aspects of a disclosure policy, whereas the enterprise that is the custodian of the information may specify other aspects. When using a rule-based approach, multiple rules (or even multiple policies), might be applicable to an incoming request. Thus, there is the need for specifying the order in which policy rules (or different applicable policies) are to be evaluated. To this end, XACML defines a set of combining algorithms, which state how to arrive at an authorization decision from multiple rules or policies. There are a number of standard combining algorithms defined, namely first applicable, only one applicable, deny overrides, permit overrides, as well as a standard extension mechanism to define new algorithms.

In XACML it is thus possible to specify a policy like "MPEG movie for adults cannot be accessed by users with age less than 18 years". Referring to this example, the subject is the user requesting an MPEG movie for downloading from a Web service. The subject can have associated an age attribute, and a predicate "age > 18 years" can be defined on it. The movie is the resource to which access must be controlled. An attribute specifying the movie category (for example 'adult only') is associated with the movie resource.

As for the request/response protocol between the PEP and the PDP, a request consists of attributes associated with the requesting subjects, the resource acted upon, the action being performed, and the environment. A response contains one of four decisions: permit, deny, not applicable (no applicable policies or rules could be found), or indeterminate (in case some error occurred during processing). In the case of an error, optional information is available to explain the error. Responses may also include obligations, which are directives from the applicable policies for the PEP to execute.

As for the security aspects, it is worth remembering that the XACML agents, that is PDP, PEP, and PIP, might reside at different hosts. Consequently, XACML assumes that the adversary has access to the communication channel between the XACML agents and is able to interpret, insert, delete, and modify messages or parts of messages. Moreover, an agent may use information from a former message maliciously in subsequent transactions. The main consequences are that rules and policies are only as reliable as the agents that create and use them, and that it is the duty of each agent to establish appropriate trust in the other agent it relies upon. Safeguard mechanisms such as mutual authentication of PEP and PDP are recommended by the XACML specification, as well the use of suitable access control mechanisms to protect the XACML policy base and the use of signature mechanisms to protect the integrity and the authenticity of an XACML policy when it is distributed between organizations. Mechanisms for trust establishment are outside the scope of the XACML specification.

OASIS XACML Profile for Web-Services [14], hereafter referred to as XACML2, is a proposal to define how to use XACML in a standard way in order to address authorization, access control, and privacy policy in a Web service environment.

XACML2 specifies a standard XACML assertion type and two specific assertions derived from it, namely an XACMLAuthzAssertion for authorization policies, and an XACMLPrivacyAssertion for privacy policies. An XACML assertion can be used to express policy requirements, policy capabilities, or both. Policy requirements describe information or behaviors that an entity requires from another party. Policy capabilities describe information or behaviors that an entity is willing and able to provide to another party. Hence, a Web service provider can use a XACML assertion to express or publish its own requirements or its capabilities for complying with requirements imposed by a Web service consumer. Conversely, a Web service consumer can use a XACML assertion to express or publish its own requirements or its capabilities for complying with requirements imposed by a Web service provider. An XACML assertion must have a scope, that is, a XACML policy, which must be explicitly referred to by the assertion or identified in some other way.

Web consumers and Web service providers XACML assertions have to be matched in order to determine whether they are compatible, that is, if what the consumer requires can be provided by the Web service and viceversa. Matching is done by computing the intersection of the requirements in each XACML assertion with the capabilities in the other XACML assertion. For each of the original XACML assertions, the result of the intersection is a new XACML assertion containing in its requirements the intersection of the original requirements with the original capabilities of the other XACML assertion, and containing in its capabilities the intersection of the original capabilities with the original requirements of the other XACML assertion.

eXtensible Right Mark-up Language (XrML)

Techniques and tools used to provide perimeter-based security, such as firewalls which limit access to the network, and access control systems that restrict access to stored data, cannot enforce business rules that control how people use and distribute the data outside the perimeter.

The control and the enforcement of digital information distribution and use have been tackled by the so-called Digital Right Management (DRM). The term is frequently referred by both copyright legislation and content owners when seeking means to control use of their intellectual property. DRM systems and related standards originated from the music industry with the goal of preventing users from illegally copying copyright-protected digital music without compensation to publishers and content owners. Central to DRM is a unified approach for specifying, interpreting, enforcing, and managing digital rights throughout the entire life cycle of digital assets. DRM systems basically accomplish two main functions. The first is a monitoring function, which allows one to track what is actually being transferred over the network and to which recipients. The second is an access and usage control function, controlling what users can or cannot do with digital contents transferred to their own computer. The description of the actions allowed to users on a digital content is conceptually similar to the description of the actions in an access control policy. The access control policy is tied to the digital content itself in a secure box [152], so that the digital content travels together with the description of the access control policy that applies to it. The DRM approach assumes that a DRM engine runs on the device (be it a PC, a mobile phone, or a PDA) where the digital content is accessed by the user. The DRM engine enforces the specific access and usage control policy associated with the digital content. Exchange of information about access rights associated with digital content is an integral part of DRM, and hence there was the need to standardize their description through a rights expression language (REL) so that potentially diverse DRM engines running on heterogeneous platforms could interpret and enforce them. The first development of a rights expression language was started at Xerox's Palo Alto Research Center (PARC) in 1994. The result of such effort has been a computer-interpretable language, called the Digital Property Rights Language (DPRL), for describing rights, conditions, and fees for using digital work. The first version of DPRL, v1.0, originally written in LISP, was released in March 1996, and the second version, v2.0, defined using the XML DTD, in November 1998.

In 1999 DPRL was renamed as eXtensible Right Markup Language^{TM} and its first version, XrML, v1.0, was introduced in April 2000 by ContentGuard Inc., an independent spin-off company of Xerox, which retains a trademark

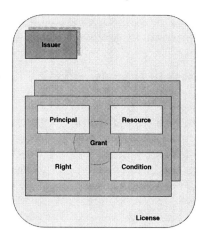

Fig. 4.16. XrML: License and Grant

on it. XrML v2.0 was released in November 2001. In November 2001, ContentGuard Inc. submitted XrML 2.0 to the Moving Picture Experts Group (MPEG) [193] working group (ISO/IEC) in response to their Call for Proposals for a Rights Data Dictionary and Rights Description Language. XrML was then selected as the basis for MPEG-21 REL [52].

XrML is a XML language which specifies how to describe rights, fees, and conditions for using digital contents (or properties), with message integrity and entity authentication. XrML was conceived to support commerce in digital contents, that is, publishing and selling electronic books, digital movies, digital music, interactive games, computer software, and other creations distributed in digital form. It was intended to support specification of access and use controls for secure digital objects also in cases where financial exchange was not part of the terms of use.

The XrML model is based on the concept that a right is granted by an issuer to a principal to use a resource under certain conditions, as shown in Figure 4.16.

The principal entity represents the subject whom one or more rights on a resource are granted. Each principal identifies only one subject. A principal can prove her identity by different authentication mechanisms, including:

- The keyHolder mechanism. It indicates that the subject is identified as possessing a secret key such as the private key of a public/private key pair. KeyHolders are represented using the KeyInfo element from XML Signature.
- The multiple credentials mechanism. In order to be authenticated the principal must present multiple credentials that must be validated simultaneously.

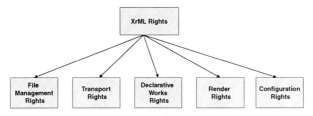

Fig. 4.17. XrML Rights

A right represents an action (or a set of actions) that a principal can perform on the granted resource, as shown in Figure 4.17.

The XrML 2.0 Core specification [293] also defines a set of commonly used, specific rights, notably rights relating to other rights, such as issue, revoke, delegate, and obtain. Extensions to the XrML Core could define rights appropriate for using specific types of resources. For instance, the XrML content extension defines rights appropriate for using digital works (for instance, play and print rights). A resource entity represents the object over which a right can be granted to a principal. A resource can be a digital work, such as an audio or video file, or an image, a service, such as an email service, or even a piece of information that can be owned by a principal, such as a name, an email address, a role, or any other property or attribute. A resource can also be a rights expression itself. A condition entity specifies the terms, the conditions, and the obligations under which a principal can exercise her rights on the resource. For example, a condition might specify a temporal interval, the number of times that the resource can be accessed, and so on. An issuer identifies a principal who issues rights. The issuer can also supply a digital signature signed by the principal to signify that the principal does indeed bestow the rights issued, and to facilitate reliable establishment of trustworthiness of the rights information by others. The license structure represents the issuance of a grant by an issuer.

4.4 Implementations of Web Services Security Standards

In this section we give an overview of the available implementations of Web services security standards provided by the most common platforms, i.e. Microsoft .NET, Java, by open software and finally by the so-called XML security appliances. This overview is not aimed at precisely identifying if a given implementation is compliant with a specific standard version, but rather at giving some indications about the adoption level of different Web service security standards.

Microsoft .NET 2.0 platform [185] supports XML encryption and XML signature. Web Services Enhancements for Microsoft .NET (WSE) [275] provides a .NET class library for building Web services which includes WS-Security, WS-SecureConversation, WS-Trust, and WS-Addressing.

As to the Java platform, Sun Microsystems and IBM have published the final release of JSR 105, XML Digital Signature APIs, to the Java Community Process (JCP) [78] and the JSR-000106 XML Digital Encryption APIs [79]. JSR 105 is available as part of the Java Web Services Developer Pack 1.6.

The Java Web Service Development Platform (WSDP) 1.5 defined the XWS-Security framework which provides security functionalities for JAX-RPC applications [171]. This framework supports the following security options:

- XML Digital Signature: The implementation uses Apache's XML-DSig implementation, which is based on the XML Signature specification.
- XML Encryption: The implementation uses Apache's XML-Enc implementation, which is based on the XML Encryption specification.
- Username Token Profile and X.509 Certificate Token Profile support, based on the OASIS WSS Username Token Profile 1.0 and the OASIS WSS X.509 Certificate Token Profile 1.0, respectively.

In June 2005, Sun launched Project GlassFish, with the goal of creating an open-source Java EE 5 application server through a developer community. The GlassFish community is developing Project Metro [181], an extensible Web service stack which will include full support of the OASIS Web service Security (WSS) 1.1 standard, and partial support of OASIS WSS Username-Token Profile 1.1, OASIS WSS X509 Token Profile 1.1, OASIS WSS SAML Token Profile 1.1, and OASIS WSS SOAP Messages with Attachments SWA Profile 1.

4.5 Standards-related Issues

Web service security standards raise several interrelated technical and management issues. Technical issues concern specific security threats posed by the Web service security standards themselves and their implementations and how to address them during the Web service life cycle, the degree of interoperability that can be really achieved by their adoption, and the performance overhead incurred when deploying software solutions implementing the standards.

Management issues are over and above technical ones. They include, to mention just some of them, the tradeoff between the organization interoperability requirements and the organization security requirement, the costs incurred when deploying and using standard compliant features provided by the development and deployment platform, the training needed to provide developers and operational management personnel the skills required to properly learn and use standardized security functions in an effective way.

Security issues

As we saw in the previous sections, Web service security standards specifications describe, to different extents, the security concerns which standards' implementers or users should be aware of. These security concerns vary depending on the purpose of the standard, and may affect the standards implementers as well as the applications using the standards implementation. As an example of the former, in XACML it is up to the implementers of the standard to duly consider and embed in the standard implementation mechanisms for protecting the protocol used by the various XACML agents (PDP, PEP, PIP, etc.). As an example of the latter, it is up to the applications using XML Encryption, and hence to the application developers, to be aware of cryptographic vulnerabilities that may arise when combining digital signatures and encryption over a common XML element [96, Section 6]. Similarly, it is up to the applications using XML Signature [97, Section 8] to be aware of the potential harm on an XML parser based on the Document Object Model (DOM) that derive from XML transformations, such as character encoding transformations [87], canonicalization instructions [97, Section 6.5], and XSLT transformations [97, Section 6.6.5] [70]. Overall, while it can be assumed that standards implementers have the competence and the knowledge needed to achieve this end, the situation can be quite different with the application developers. Hence, the adoption of a Web service security standard requires us to educate and train application developers not only on security fundamentals, but also on how to use the standard itself.

Interoperability issues

Web service standards specifications can be very rich and complex, due to the extensibility mechanisms they provide and their evolving nature. Moreover, not all the features of a given standard specification need to be implemented in order for the implementation to conform to the standards specification[2]. A possible consequence is that different implementations of the same standard specification might not be completely interoperable. To help solve these problems, the Web Services Interoperability organization (WS-I), an industry consortium whose primary goal is to promote Web Services interoperability across many technology substrates (platforms, OSs, languages, and so forth), was established. The approach of WS-I is based on the use of profiles. A profile of a single standards specification basically consists of an agreed-upon subset and interpretation of the specification that provides guidelines to the standards specification implementers and users to achieve an effective interoperability. The profiles developed by WS-I apply to a specific group of non-proprietary Web service specifications at specific version levels. The first one is WS-I Basic Profile 1.1, which covers aspects of SOAP, WSDL, UDDI, and HTTPS by providing clarifications and amendments to those specifications that promote

---

[2] In any specific standards specification, normative statements that conforming implementations must adhere to are labeled MUST, while the implementation of statements labeled as SHOULD or MAY is left to the discretion of the implementer.

interoperability. As for Web service standards related to security, interoperability of different WS-Security implementations is crucial due to the roles played by SOAP messages and by SOAP message security. To this end, WS-I has defined the WS-I Basic Security Profile (WS-I BSP) [174], which covers transport layer security (HTTP over TLS) and SOAP message security. WS-I BSP defines proper, interoperable usage of security tokens (specifically username/password and X.509 certificates), timestamps, id references, security processing order, SOAP actors, XML signature and XML encryption, and security of SOAP attachments. In addition to the above mentioned profiles, WS-I provides testing tools used to determine whether the messages exchanged with a Web service conform to WS-I guidelines. These tools monitor the messages and analyze the resulting log to identify any known interoperability issues. In addition to testing tools, WS-I provides sample applications as examples of applications that are compliant with WS-I guidelines.

Another interoperability issue derives from possible overlaps among different standards specifications, and from a specification of a standard at a given layer being sometimes developed by a standardization body different from the one specifying the standard at another layer. Such a situation requires verification and alignment of the specifications, which involves further iterations within each standardization body. Moreover, such an alignment might be further constrained by the fact that one of the standards involved is more stable and mature and is already implemented by some manufacturers.

Performance issues

Performance issues mainly stems from the characteristics of the XML language itself, the increasing number of software layers needed to fully process XML messages an payloads, and finally from encryption and decryption. Processing XML-encoded messages can require a very large amount of bandwidth with respect to traditional binary messaging protocols. The overhead induced by XML has been addressed by the World Wide Web Consortium, which recently released three W3C Recommendations to improve Web services performance by standardizing the transmission of large binary data: XML-binary Optimized Packaging (XOP) [122], SOAP Message Transmission Optimization Mechanism (MTOM) [123], and Resource Representation SOAP Headers Block (RRSHB) [148]. These recommendations are intended to provide ways to efficiently package and transmit binary data included or referenced in a SOAP 1.2 message. Processing requirements of XML (for example, XML parsing) can also induce a performance overhead on the software implementing Web services security standards. As for security, it adds the additional overhead due to the processing required by XML Encryption and XML Signature.

XML appliances

In order to improve the performance of XML message processing and to ease and reduce the cost of XML-related security functions, several manufacturers introduced in the market specialized products referred to as *XML appliances*. XML appliances can be based on proprietary hardware and operating systems or on standard operating systems and include the so-called *XML accelerators* and *XML firewalls*. An XML accelerator appliance is a customized hardware and software performing the XML/SOAP parsing, XML schema validation, XPath processing, and XSLT transformation functions. XML firewalls, also known as XML security gateways, are devices that, in addition to the functions of an XML accelerator, support a range of security-related functions such as content or metadata-based XML/SOAP filtering functions; XML message encryption/decryption at the message or element level; XML signature verification and XML message signing; authentication and authorization functions; and auditing and accounting functions. XML firewalls implement XML message encryption and signing according to the XML Encryption and XML Signature standard. The advantage of using XML appliances is that they can be deployed with other firewalls in the DMZ, serving as the first line of defense. Another advantage is that they are optimized for XML handling so the performance impact of the appliances is lower with respect to self-coded solution. Disadvantages of hardware XML firewalls are the setup costs and the increased maintenance complexity which comes from managing an additional hardware type.

Bibliographic notes

An extensive analysis of extensibility issues and their relationships with versioning for XML-based languages can be found in the personal notes of Tim Berners-Lee [30, 31] and in [213].

A detailed discussion of the WS-I Basic Interoperability Profile, together with a worked out example of its application, is provided in [118, Chapter 13 Web Services Interoperability].

5

Digital Identity Management and Trust Negotiation

As more and more activities and processes such as shopping, discussion, entertainment and business collaboration are conducted in the cyber world, digital identities, be them user names, passwords, digital certificates, or biometric features and digital identity management have become fundamental to underpinning accountability in business relationships, controlling the customization of the user experience, protecting privacy, and adhering to regulatory controls. In its broadest sense, identity management revolves around the enterprise process of adding or removing (provisioning) digital identity information and managing their authentication and associated access rights (policy) to information systems and applications ("access management"). Hence, digital identity management is strictly intertwined with identification technologies, such as biometrics, and authorization and access control technologies. Moreover, digital identity management requires us to consider at the same time aspects and technologies related to usability and management. Digital identity is not a static information too. It may evolve over time, and hence digital identity management requires us to consider and apply change management techniques to digital identity representations.

Digital Identity management is an emerging research field which addresses the aspects mentioned above. Moreover, the emergence of SOA and Web services-based enterprise information systems requires us to consider not only the technical aspects of distribution but also the impact of service autonomy on identity management solutions.

This chapter covers all relevant notions related with identity management and then discusses how digital identity management can be combined with negotiation techniques to provide a more flexible but still privacy-preserving solution.

The chapter first provides an overview of the main concepts related to digital identity management, focusing on recent federated approaches, namely Liberty-Alliance initiative [166], WS-Federation [170], the Shibboleth System [138], and Microsoft CardSpace. Issues related to identity management in the context of grid computing systems are discussed, in that these systems

E. Bertino et al., *Security for Web Services and Service-Oriented Architectures,*
DOI 10.1007/978-3-540-87742-4_5, © Springer-Verlag Berlin Heidelberg 2010

represent a significant application context for SOA and digital identity management. The chapter also presents the trust negotiation paradigm, its main concepts and protocols, and possible applications of it in the context of federated identity management systems. Finally, to show the advantages of the digital identity management and trust negotiation approaches, the chapter presents a federated attribute management and trust negotiation solution, which provides a truly distributed approach to the management of user identities and user attributes with negotiation capabilities.

5.1 Overview of Digital Identity Management

Digital identity management is the set of processes, tools, social contracts, and a supporting infrastructure for creating, maintaining, utilizing, and terminating a digital identity. These tools allow administrators to manage large populations of users, applications, and systems securely and efficiently. They support selective assignment of roles and privileges that makes it easier to comply with regulatory controls and contribute to privacy-sensitive access controls. Identity management systems (IdM systems, from now on) have strong links with the management of security, trust, and privacy in a given system. Traditionally, identity management has been a core component of system security environments for the maintenance of account information to control log in access to systems or to a limited set of applications. Additionally, the identity of users has been the core of many authentication and authorization systems.

Recently, however, the scope of identity management has expanded, with its becoming a key enabler for electronic business. Identity management systems are now fundamental to underpinning accountability in business relationships, controlling the customization of the user experience, protecting privacy, and adhering to regulatory controls.

In this section we discuss the main concepts related to IdM systems. We begin with a brief overview of the notion of digital identity and identifiers, and then outline the most significant identity management frameworks.

Digital identity and identifiers

Digital identity can be defined as the digital representation of the information known about a specific individual or organization. Such information can be represented and conveyed in various ways, from log in names and passwords to digital credentials and biometric features.

IdM systems, according to the typical representation in SOA architectures, define identities by profiles of attributes associated with an individual. Identity attributes are typically stored at ad hoc *Identity Providers* (or IdPs, for short) which disclose identifiers as dictated by the authentication or authorization protocols in place.

Identity attributes, also referred to as *identifiers*, can encode demographic information about an individual or attest that an individual belongs to a particular group (such as military veterans or U.S. citizens).

Identifiers can be classified on the basis of their nature and uniqueness. An important distinction in fact lies in the ability of an identifier to uniquely represent an individual within a certain identity domain. Identifiers of this type are typically known as *strong identifiers*. *Weak identifiers* are instead associated with many individuals in a population. Whether an identifier is strong or weak depends upon the size of the population and the uniqueness of the identity attribute. The combination of multiple weak identifiers may lead to a unique identification [247]. Examples of strong identifiers are a user's passport number or social security number. Weak identifiers are attributes like age and gender.

Identity framework classification

In the past few years, several approaches to identity management have been proposed. An interesting categorization, [8], distinguishes *isolated, centralized*, and *distributed* identity management frameworks. The isolated model is based on the independent and autonomous management of identities among service providers (SPs for short) and is the oldest approach. Users have different identities at each SP, risking inconsistency, replication; and additionally, they have to remember log in names and password for each site. The centralized model assumes the existence of a single IdP and of a "circle of trust" among the IdPs and a set of participating members or SPs. A "circle of trust", according to the Liberty Alliance [166] initiative, is a federation of SPs and identity providers that have business relationships based on operational agreements, and with whom users can transact business in a secure and apparently seamless environment. The IdP has centralized control over the identity management task, providing access to all SP domains with simplicity of management and control. The obvious drawback of this approach is that the IdP may represent a bottleneck and a single point of failure that could result in enormous damage if compromised.

The distributed federated identity management model is based on the notion of federated IdPs, and on a distributed authentication process. The main idea underlying such a model is that some identity information exists beyond the corporate firewalls, and is therefore at least partially beyond any one corporation's individual control. In this model, every member of the federation agrees to trust user identities vouched for by other members of the federation without needing to adopt the same security technologies or maintain a shared, centralized system for managing identities. Such an approach results in a protected environment through which members can provide integrated and complete services to qualified groups of individuals across organizational boundaries.

Federated Identity Management Systems

Federated Identity Management (FIM) Systems represent the most recent and powerful model among the ones previously discussed, because of its ability of capturing a rich notion of identity which can be shared among members in a controlled fashion. At a higher level, FIM's members are organizations sharing identity profiles according to specific rules of sharing and contractual agreements.

Technically, an FIM system consists of software components and protocols that handle the identity of individuals. An FIM system involves three main types of entities, namely users, IdPs, and SPs. Such entities may, and typically are, implemented using SOA architectures. The IdPs manage and provide user identities and may also issue user credentials. The SPs (also known as relying parties) are entities that provide services to users based on their identity (attributes). A FIM system is characterized by a user having identity information certified by one or more IdPs. An important aspect of FIM systems is that the various management components are distributed amongst entities adopting independently established authentication policies: a relying party may accept identities according to its authentication policy, although such an authentication policy may not be shared or agreed upon with the other entities of the federation.

An important benefit of FIM systems is that they help in sharing personal information in a protected way and in facilitating Single-Sign-On [227] (SSO), based on the contractual and operational agreement existing among the FIM members. SSO allows a user to sign on once at a SP site and then to be seamlessly signed on when navigating to another site, without the need to authenticate again.

Having a federation prevents the problem of a single point of failure, but requires that a trusted IdP be chosen. Typically, the individual relies on an online IdP to provide the required credentials, and hence these systems are referred to as *provider-centric*. In some cases individuals have very limited control over their credentials, and this is considered as one of the factors hindering the widespread use of technologies for federated identities.

As a result, a currently emerging paradigm in federated IdM systems is that of *user centricity*, where the idea is to provide the individual full control of transactions involving his identity data. This paradigm, discussed later, is embraced by multiple industry products and initiatives such as Microsoft CardSpace [282], SXIP [180], and the open source Higgins Trust Framework [129].

5.2 Overview of Existing Proposals

Identity management is being investigated extensively in the corporate world and several standardization initiatives for identity federation are being developed. Table 5.1 summarizes some of the most significant ongoing projects. In

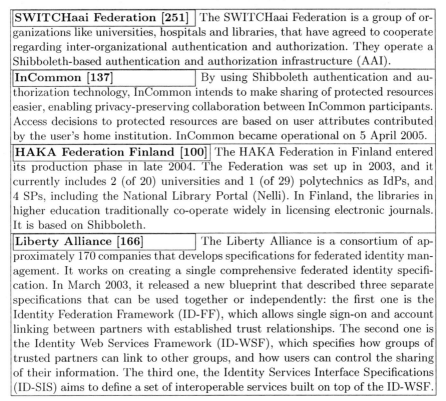

| **SWITCHaai Federation [251]** | The SWITCHaai Federation is a group of organizations like universities, hospitals and libraries, that have agreed to cooperate regarding inter-organizational authentication and authorization. They operate a Shibboleth-based authentication and authorization infrastructure (AAI). |

| **InCommon [137]** | By using Shibboleth authentication and authorization technology, InCommon intends to make sharing of protected resources easier, enabling privacy-preserving collaboration between InCommon participants. Access decisions to protected resources are based on user attributes contributed by the user's home institution. InCommon became operational on 5 April 2005. |

| **HAKA Federation Finland [100]** | The HAKA Federation in Finland entered its production phase in late 2004. The Federation was set up in 2003, and it currently includes 2 (of 20) universities and 1 (of 29) polytechnics as IdPs, and 4 SPs, including the National Library Portal (Nelli). In Finland, the libraries in higher education traditionally co-operate widely in licensing electronic journals. It is based on Shibboleth. |

| **Liberty Alliance [166]** | The Liberty Alliance is a consortium of approximately 170 companies that develops specifications for federated identity management. It works on creating a single comprehensive federated identity specification. In March 2003, it released a new blueprint that described three separate specifications that can be used together or independently: the first one is the Identity Federation Framework (ID-FF), which allows single sign-on and account linking between partners with established trust relationships. The second one is the Identity Web Services Framework (ID-WSF), which specifies how groups of trusted partners can link to other groups, and how users can control the sharing of their information. The third one, the Identity Services Interface Specifications (ID-SIS) aims to define a set of interoperable services built on top of the ID-WSF. |

Table 5.1. Federation initiatives

this section we analyze and compare two emerging standards from the corporate world, Liberty Alliance [166] (LA) and WS-Federation [170]. Then we provide an overview of other relevant approaches, namely, Shibboleth [138] and Microsoft CardSpace.

5.2.1 Liberty Alliance

The Liberty Alliance [166, 167] was formed in December 2001 to serve as an open standard organization for federated network identity management and identity-based services. The main aim of Liberty Alliance is to provide the specification of a federated identity infrastructure in which *individuals and businesses can more easily interact with one another, while respecting the privacy and security of shared identity information* [166]. The framework for such an infrastructure is based on the *circle of trust* concept. A circle of trust is constituted by mutually trusting SPs and Identity SPs (IdPs). SPs are organizations offering Web-based services to users. IdPs are SPs offering business incentives so that other SPs will affiliate with them.

Objectives

Liberty Alliance objectives are twofold. The first objective is to establish a standardized, multi-vendor, Web-based single sign-on based on federated identities. The second one, which raises a number of interesting technical challenges, is to enable businesses to maintain and manage their customer relationships without third-party participation.

Requirements

Liberty Alliance outlined a number of requirements that an identity solution must satisfy. In the following we summarize the most relevant ones:

- IdPs must support identity federation by giving the user a notice upon federation (sharing with other federation members) or de-federation (stopping to share with other federation members) of his identity. Both SPs and IdP must notify each other about identity de-federation. Each IdP should notify the appropriate SPs of user account terminations at the identity provider. Each SP and/or IdP should give each of its users a list of the user's federated identities at the identity provider or SP.
- Authentication between IdPs and SPs on the part of the user, that is, how the user navigates from SP A to SP B (including click-through, using favorites or using bookmarks, URL address bar, etc.) must be supported. Confidentiality, integrity, and authenticity of information exchanged between IdPs, SPs, and user agents, must be guaranteed. Additionally, mutual authentication of the identities of the IdPs and SPs during the authentication and single sign-on processes must be supported.
- A range of authentication methods must be supported, as well as extensible identifying authentication methods; also coalescing authentication methods into authentication classes and citing and exchanging authentication classes must be supported. The following minimum set of authentication information with regard to a user must be exchanged: authentication status, instant, method, and pseudonym. SPs must have the capability of causing the identity provider to re-authenticate the user using the same or a different authentication class.
- The use of pseudonyms must be supported, which must be unique on a per identity federation basis across all IdPs and SPs.
- Global logout must be supported, by handling the notification of SPs when a user logs out at the identity provider.

Technical Specification

The Liberty Alliance's specifications build on OASIS's Open Standard Security Assertion Markup Language [222], an XML-based security standard that provides a way of exchanging user authentication information. We refer the interested reader to Chapter 4 for a detailed presentation of SAML.

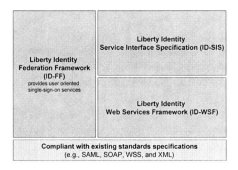

Fig. 5.1. Liberty Alliance architecture

Architecture

As reported in figure 5.1, Liberty Alliance architecture is organized around three building blocks: (1) the Federation Framework (ID-FF); (2) the Identity Web Services Framework (ID-WSF); (3) the Identity Services Interface Specifications (ID-SIS). ID-FF enables identity federation and management, and it supports, among others, a simplified SSO and anonymity. In the ID-FF framework, users' accounts are distributed and maintained at each site. In order to federate these accounts while respecting user privacy, the IdPs and SPs establish a pseudorandom identifier that is associated with a real name identifier at each site. The process of federating two local identities for a user between SPs and IdPs is triggered by the users with the consent of the SPs, so to map the established pseudonyms into their local account identifiers [166]. When the authentication of a user is requested by an SP, the IdP authenticates him and then issues an authentication assertion. If the IdP has already authenticated the user, then it can just issue an assertion without necessarily requiring the user to present his credentials again. Each SP validates the assertion issued from the IdP, and determines whether or not it should be accepted. As the IdP can issue multiple assertions to different SPs based on a single authentication action by the user, the user is able to sign on to these other service sites without needing to be re-authenticated at each site. ID-FF defines how data must be exchanged between IdPs and SPs.

The ID-WSF (IdentityWeb Services Framework) defines a framework for Web services that allows SPs to share users' identities and attributes according to permissions, and to create, discover, and request identity services. It also supports discovery of services and security mechanisms to transmit messages. ID-WSF operates on open protocol standards.

ID-SIS (Identity Service Interface Specifications) defines service interfaces for each identity-based Web service so that SPs can exchange different aspects of identity (i.e., a user's profile) in an interoperable manner [166]. ID-SIS serves to build security services of higher level (application services) based on the ID-WSF framework. Examples of ID-SIS services include personal information request, geo location services, and directory services.

5.2.2 WS-Federation

WS-Federation is a collaborative effort of BEA Systems, BMC Software, CA, IBM, Layer 7 Technologies, Microsoft, Novell, and VeriSign. It is elegantly integrated into a series of other Web service specifications such as WS-Trust[13] and WS-Security[170].

WS-Federation [170] describes how to manage and broker the trust relationships in a heterogeneous federated environment, including support for federated identities, sharing of attributes, and management of pseudonyms.

The WS-Federation approach to a federation framework is based on the consideration that a federation framework must be capable of integrating existing infrastructures into the federation without requiring major new infrastructure investments. As a consequence, the framework should allow us to manage different types of security tokens and infrastructures, as well as different attribute stores and discovery mechanisms. Additionally, the trust topologies, relationships, and mechanisms can also vary, requiring the federation framework to support the resource's approach to trust rather than forcing the resource to change.

In WS-Federation, users obtain security tokens from their IdPs and can pass them to SPs in order to get access to resources. WS-Federation, in addition, defines a request-response protocol which can be used by SPs to acquire security tokens containing the attributes they actually need. WS-Federation specifies mechanisms that can be used by Web service (SOAP) requesters as well as by Web browser requesters. The Web service requesters are assumed to understand the WS-Security and WS-Trust mechanisms and be capable of interacting directly with Web SPs. The Web browser mechanisms describe how the WS-* messages (e.g., WS-Trust messages) are encoded in HTTP messages such that they can be passed between resources and Identity Provider (IP) and Security Token Service (STS) parties by way of a Web browser client.

The defined Web browser mechanisms support the full richness of WS-Trust, WS-Policy, and other WS-* mechanisms to be leveraged in Web browser environments. The WS-Federation framework also leverages the WS-* specifications to create an evolutionary federation path allowing services to use only what they need and leverage existing infrastructures and investments. It also has the advantage of allowing identities and attributes to be brokered from identity and security token issuers to services and other relying parties without requiring user intervention. In addition, it provides authenticity and secure channel establishment in a realistic trust scenario.

Objectives

WS-Federation has been created with the goal of standardizing the way companies share user and machine identities among disparate authentication and authorization systems spread across corporate boundaries. Such a goal translates into mechanisms and a specification to enable federation of identity, attribute, authentication, and authorization information, but it does *not* include the definition of message security or trust establishment or verification protocols and/or specification of new security token formats or new attribute store interfaces.

Requirements

The requirements for WS-Federation, described in the specification, are summarized as follows:

- Enable appropriate sharing of identity, authentication, and authorization data using different or like mechanisms.
- Allow federations using different types of security tokens, trust topologies, and security infrastructures.
- Facilitate brokering of trust and security token exchange for both Simple Object Access Protocol (SOAP) requesters and Web browsers using common underlying mechanisms and semantics.
- Express federation metadata to facilitate communication and interoperability between federation participants.
- Allow identity mapping to occur at a requester, target service, or any IdP or Security Token Service (STS).
- Provide identity mapping support if target services choose to maintain optional local identities, but do not require local identities.
- Allow for different levels of privacy for identity information and attributes (e.g., different forms and uniqueness of digital identities).

WS-Federation Model

The WS-Federation framework builds on the WS-Security, WS-Trust, and WS-SecurityPolicy family of specifications, providing a rich extensible mechanism for federation. The WS-Security and WS-Trust specifications allow for different types of security tokens, infrastructures, and trust topologies. WS-Federation defines additional federation mechanisms that extend these specifications and leverage other WS-* specifications.

WS-Federation assumes the existence of Attribute Services (ASs), Security Token Services (STSs), Authorization Services, and Validation Services (VSs). An AS is a Web service that maintains information (attributes) about principals within a trust realm or federation. An STS is a Web service that provides issuance and management of security tokens. A security token is a collection of security assertions (or claims) and can be signed by the STS. Security assertions are based on the receipt of evidence that the STS can directly verify, or on security tokens from authorities that it trusts. An AS is a specialized type of Security Token Service (STS) that makes authorization decisions. A VA is a specialized form of a Security Token Service that uses the WS-Trust mechanisms to validate the tokens provided and assess their level of trust.

In WS-Federation, an IdP, typically an extension of a Security Token Service, is an entity that acts as an entity authentication service to end requesters and as a data origin authentication service to SPs. IdPs are trusted parties which need to be trusted by both the requester and the SP.

The goal of a federation is to securely share principal's identity information across *trust* boundaries, by making it brokered from IdP and STS issuers to services and other relying parties without requiring user intervention. This process involves the sharing of federation metadata which describes information about the federated services, and the policies describing common communication requirements, and the brokering of trust and tokens via security token exchanges (issuances, validations, etc.).

WS-Federation considers the possibility of dynamically establishing a federated context, which is a group of realms to which a principal has presented Security Tokens and obtained session credentials. The federated context lasts when the principal performs a sign-out action.

Hence, the federation context is related to the (dynamic) principal request. To establish a federation context for a principal, WS-Federation provides two possibilities. In the first one the principal's identity is universally accepted. The second one requires that the principal's identity be brokered into a trusted identity relevant to each trust realm within the federation context.

This approach requires identity mapping that consists of the conversion of a digital identity from one realm to a digital identity valid in another realm by a party that trusts the starting realm and has the rights to speak for the ending realm or make assertions that the ending realm trusts. Identity mapping, that is, brokering, is typically implemented by an IdP or STS when initially obtaining tokens for a service or when exchanging tokens by the IdPs or STS. A principal's digital identity can be represented in different forms requiring different types of mappings. For example, if a digital identity is fixed, it may only need to be mapped if a local identity is needed. Fixed identities make service tracking (e.g,. personalization) easy, but this can also be a privacy concern. This concern is lessened if the principal has multiple identities and chooses which one to apply to which service, although collusion is still possible.

Another approach to identity mapping is pairwise mapping, where a unique digital identity is used for each principal at each target service. This approach simplifies service tracking, since the service is given a unique ID for each requester, and prevents possible collusion issues (if the mapping is performed by a trusted service). While addressing collusion, the use of pairwise mapping requires the principal's IdP or STS to drive identity mapping. A third approach is to require the service to be responsible for the identity mapping. That is, the service is given an opaque handle which it must then have mapped to an identity it understands, assuming it cannot directly process the opaque handle. More specifically, the requester's IdP/STS generates a digital identity that cannot be reliably used by the target service as a key for local identity mapping. The target service then uses the requester's mapping service, referred to as pseudonym service, to map the possibly random digital identity to a constant service-specific digital identity which it has registered with the requesters mapping service. This approach addresses the collusion issue. However, it shifts the mapping burden onto the service. The WS-* specifications are used and extended to create a federation framework to support these concepts.

5.2.3 Comparison of Liberty Alliance and WS-Framework

Liberty Alliance and WS-Framework are two of the most significant initiatives that have recognized the value and the importance of identity in the digital era. The common objectives of these initiatives have been primarily to reduce the number user-business interactions and exchange of information and ensure that critical private information is only used by appropriate parties. However, the analysis of how to manage and represent digital identities was conducted from very different perspectives. Liberty Alliance is a commercially funded and oriented project. Its research has been aimed at specific commercial goals related to identity management and federation, in contrast to the more technical motivation of much of the WS work. Liberty Alliance has made far more progress in defining how to manage and exchange personal information across Liberty Alliance networks. These different views have led to the specification of separate comprehensive frameworks for digital identity management.

However, a number of similarities among these two initiatives exist. Highlighting some common factors is important to fully understand the future trend in the area of digital identity, and help foresee how the next generation solutions will be more likely developed.

Common advantages

- Both Liberty Alliance and WS-Federation make user identity information available to the SPs on demand, online, and with low delay. Thus, user data is more up-to-date and consistent compared to the case where each user has to maintain her data in multiple places.
- Both frameworks enable fewer and stronger authentication events, so as to help in minimizing the risk of ID theft and hence increasing system security.
- Both frameworks reduce costs and redundancy because organizations do not have to acquire, store, and maintain authorization information about all their partners' users anymore.
- Both frameworks satisfy the minimal disclosure information security requirement, in that only data required to use a service has to be transmitted to a business partner.

Common shortcomings

- Both approaches enable inter organizational Web SSO, but neither of them can be applied to services which are not yet or cannot be fully Web-enabled, e.g., e-mail and file storage. Although Web interfaces exist for both frameworks, access through conventional protocols, such as FTP for accessing files, is much more popular and cannot be given up. As there is no support for such legacy protocols, conventional user registration and system provisioning would be required [134].
- Although an SP can request arbitrary attribute information from a user's identity provider while the service is being used, neither approach offers the means to notify the SP about changes in this data later on.
- The only security issue considered in both LA and WS-Federation is communication security. Although a PKI-based solution is feasible in theory, it is not trivial to realize. In practice building a common single-purpose PKI for a lot of federation partners, e.g., in supply chain management, would require enormous resources for both setup and maintenance. Furthermore, neither a holistic security view nor methods for the correlation of security-related events across organizational boundaries exist yet in both frameworks.
- As for privacy, the users must be able to regulate what information about them is allowed to be sent to which providers. However, there are yet no concrete definitions of such *attribute release policies* (ARPs) in the specifications.
- Both frameworks support the exchange of arbitrary attributes, i.e., pairs of keys and values. But they do not provide mechanisms to help find a common data scheme which should be used within an identity federation, including the definition of syntax and semantics. In the real world, finding a common data scheme for inter organizational cooperation is not trivial: each organization internally uses slightly different terms and changes are not easy because of organizational and financial costs. Neither standard supports the process of finding a federation-wide data scheme; nor does it offer methods to deal with provider-specific semantics. So far, Liberty Alliance has attempted to define a common set of user attributes within ID-SIS. But employing such a common set of attributes likely require substantial application and federation specific extensions, which does not seem to be straightforward.

5.2.4 Other Digital Identity Management Initiatives

Shibboleth [138] is a project run by the Internet2 consortium in the USA. It is a standards-based, open source middleware architecture providing both intra-domain and inter-domain SSO capability. Shibboleth implements the SAML standard specification, and is currently interoperable with Microsoft's Active Directory Federation Services (ADFS).

A Shibboleth Federation is an agreement between resource (service) providers and institutions wishing to access those resources or services. For sharing to occur, all parties need to agree on a common set of acceptable authorization attributes for their users and a schema to describe them.

User attributes are stored at the IdPs of the user home institution. Attributes can be encoded in Java or pulled from directories and databases. Standard X.520 attributes are most commonly used, but new attributes can be arbitrarily defined as long as they are understood and interpreted similarly by the Identity Provider (IdP) and SP in a transaction. Origin sites are responsible for authenticating their users through IdPs. Figure 5.2 shows the

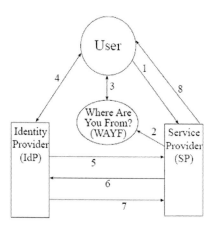

Fig. 5.2. Typical Shibboleth flow of messages

message flow of a typical Shibboleth-enabled transaction, with the browser user arriving at the SP site without an existing session, and without any information about the user's home institution being known by the SP.

1. The user attempts to access a Shibboleth-protected resource on the SP site.
2. The user is redirected to the federation WAYF. WAYF (acronym for 'Where Are You From') is a service guiding a user to his IdP.
3. The user selects his home institution (the IdP) from the list presented by the WAYF.
4. The IdP ensures that the user is authenticated using the internal authentication method.
5. After successful authentication, a one-time handle (session identifier) is generated for this user session and sent to the SP.

6. The SP uses the handle to request the user's attribute information from the IdP. The required attributes are needed to ensure that the user can be authorized to access the requested resource.
7. The IdP allows or denies attribute information to be made available to the SP.
8. Based on the attribute information available to it, the SP allows or refuses the user access to the resource.

There are many variations on this flow, most of them simpler. In addition, later versions of Shibboleth are able to operate in other ways.

A key aspect of Shibboleth is the emphasis on users' privacy. At step 7, the SP releases user attributes on the basis of the users' specified ARPs. ARPs dictate the conditions according to which attributes can be released. As such, the target SP only knows the attributes and information necessary to perform an access control decision, protecting users' anonymity in cases where their identity is not necessarily important. This approach gives users a large amount of control and flexibility about how their attributes are released and known and enables simple and anonymous access control.

CardSpace [282] is part of Microsoft's implementation of an identity meta-system based on standard protocols and composes seamlessly with the WS-* security protocol family (including WS-Security, WS-Secure Conversation, WS-SecurityPolicy, WS-MetadataExchange, and WS-Trust). CardSpace functions as a sort of "digital wallet" that stores authentication information for a number of different Web sites and Web services. More specifically, it securely stores pointers to digital identities of an individual, and provides a unified interface for choosing the identity for a particular transaction, such as logging in to a Web site or accessing some Web service. A use case of CardSpace is described as follows:

1. A CardSpace-enabled user first enrolls with one or more IdPs of his choice. That could be for instance, an ISP, a bank, a site like eBay or Slashdot. This process is entirely outside of CardSpace, but of course the IdPs must support their portion of the CardSpace protocol.
2. The user visits a CardSpace-enabled relying Web site, such as a CardSpace-enabled Bestbuy, that requires certain identity information from the user, say, a shipping address. The website sends the client a web page which contains an HTML OBJECT tag, which triggers a DLL that invokes the CardSpace system at the client.
3. The CardSpace system determines what personal information is requested by the Web site, and matches it to the identities (i.e., Information Cards) that are in possession of the user. It then displays to the user the applicable cards, such as: driver's license (if the government is a CardSpace-enabled identity provider) or a credit card from BankOne. The CardSpace selector runs on the user's computer and is not downloaded.
4. The CardSpace user interface enables users to create personal cards (aka self-issued cards) associated with a limited set of identity data. As a result

of the selection, the CardSpace process contacts the selected IdP and obtains essentially a digitally signed XML document that contains the requested identity information. The signature is of the IDP.

5. The CardSpace client then forwards the obtained document to the relying party (the Web site).

Note that the key difference with other identity management systems, such as Shibboleth, is that identity information is not recorded at a server owned by Microsoft. Additionally, while other initiatives have been mostly designed with the goal of enabling interoperability of identities among different administrative domains (e.g., Liberty Alliance) and to protect individual's privacy (e. g., Shibboleth), CardSpace's main effort is to alleviate some of the usability problems that individuals face today in terms of online identity abuse. To this extent, the designers of CardSpace focused on an approach that reduces the reliance on username/password authentication with cryptographically strong claims-based authentication. The goal is to mitigate the risks of the most commonly deployed identity attacks, such as compromised accounts and stolen passwords, and to reduce the likelihood of personal information being lost via phishing schemes.

5.3 Discussion on Security of Identity Management Systems

Identity managements systems' main resources are represented by identity attributes, thus *security* of such resources should always be assured. Security includes a comprehensive set of properties, dealing with integrity, confidentiality, revocability, and unlinkability of identity attributes. Integrity requires data not to be altered in an unauthorized way. To preserve the integrity of an individual's identity attributes the IdPs should collaborate with one another for efficient updates and deploy appropriate mechanisms for maintaining a consistent view of the individual's identity. Confidentiality is also an important requirement for the secure management of identities. Specifically, confidentiality deals with the protection of sensitive identity information from unauthorized disclosure. Identity information should only be accessible by the intended recipients. If an attacker can retrieve someone's information, then the user loses control (at least partially) on her attributes' release and usage. It is therefore essential that mechanisms for confidential release of the individual's attributes be provided and identity information be protected accordingly at all times. Revocability is also essential, to ensure that no longer valid information is recognized as such, and not used for identification purposes. Finally, unlinkability of two or more identities or transactions—or, generally, of items of interest—means that the attacker after having observed transactions, should not be able to infer sensitive information based on observed information.

Despite the growing interest in solutions to digital identities, in today's Internet environment, many developers still fail to see and understand the central place of identity in the applications. Mostly, the current initiatives, such as Shibboleth and WS-Framework, are primarily an attempt to improve in flexibility and interoperability of users identities and profiles. As a result, despite their potential, they still have significant shortcomings.

First, most approaches do not provide information about the verification of the identity data of the individuals enrolled and stored at the IdPs. If an IdP has such information, then the SPs are in a position to make a more accurate judgment concerning the trustworthiness of such identity information.

The second major drawback is that no specific techniques are provided to protect against the *misuse of identity attributes* stored at the IdPs and SPs. Even the notion of misuse of such attributes has not been thoroughly investigated yet. Dishonest individuals can register fake attributes or impersonate other individuals of the federation, leading to identity theft. Digital *identity theft* occurs when attackers impersonate other identities without their consent or knowledge. These attacks are launched to obtain fraudulent credit or to commit crimes like accessing classified records without the proper authorizations. Digital identity theft in cyberspace is especially hard to prevent because digital information can be copied, and hence stolen unnoticed. Additionally, it is difficult to find or prosecute the Internet thieves. The most common identity theft attacks are perpetrated through passwords cracking, pharming, phishing, and database attacks. The intuitive solution of maintaining confidentiality through cryptographic techniques is inadequate or not sufficient when dealing with identity. Identifiers often have to be released to third parties and validated each time authentication is required or an access control policy needs to be enforced.

To mitigate this threat, *strong authentication* is an upcoming trend. Strong authentication refers to systems that require multiple factors, possibly issued by different sources, to identify users when they access services and applications. However, current approaches to strong authentication (deployed by banks, enterprises, and governmental institutions) are neither flexible nor fine-grained. In many cases, strong authentication simply requires two forms of identity tokens, for example a password, and a biometric. By having prior knowledge of these token requirements, an adversary can steal the required identity information to compromise such authentication. Moreover if the same tokens are repeatedly used for strong authentication at various SPs, then the chances of these tokens being compromised increase. Thus, as of today, the strong authentication implemented does not meet the stronger protection requirements of identities in a federation. Individuals should be able to choose any combination of identity attributes to perform strong authentication, provided that the authentication policies defined by the verifying party are satisfied.

An additional limitation is represented by the difficulty for individuals to monitor whether their privacy requirements are in fact satisfied, and to fully control their identity information. Additionally, existing approaches for federated identities do not support *biometric data*; in that digital identities are defined by digital attributes and certificates. The use of biometrics as an integral part of individual identity is, however, gaining importance. At the same time, because of the nature of the biometric data, it is not trivial to use this data as digital attributes.

Finally, a potential security breach in current federated IdM systems is caused by the lack of practical and effective revocation mechanisms. To enable consistency and maintain correctness of an individuals identity information, revocation should be feasible. Revocation in IdP-centric systems, where the issuer is providing the required credential to the user each time, is relatively simple to support. Such credentials are typically short term, and cannot be used without consulting the issuer again. If, however, the credentials are indeed stored with the user, such as a long-term credential issued by the appropriate authority, then building a revocation system becomes more challenging and critical.

5.4 Business Processes

Business processes are built from composable services (component services), that may belong to different domains. Each of the services is deployed using SOA architectures. Precisely, processes are typically specified using WS-BPEL[5] business processes language. Business processes represent an example of SOA applications where flexible multi-domain identity management solutions are crucial for increased security and user-convenience. In particular, it is important that during the execution of a business process the component services be able to verify(at least partially) the identity of the client to check that it has the required permissions for accessing the services. Clients identity consists of data, referred to as identity attributes, that encode relevant-security properties of the clients.

Managing and verifying clients identity in business processes raise a number of challenging issues. A first issue is related to how the clients identity attribute have to be managed within the business process. The client of a business process is not aware that the business process that implements the required service invokes some component services. The client thus trusts the composite service but not the component services. Therefore, every time the component services have to verify the clients identity, the composite service has to act as an intermediary between the component services and the client. Moreover, since the clients identity attributes may contain sensitive information and clients usually do not trust the component services, the clients identity attributes should be protected from potential misuse by component services. Another issue is related to how the identity verification process is performed. Because component services belong to different domains, each with its own identity verification policies, the sets of identity attributes required to verify clients identity may partially or totally overlap. Therefore, the client has to prove several times the knowledge of the same subset of identity attributes.

It is thus important to take advantage of previous client identity verification processes that other component services have performed. finally, another issue is the lack of interoperability because of naming heterogeneity. Naming heterogeneity occurs when component services define their identity verification policies according to a vocabulary different from the one adopted by clients. Therefore, component services and clients are not able to have meaningful interactions because they do not understand each other. Thus, it is also necessary that client identity verification process supports an approach to match identity attribute names of component services and clients vocabularies.

5.4.1 Deploying Multifactor Authentication for Business Processes

In this section we provide a solution that provides multifactor authentication for SOA architecture, focusing on the business process domain. To enable multi-factor identity attribute verification, clients have to register their identity attributes to a trusted server, namely the registrar. The registrar stores and manages information related to identity attributes. For each client's identity attribute, the registrar records an identity tuple. Each identity tuple consists of tag, an attribute descriptor, and a commitment m computed using zero knowledge proof protocols. Weak identifiers are used to denote identity attributes that can be aggregated together to perform multi-factor authentication. The identity tuples of each registered client can be retrieved from the registrar by the component services or the registrar can release to the client a certificate containing its identity record. Each component services defines its identity verification policies by specifying a set of identity attribute names that have to be required from the client. Because of naming heterogeneity, clients may not understand component services identity verification policies. The type of variations that can occur in clients and component services identity attribute names can be classified in: syntactic, terminological and semantic variations. Each of these variations can be addressed using different techniques: for syntactic variations, that arise because of the use of different character combinations to denote the same term, look up tables can be used. In detecting terminological variations, dictionaries or thesaurus such as WordNet[288] can be exploited. Finally, semantic variations can be determined by using ontology matching techniques. The identity matching protocol is executed at component service in a privacy-preserving fashion, so that the values of the identity attributes of the client cannot be learned, and therefore there is no incentive to lie about the verified identity attributes.

The matching process consists of two main phases. The goal of the first phase is to match the identity attributes that have syntactical and terminological variations, using ontologies or look-up dictionaries. During the second phase the client sends the set of its proof-of-identity certificates to the composite service that forwards them to the component service. Thus, in the second phase of the matching process the component service tries to match the concepts corresponding to the identity attributes the client is not able to

provide with concepts from the ontologies of the services which have issued
the proof-of-identity certificates. Only matches that have a confidence score
greater than a predefined threshold are selected. The acceptance threshold
is set up by the component service to assess the matches validity. Once the
client receives the set of matched identity attributes from the composite service, it retrieves from the registrar the commitments satisfying the matches
and the corresponding signatures and combine them together for verification
using aggregate zero-knowledge proof protocols.

5.4.2 Architecture

In order to provide a concrete representation of how the discussed approach
can be effectively deployed using SOA architecture, we provide a brief description of a representative architecture supporting this type of solutions. Figure
5.3, reports a graphical representation of the system's most important components. As illustrated, the main components of the architecture are: the BPEL
engine, the Identity Attribute Requester module, the Client, the Registrar,
the Identity Verification Handler module, and the component Web services.
The WS-BPEL engine is responsible for scheduling and synchronizing the
various activities within the business process according to the specified activity dependencies, and for invoking Web services operations associated with
activities. The Identity Attribute Requester module extends the WS-BPEL
engines functions by carrying on the communication with the client asking
for new identity attributes whenever necessary. The Identity Attribute Requester keeps in a local repository the mapping certificate associated with
previous clients identity verifications. The Client supports the functions to
trigger the execution of the WS-BPEL business process, to select the identity
attributes matching the ones requested by the component services, and to generate the aggregate ZKP of the matched attributes. The Registrar component
provides functions for storing the clients identity records and retrieving the
public parameters required in the aggregate zero-knowledge proof protocol.
The Identity Verification Handler intercepts the components services invocation messages and provides functions for matching client identity attribute
names and performing the aggregate ZKP verification. finally, the component
Web service supports the operations that are orchestrated by the business
process. The Identity Attribute Requester, the Identity Verification Handler
modules, and the component Web service can be implemented in JAVA.

5.5 Digital Identity Management in Grid Systems

The problem of digital identity management is particularly compelling in some
specific domains, for example, grid systems. By their nature, grids span multiple institutional administration boundaries and aim to provide support for the

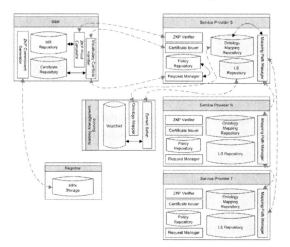

Fig. 5.3. Business Process Architecture.

sharing of applications, data, and computational resources in a collaborative environment.

The grid introduces additional challenges to the problem of identity management since it aims to facilitate the sharing of resources in a collaborative environment across boundaries. A grid environment has thus to facilitate user's access to resources at disparate institutions, while enforcing authentication and authorization policies set forth by the different institutions.

Traditional access control mechanisms for the grid were designed for scenarios in which a strong trust relationship exists between users and resource providers. In such scenarios, resource providers control the identities of all their users ahead of time to allow access based on authentication of the individual user.

Since grid environments are gaining visibility and interest of researchers and scholars, the number of individuals joining the grid is growing higher[1]. Because of the large size of Grid's population managing users, and creating and managing their grid identities, become very challenging to support. Also, it is not trivial to support authentication such that grid services can be accessed securely. In this context, it is not desirable nor tractable to have a centralized identity management system. It is unpractical to require that each shared service or group of services in the grid maintain separate identity management and authentication mechanisms. Therefore, grid-enabled infrastructures are needed to facilitate the federation of institutional identities. Another important issues the grid needs to face is that of mapping identities with local accounts at servers and resource providers while still being able to maintain a unique federated identity.

---

[1] In the presence of about a hundred institutions, the number of users can be in the order of ten thousands

Shibboleth, as discussed in Section 5.2.4, provides the infrastructure for federation of identities across boundaries, and thus it can be employed for managing identities. However, Shibboleth cannot be plugged in as it is, since it does not provide any specific authentication mechanism, lacks some security features and was primarily designed for Web applications. As a result, several projects developing technologies for leveraging Shibboleth to support grids [124, 263, 261] have been undertaken.

As a representative example, we briefly overview the well-known GridShib [124] project. The GridShib project's goals [124] include ease of access for users, improved scalability (resulting in improved security), reduced cost and overhead for providers, and better integrating of a national-scale cyberinfrastructure with campus cyberinfrastructure, further reducing the administrative overhead faced by campus users in accessing national resources. More specifically, Gridshib's objective is to integrate Public Key Infrastructures [279] with Shibboleth, in order to achieve large-scale multi-domain PKIs for access control. The protocol is very similar to the original Shibboleth, in that it involves both SPs and IdPs. However, in GridShib the grid client and the grid SP each possess an X.509 credential. The grid client has an account with a Shibboleth IdP. The IdP is able to map the grid client's X.509 Subject Distinguished Name (DN) to one and only one user in its security domain. The IdP and the Grid SP each have been assigned a globally unique identifier.

When the user tries to access a resource the Grid Client authenticates using his X.509 credentials to the Grid SP. The Grid SP authenticates the request and extracts the clients DN from the credentials. It then contacts the user IdP to obtain attribute assertions necessary to authorize the user.

The IdP authenticates the attribute request, maps the DN to a local principal name, retrieves the requested attributes for the user (suitably filtered by normal Shibboleth attribute release policies), formulates an attribute assertion, and sends the assertion to the Grid SP. Finally, the Grid SP parses the attribute assertion, caches the attributes, makes an access control decision, processes the client request (assuming access is granted), and returns a response to the grid client.

GridShib is an ongoing project which has the potential to radically change the way access control and authentication are performed in grid systems. Coupling PKI based systems with attribute based access control methods has great benefits for both users' and site administrators, in that it supports fine-grained access protocols not purely based on cryptographic keys. There are, however, several scalability issues to address before actual deployment in large-scale settings can be achieved. An important issue to address is that there are currently no unified standards for attribute transfer from the attribute authority to the relying services and no policies regarding the attributes; thus, different IdPs use different name forms and name values to identify the same user. The GridShib team had to overcome this incompatibility issue by introducing the DN mapping plug-in for the Shibboleth, which significantly constrained the scalability of the project and is still a major issue that needs to be resolved.

To be successfully deployed, GridShib needs to be integrated with current systems used for authentication services, such as MyProxy. The integration requires overcoming the problem of naming schema, in that multiple schemas are employed at different sites. Finally, an important issue is represented by the recent usage of gateways of portals available to users for access to the grid. Compatibility with such type of Web based protocols is still being tested, and requires extensions to existing portals.

In addition to Gridshib, two similar projects are the U.K.-based Shibboleth Enabled Bridge to Access the National Grid Service (SHEBANGS) project [263] and the ShibGrid project [261]. Both of these projects are developing prototypes for access to the UK National Grid Services via Shibboleth, which is being heavily deployed in the UK SHEBANGS uses a trusted intermediary service, known as the Credential Translation Service (CTS), to create an X.509 credential for the user in MyProxy, while ShibGrid is developing support for processing Shibboleth authentication in MyProxy itself. SHEBANGS requires less modification to other software, but requires the user to be more aware of the process since it must use a username: password: server triplet from the CTS to authenticate him to the application portal.

5.6 The Trust Negotiation Paradigm and its Deployment using SOA

Integrity and confidentiality of identity attributes are two key requirements of digital identity management systems. Users should have the maximum control possible over the release of their identity attributes and should state under what conditions these attributes can be disclosed. Moreover, users should disclose only the identity attributes that are actually required for the transactions at hand.

One approach to achieve such a level of flexibility and fine-grained access in identity management systems is to enhance IdM technology with automated trust negotiation (ATN) techniques [38, 238]. Trust negotiation is an access control approach for establishing trust in open systems like the Internet. The idea of trust negotiation is to establish trust on-line between (generally) two negotiating parties through bilateral credential disclosure. Digital credentials are assertions stating one or more properties about a given subject, referred to as the "owner", certified by trusted third parties. The goal of such a negotiation is to establish a sufficient level of trust so that sensitive resources, which may be either data or services, can be safely released. A key aspect of trust negotiation is that sensitive credentials may be protected by *disclosure policies* specified by credential holders. Disclosure policies state the conditions under which a resource can be released during a negotiation. Conditions are usually expressed as constraints against the credentials possessed by the interacting parties and their properties.

To carry out a trust negotiation, parties usually adopt a strategy, which is implemented by an algorithm defining what credentials to disclose, when to disclose them and whether to pass or fail the negotiation. There are a number of strategies for negotiating trust [239], each with different properties with respect to the speed of the negotiations and the necessary caution in releasing credentials and policies.

Trust negotiations represent an important example of an emerging research field which builds upon SOA. The decentralized and expressive nature of trust negotiation makes it a natural fit for Web services computing environments. To date, some initial trust negotiation architectures were deployed using client-service architectures. However, this architecture did not well represent the trust negotiation paradigm, and required one of the two parties (implemented as a server) to control the negotiation, in contrast with the peer-to-peer nature of the trust negotiation paradigm. Additionally, client-server architectures were demanding in terms of resource consumption, and very inefficient. Currently, the most well-known and successful ATN systems are now deployed using Web services. Each Web service offers the services required to carry on a negotiation. Additionally, recently Lee et al [161] have investigated how to fully integrate ATN with the WS-stack, and support policy specification using WS-Policy and credentials encoded as SAML certificates. In particular, [161] showed that after defining a rudimentary claims dialect which is fully-compliant with the WS-Trust standard the WS-Policy and WS-SecurityPolicy standards can be used to define a range of expressive trust negotiation policies. They also show that WS- Trusts negotiation and challenge framework can be extended to act as a standards-compliant transport mechanism within which trust negotiation sessions can occur. Furthermore, Lee and colleagues examined the systems aspects of this process and showed that trust negotiation policies specified using the WS-Policy and WS-SecurityPolicy standards can be complied into a format that is suitable for analysis by CLOUSEAU, an efficient policy compliance checker for trust negotiation systems. This not only eases the development of trust negotiation solutions for the Web services domain, but shows that it is possible to design a single compliance checker namely CLOUSEAU that is capable of analyzing Datalog-style policy languages, as well as other industry standard policy languages.

5.7 Trust Negotiation and Digital Identity Management

As digital identity management systems and trust negotiation systems are two technologies with many common goals, it is important to clearly assess their differences and their similarities in order to better understand the potential advantages deriving from their integration. In the rest of the chapter we develop such a comparison according to a number of relevant criteria. Based on our analysis we discuss our solution to integrate federated IdM with trust negotiation techniques, such as those provided as part of the Trust-χ [38]

system. More specifically, we discuss a framework, referred to as FAMTN[2] [44], supporting trust negotiation between federated SPs (FSP) in a federation, and between users and SPs. Users' interacting with FSPs can be of two types. A user who is affiliated with an organization within the Identity Management federation is a *member user* of the federation. In contrast, a users not affiliated with any FSP is a non-member. A key aspect of the FAMTN framework is that the user does not have to disclose a federated attribute[3] more than once to a given federation. Member users are able to perform negotiations by exploiting their SSO id without having to repeat any identity verification process. Further, an FAMTN system supports temporary SSO, so that non-member users can perform different negotiations with the federation by taking advantages of the federated framework to reduce the amount of identity information they need to provide during their interactions with the federation.

The FAMTN approach relies on the use of special-purpose tickets, that is, signed assertions that are released by the federation members to users upon successful negotiation. Two different types of ticket are supported. The first type, referred to as *trust ticket*, encodes the list of federation SPs with which a user not part of the federation has successfully negotiated. The second type, referred to as *session ticket*, is used by member users to speed up negotiations. FAMTN takes advantage of the fact that most attributes do not change in a short period of time; thus, if a user recently received a service, she is most likely eligible for the service again.

5.7.1 Automated Trust Negotiation and Digital Identity Management Systems: Differences and Similarities

The automated trust negotiation (ATN, for short) paradigm has several similarities with federated identity management. It has been argued that the two models might substitute for each other as they both aim at better handling user-sensitive information. However, the two paradigms have been designed for addressing specific and different goals: the goal of trust negotiation systems is to handle introductions between strangers, while the intent of identity management systems is to manage and protect identities of known users, within closed environments. The underlying goals being so distinct, it is easy to identify several architectural and design differences, which we summarize in what follows.

1. **Open vs. closed environment.** ATN techniques [128] have been developed for use in open systems and aim at providing protocols for stranger introduction to each other. This is in contrast to identity management frameworks which are typically in closed systems. ATN work suggests

---

[2] Federated Attribute Management and Trust Negotiation.

[3] Attributes the user is willing to share in a federation are called federated attributes.

Criteria	ATN Systems	IdM Systems
Environment	Open environment	Closed Environment
Credential management	User centric	Poly centric
Attributes used	Certified attributes or credentials	Certified and uncertified attributes
Attribute Encoding	X.509 certificates, XML certificates	username, SAML assertions, X.509 certificates, Kerberos tickets
Architecture	P2P	Client server
Policies	Privacy policies, Access control Policies	Privacy policies, authorization policies
Policy language	X-TNL, RT, PROTUNE etc.	XACML
Trust Model	Pairwise Trust (some brokered trust)	Pairwise Trust, Brokered Trust, Community Trust
Unique identification	Optional	SSO required
Credential discovery	Credential chain management protocols	Discovery service protocols

Table 5.2. Comparison of ATN and IdM systems

that the techniques may be interesting for the initial trust establishment
process between users and IdPs or to automatically manage introductions
between different federation groups.

2. **Credential and identity attribute management.** In a typical ATN
system the IdPs issuing identity attributes are certification authorities
(CAs). Such credentials are stored and provided by a client on behalf of
a user with the help of negotiation. Although there has been recent work
on storing user credentials with SPs using anonymous credentials [60], the
majority of ATN systems assume that users directly manage their own
credentials. In IdM systems, on the other hand, the IdPs save the user
profiles for future use in the federation according to the privacy preferences of the owner of the profile which is the user herself. Even the user
centric IdM systems discussed earlier in the chapter that emphasize the
role of the user during identity disclosure or attributes sharing do not man-
date identities to be locally stored at the user end. Regarding attribute
certification, ATN's typically negotiate certified attributes or credentials.
In IdM systems, uncertified attributes are widely used, along with certified attributes. IdM systems most used encoding assertions' language
is SAML, whereas in ATN systems attributes are encoded in digital attribute certificates represented according to the X.509 certificate format
or similar.

3. **Architectural differences.** An ATN system is typically used in peer-to-
peer systems. As such, the basic architecture of clients and SPs is identical.
Any entity playing the role of provider in a trust negotiation can act as
a client in different negotiations, if needed. In this respect, ATN systems

differ to a great extent with respect to IdM frameworks in which IdPs, SPs and clients all have different architectural components depending on the functionality of the entity. Due to the peer-to-peer nature of ATN systems, the integration of an ATN architectural component becomes simpler with the existing IdM systems.

4. **Policies.** In both IdM and ATN systems one of the goals is to satisfy user privacy preferences for their personal data and to make sure that access control policies are stated and enforced. Therefore, both types of system support privacy and access control policies. However, in ATN systems access control policies play a key role in the trust negotiation processes, whereas so far they have been considered as a marginal aspect in IdM systems. As such, ATN policies provide various alternative ways of expressing the requirements for access to a given resource or for different usage conditions. This approach ensures soundness for any transaction, meaning that if user preferences and the SPs requirements are compatible, then the transaction will certainly succeed. Soundness is not guaranteed in current IdM systems because of the lack of formal negotiation procedures and corresponding expressive policy languages. IdM systems, however, provide mechanisms for policy verification which could be used by additional negotiation modules to provide ATN functions.

5. **User identity.** Both ATN and IdM systems require users to be identified. Such a requirement is particularly relevant in IdM systems, which actually aim at uniquely identifying users within federations. In contrast, unique identification of users is usually a secondary aspect in ATN systems as authentication is mainly based on properties of the user rather than on a unique identifier. However, real case scenarios show that authentication is often a first class requirement in specific negotiations, such as in business transactions or negotiations of individuals' data. Another aspect to highlight is that IdM systems that rely on SSO to identify users do not need to certify user identities in other ways. In ATN systems, instead, identification is obtained by credential combinations, although SSO might be employed in specific contexts. There is no need to link multiple negotiations to the same identity as identification is (if required) executed on the fly, while the negotiation process is taking place.

6. **Trust model.** There are three main types of trust models in a typical IdM system [168], namely pairwise, brokered, and community trust models. The pairwise model is related to the case where two entities have direct business agreements with each other. The brokered trust model is related to the case of two entities that do not have a direct agreement with each other, but have some agreements with one or more intermediaries so as to enable a business trust path to be constructed between them. finally, community trust model supports the cases where multiple entities have common business agreements within the community or federation. Although all three trust models can use ATN systems, the brokered trust model integrated with ATN is particularly interesting, since it provides a

unique feature to existing IdM systems, in that it supports interactions also among unknown entities and is the one model which requires fewer assumptions on pre existing agreements.

Despite the differences discussed above, there are many common aspects between IdM and ATN systems. For instance, a relevant aspect is related to credential discovery, which is required in both the environments, although in a different manner. Using the discovery service mentioned earlier, the IdMs collaborate in order to be able to make assertions about a user from a local IdP to a remote IdP. Similarly, in ATN systems, credential discovery is extensively used to retrieve remote credentials not available at the negotiating parties. Another common aspect is delegation. Although not a main issue in trust negotiations, delegation is achieved through ad-hoc protocols and credentials, enabling entities to negotiate on behalf of third parties. In IdM systems the brokered trust model can be used to delegate the responsibility for attribute assertion to another IdP which the user may trust more. Table 5.2 summarizes the discussion. It is, however, important to note that such analysis is based on the pure IdM and TN models, as originally designed. Variations to both approaches have been proposed in the last few years, which make the evaluation results slightly different.

5.8 Integrating Identity Management and Trust Negotiations

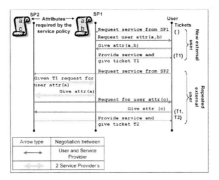

Fig. 5.4. External user negotiating with two SPs of a federation. A user who has already provided attributes to any SP in the federation might not need to provide them again when another SP in the federation requires them.

To combine the advantages of the IDM and ATN approaches, a Federated Attribute Management and Trust Negotiation (FAMTN) solution, which provides a truly distributed approach to the management of user identities and user attributes with negotiation capabilities [44] has been proposed. A FAMTN federation essentially involves two type of entities: FAMTN FSPs and users. FSP's support identity and attributes provisioning, as detailed later in this section.

The FAMTN supports two types of negotiation. The first type is between an FSP and the user, and the second is between two FSPs in the same federation. The protocol for negotiations between FSPs and users depends on the interacting user's type. The distinction is based on the user's membership in the federation. Member users do not have to provide their identity attributes multiple times. The federation is more likely to have information about a member user even if the member has not accessed any of its services. The information known to the federation changes also according to the policy of the member organization that defines which of the user attributes are federated. The member will be identified among the federation with an SSO user identification.

In contrast, non-member users have to provide all required attributes during their first negotiations. The first negotiation between a non-member user and an FSP includes identity provisioning, since the provider issues a temporary user-id to be used within the federation. The use of a time-limited SSO id for non-members ensures identity linkability.[4] Of course, users might have multiple identities and choose which one to adopt for requesting access to a service. We do not elaborate on multiple identity issues since they go beyond the scope of this discussion. By interacting further with the federation, the amount of information about users they disclosed to the federation increases. This information can be linked to the user (who is then called *repeated non-member user*) and thus reused in the subsequent negotiations. As a result, faster negotiations with fewer exchanges of user's attributes are executed. An example is given in the figure 5.4. User U requests service from SP SP1. SP1 requires user attributes (a,b) to satisfy its service policy. U provides (a,b) and gets the service. Suppose that U, at the end of this successful negotiation, opts for sharing attribute (a,b) within the federation, and suppose that then U requires a service from another provider SP2 in the same federation. Suppose that the attribute requirements there are (a,c). In this case, U only has to provide the attribute c to receive the service.

At the end of a successful negotiation, users receive one of two types of ticket. The first, referred to as *trust ticket*, is issued to non-member users to provide information about the previous services and FSPs the user has accessed. The other type of ticket, referred to as *session ticket*, is issued to non-member users. We show a detailed negotiation process using the described user cases in Section 5.9.3.

---

[4] We can reasonably assume that the time interval duration is defined by the federation policy.

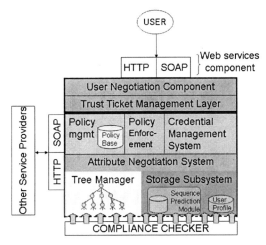

Fig. 5.5. Architecture for FAMTN SP.

The second type of negotiation occurs between two FSPs. Such a type of negotiation is useful when a user successfully negotiates a service from one FSP, and automatically becomes eligible to receive service from another FSP. As such, when the user asks for a service the FSP providing it can directly negotiate user-related attributes with the FSP holding such attributes from previous negotiations. Also, negotiations among FSP's might be required for verifying external user identities. As FAMTN does not rely on a single IdP, an IdP might not be aware of the last registered users. When a request from a locally unknown user Id is received, an FSP can directly interact with the FSP that has issued the claimed user Id to double check its validity.[5]

5.8.1 Architecture of a SP in FAMTN

An FAMTN framework is composed of FSP that contains the necessary components required to execute: 1) trust negotiation among users and FSP's; and 2) federation of user attributes. The architecture of FSP is sketched in figure 5.5. FSP is equipped with components deriving from the two underlying frameworks of automated trust negotiations and federated identity management. Each FSP can perform the functionality of an IdP and SP.

The FSPs main components are:

- the *Web services* component, which enables secure communication within the federation and with the users;
- the *user negotiation* component, which contains the modules executing the negotiation, depending on whether the user is a member or nonmember (this component is directly related to the trust ticket management layer).

---

[5] For simplicity we assume user Id contains an FSP information to easily identify the issuer.

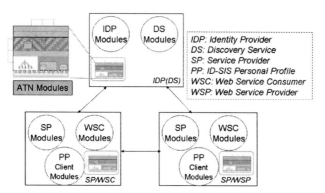

Fig. 5.6. Liberty Alliance ID-WSF and FSP Example: Three websites and system modules

Other parts of the FSP include the trust ticket management layer which manages the trust tickets and the session tickets required for the negotiation. The *policy base* in the policy management component stores the authentication and access control policies. The *credential management* system is in charge of managing and validating certificates and user tickets by verifying the FSP's signatures. It is also responsible for revocation when required.

The *attribute negotiation* system consists of the main components required for negotiation, including the *tree manager*, storing the state of the negotiation; the *sequence prediction module*, caching and managing user profile information; and the *compliance checker*, policy compliance testing and determining request replies during a negotiation.

5.8.2 An Example of a Use Case: FSP in Liberty Web Services Framework

Figure 5.6 gives an example scenario of the Liberty Alliance Web Services Framework (WSF) [167] with additional FSP components. For details about the original Liberty-ID WSF example we refer the reader to Section 6.1 of [167]. We now discuss how ATN comes into play in a typical identity framework.

1. User Joe attempts access to SP1 using SSO.
2. Using redirection and IdM system protocols, IDP transmits to SP1 an SAML assertion authenticating Joe.
3. SP1 requires a certificate from Joe to verify that he is older than 21 and his address for delivery.
4. Joe does not trust SP1 and therefore he is not willing to reveal to SP1 his certified credential. He therefore negotiates with IDP, and reveals his credential to IDP instead.

5. SP1 now negotiates with IDP which finally sends an SAML assertion stating whether Joe satisfies SP1's age criteria or not. Joe does not thus have to reveal the actual credential to SP1, ensuring that the credential is only stored with a party he trusts.

6. Joe also registers his address with SP1 for delivery but requires that his address be released to a member of the federation only when the address is required for a purchased product delivery and if the member is certified by Better Business Bureau (BBB).

7. Joe subsequently attempts access to SP2 to rent a movie. Due to SSO he gets seamless access.

8. SP2 asks Joe for his address. Joe[6] replies to SP2 to retrieve his profile from other sites in the federation. Using the discovery service, SP2 contacts SP1, who first negotiates with SP2 to verify that the conditions for Joe's attribute release are met. If they are, SP2 receives the required information and can make the appropriate delivery.

The example demonstrates how additional privacy and flexible policies can be implemented with ATN. Also not all components of the FSP are required in a typical IdM system. An FSP can benefit from modules that are part of the Liberty Alliance Framework or other IdM systems, such as the DS, PP, policy, and credential management systems. In figure 5.5, the striped color components denote the ATN-specific parts used for ATN in the Liberty WSF framework.

5.9 Negotiations in an FAMTN Federation

In this section we elaborate on the approach for negotiating trust in FAMTN. We first introduce the notion of trust tickets and session tickets, as they are the main building blocks in the FAMTN trust negotiation protocols. A possible implementation of trust tickets through cookies is then proposed.

5.9.1 Ticketing system in an FAMTN Federation

The two types of tickets supported by the FAMTN framework have a fixed lifetime. Loosely synchronized clocks in the federation are assumed. The SSO ID is given by the user ID in the tickets. The structure and functions of the tickets are discussed in what follows.

Session ticket
   A session ticket ensures that if the negotiation ends successfully and the

---

[6] Note that in this case, it is actually an agent operating at the client on behalf of Joe that actually suggests request re-directions. We use Joe to simplify the presentation of the example.

same user requests the same SP for the same service in a subsequent session, the service can be granted immediately without unnecessarily having to repeat the trust establishment process. A session ticket therefore contains the following fields:

$$Signed_{SP} < \tau(s_{req}), u, \ T, \ R>$$

where $\tau(s_{req})$ denotes the service requested, u is the user ID, and T is the ticket time stamp. R denotes the result of the negotiation. R can be either a simple statement or a structured object. The use of structured objects is particularly interesting for tracing intermediate results of negotiations of aggregated services. A session ticket is signed by the SP, which authenticates it by giving it a receipt of the trust establishment. Since session tickets are encrypted with the SP's private key, they are tamper- proof and can be verified. The timeout mechanism depends on the type of user attributes required for the service and the security level of the service.

Trust ticket

The purpose of the trust ticket is to determine the previous services external users have accessed. Assuming that all the SPs are members of the same federation, the signature of a member provider can be verified by any other member provider. Such a ticket has the following form:

$$Signed_{SP_{last}} < list\{\tau(s), FSP, T\}, u, T\text{-}I >$$

Every 3-tuple in the list contains the type of service, the corresponding SP, and the timeout. u corresponds to the temporary user identification, and $T\text{-}I$ is the expiration date for this ID. The ticket is signed by the last SP with which the user had a successful transaction. At the end of a successful transaction, the SP takes the current user trust ticket, removes all *timed out* entries, appends its information, signs the ticket and sends it to the user.

5.9.2 Implementing Trust Tickets Through Cookies

Cookies may be used with many IdM systems to make information about the users available to servers. State information is stored at the client and is sent to the server the next time the user accesses the server. Like the tickets described in the previous section, cookies can be valid only for the session for which they have been issued or can persist beyond the end of the session. A persistent cookie is typically written to a file on the browser's hard drive if its lifetime has not elapsed when the browser is shut down, and therefore can be used for a longer period of time. In a truly distributed federation if there is more than one IdPs, an SP needs a mechanism to determine which IdP has the user information. This problem is known as the "Introduction Problem" in the Liberty Alliance approach. The current approach is to rely on cookies for redirecting IdPs. There are several advantages of using cookies. Implementing them is efficient, as there is no requirement of new software installation for their use, and they can be used independently from any authentication mechanism. They also provide dynamic state information, helpful to prevent several security threats. One such threat is an impersonation attack, which arises because when a user has successfully logged into one SP, the SPs in the federation do not re-authenticate her. Thus, if the authentication is no longer valid because of attacks or other failure there is no straightforward way to detect it. Cookies help in checking whether the authentication ticket is associated with the user identity as well as in checking the validity of the IdP session of that user. Alternatives to the use of cookies for the "Introduction Problem" are based either on interactions with the user actively or on the use of a statically hand-configured list of the possible IdPs. Such approaches inhibit the seamless SSO process and are not as efficient.

Cookies, however, have some security problems [227]. Firstly, they are usually in clear text. Their headers are generally unprotected, and even the encrypted cookies are vulnerable to replay attacks. Second, since the cookies are stored on the local machines, they can be easily read by anyone using the machines. Thirdly, there is a need to control where cookies are sent, because it is not desirable to send a user cookie to an untrusted SP. For example, several spyware applications exploit user cookies, and therefore better control on the destination of cookies is needed. As a consequence, cookies should not store any personal identifiers or any sensitive information. In real applications, however, a cookie typically stores the SSO user ID, or other tracking record which may leak information about the user. Most of these security vulnerabilities can be addressed by better storage and usage protocols and mechanisms. An approach has been suggested in [44] for implementing trust tickets using cookies in IdM systems, in order to exploit the advantages and prevent several of the vulnerabilities. Indeed, the timeouts and signed information given by the session and trust tickets give reliable and dynamic state information. To further increase the security of cookie usage in a federation, mechanisms enabling *selective download of cookies* should be employed. Browsers typically give users limited choice about how to handle cookies. There is only coarse grained control on cookies: either no cookies are to be downloaded or all cookies have to be accepted. The case where a user can choose cookies from a Web site that uses a single domain rather than multiple domains may cause problems in a federation which is typically a multiple domain environment. Building server filters is currently complicated and they are not usable by average users. As with privacy preferences, a user should be able to set preferences for the cookies, specifying more fine-grained conditions. The following are examples of selective use of cookies:

1. Accept only signed cookies from a given federation SP.
2. Accept cookies from members certified by BBB by negotiating servers' attributes.

3. Send the cookie which does not contain personally identifying information.
4. Send the cookie to an SP which is not in a class with a conflict of interest with the SP which set this cookie.

Algorithm 1: FAMTN negotiation process

Input: $userID, userAuthenticationInfo$
Output: $IsRegistered(userID)$
(1) $userRequest \Leftarrow getRequest(userID)$
(2)   **if** $userRequest \notin Services_{FSP}$
(3) $return$ Abort-Negotiation
(4)   ***Comment: For Members***
(5)   **if** $isValidMember(userID) = true$
(6) $sessionTicket \Leftarrow getSessionTicket(userID)$
(7)   **if** $sessionTicket \neq NULL \land sessionTicket.time < timeout$
(8) $return$ OK
(9) $M_{FSP} = getMemberFSP(userID)$
(10) $remAttrList1 \Leftarrow NEGOTIATE_{FSP}(Curr_{FSP}, M_{FSP}$
(11) $userID, userRequest)$
(12)   **if** $remAttrList1 \neq NULL$
(13) $remAttrList2 \Leftarrow NEGOTIATE_{User}(Curr_{FSP},$
(14) $userID, CurrPolicy_{FSP})$
(15)   **else**
(16) $send(SessionTicket) \Rightarrow userID$
(17) $return$ OK
(18)   **if** $remAttrList2 \neq NULL$
(19) $return$ Abort-Negotiation
(20)   **else**
(21) $send(SessionTicket) \Rightarrow userID$
(22) $return$ OK
(23)   ***Comment: For Non-Members***
(24) $FSPlist \Leftarrow getTrustTicket(userID)$
(25)   **while** $FSPlist \neq EmptyList$
(26) $M_i = rmHeadOfList(FSPlist)$
(27) $remAttrList3 \Leftarrow NEGOTIATE_{FSP}(Curr_{FSP}, M_i$
(28) $userID, userRequest)$
(29)   **if** $remAttrList3 = NULL$
(30) $send(TrustTicket) \Rightarrow userID$
(31) $return$ OK
(32)   **if** $remAttrList3 \neq NULL$
(33) $remAttrList4 \Leftarrow NEGOTIATE_{User}(Curr_{FSP},$
(34) $userID, CurrPolicy_{FSP})$
(35)   **if** $remAttrList4 \neq NULL$
(36) $return$ Abort-Negotiation
(37)   **else**
(38) $send(TrustTicket) \Rightarrow userID$
(39) $return$ OK

5.9.3 Negotiation in Identity Federated Systems

The negotiation process for trust establishment depends on the type of user involved and the history of her interaction with the federation members. Algorithm 1 reports the complete negotiation process developed for FAMTN, which includes all user cases, assuming one federation is in place. Multiple federations with non empty intersection are outside the scope of FAMTN. The two main types of negotiations are between the user and the FSPs, and between the FSPs. The four different user cases give the basis for the design and analysis of the user-FSP negotiation process.

Intuitively, a recent user should obtain service access faster than a new user. This is achieved with the help of the short-term session tickets. Similarly, a repeat user, who has already received services from different FSPs of the federation, should get service access faster than a new external user. The reason is that the new external user directly negotiates all the required attributes with the FSP, whereas for a repeat user some of the attributes can be retrieved from the other FSPs she has visited before. The information about the previously visited FSP's is given in the list of trust tickets which are retrieved iteratively until the user attribute requirements are satisfied. At each iteration, the FSP requiring the user attributes to satisfy its service disclosure policy negotiates with the FSP indicated in the trust ticket. If the retrieved attributes do not suffice, the FSP negotiates with the user herself. finally, a member user, internal to the federation and thus more trusted, should have advantage in the negotiation process compared to a new external (non-member) user. Indeed, member user attributes are directly retrieved from the organizations in the federation within which users are affiliated with each other. This provides an efficient mechanism for retrieval of users attributes, as it avoids iterated negotiations between all the SPs a user has interacted with. Here we assume that all of the member users' attributes are stored and possibly certified by organizations they are affiliated with. Member users can also use the session tickets just like the external users.

5.10 Bibliographic Notes

Digital identity management is being investigated in both the corporate world and academia. In [126], readers can find an interesting reading presentation of guidelines and advices for identity management system designers looking to build privacy-protective systems. Biometric technologies have been suggested as a natural tool in identity management systems for enhancing privacy and assuring a one-to-one correspondence between people and records. An interesting discussion on challenges and drawbacks appear in [272]. Additional information related to the Liberty Alliance Initiative is found online at http://www.projectliberty.org, where white papers and technical specifications are available. Regarding WS-Federation, technical specifications are available online at http://www.ibm.com/developerworks/library/specification/ws-fed/.

Trust negotiation is acknowledged as a relevant and challenging research topic in the wider field of trust management. Interested readers can find a well-written introduction in [37], where a high level discussion of the main concepts related to trust negotiation is presented. In [232], an interesting analysis of the main requirements for trust negotiation systems is presented. More technical and detailed presentation of trust negotiation system prototypes can be found in [159, 161, 38].

A large body of work on trust negotiation has focused on the issue of policy sensitivity, that is, on how to make sure that the disclosure policies driving the negotiation do not intentionally leak any sensitive information. We suggest [283] for a presentation of ad hoc logic based system, and [165] for one trust negotiation system in which protection is based on a wide array of crypto-based techniques.

6

Access Control for Web Services

An access control model restricts the set of service requestors that can invoke Web service's operations. While access control has been widely investigated, especially in database systems [42], only recently work on security for Web services emerged as an important part of the Web service saga [285, 237, 41]. However, most approaches assume that the Web services are stateless.

Access control enforcement approaches for stateless and stateful Web services have similarities. Since in SOA the relation between Web service requestor and Web service provider is much more loosely coupled than in traditional client-server applications, the enforcement is based on the definition of access control policies that are expressed based on relevant characteristics of service requestors, known as *attributes*, that service requestors provide to the Web service. Access control policies can be defined at different levels of granularity: the object of an access control policy can be a class of Web services managed by the same service provider, a single Web service, a single operation, or operation's parameters. The main difference in access control enforcement for stateless and stateful Web services is in the way access control decisions are made. With respect to stateless Web services, the decision to grant or not grant the execution of an operation to a service requestor is based on the access control policy that applies to the operation; if the service requestor's attributes satisfy the conditions in the policy, the operation is invoked and the result is returned to the service requestor. In contrast, for stateful Web services the decision about whether a service requestor can invoke an operation or not is made not only on the basis of access control policy fulfillment but also of the state of the interaction between the service requestor and the Web service.

Other issues related to access control enforcement arise when Web services (called *component services*) are composed together to build a new Web service (referred to as *composite service*) to satisfy a user request. As single Web services, a composite Web service has an interface that provides a set of operations. The fact that the Web service is composite is totally transparent to its service requestors. A first issue with a composite Web service is related

E. Bertino et al., *Security for Web Services and Service-Oriented Architectures*,
DOI 10.1007/978-3-540-87742-4_6, © Springer-Verlag Berlin Heidelberg 2010

to the management of service requestors' identity attributes. The credential ownership can be verified by the composite service or its verification can be delegated to the component services. In the second case there is the problem of assuring that a service requestor's credentials are used in ways that he intends. In fact, a service requestor may trust the composite service, but not the component Web services of which it is not aware. Another issue concerns access control policy definition and enforcement. The component Web services have their own access control policies to protect their operations from unauthorized use. These policies may represent conflicting requirements. Therefore, a mechanism is needed to combine the component Web services' policies to derive a policy to be enforced at the level of the composite service. Another approach is to define new access control policies for the composite service that may or may not take into account the policies of the component services. Finally, the enforcement can be centralized or decentralized. In the centralized approach, when a service requestor invokes an operation, the composite Web service makes the decision about the service invocation on the basis of a policy resulting from the combination of component Web services' access control policies or on the basis of a newly defined policy for the composite service. Such an approach limits unnecessary invocations ending in rollback operations if particular permissions for invoked component Web service operations are missing. In contrast, in the decentralized approach it is the component Web service providing the invoked operation that decides about the invocation on the basis of its own local policies.

6.1 Approaches to Enforce Access Control for Web Services

In this section, the main approaches to access control for Web services are categorized according to the following parameters: a) whether the focus is on enhanced policy specification features or on enforcement; b) the basic mechanism for access control (role-based vs. attribute-based); c) applicability to single or composite Web services; d) stateless vs. stateful Web service interactions. Among all the proposals for access control enforcement for Web services, the most relevant ones are the following one:

- Gun et al. [237] propose an approach for specifying and enforcing security policies based on the temporal logics-based WebGuard language. They propose an enforcement engine that processes the security policies and generates platform specific code to enforce them. The enforcement code is integrated in the Web service code and is executed when a Web service's invocation starts and ends.
- Feng et al. [103] present a context-aware service-oriented role-based access control model. In this model, access control decisions are taken by capturing security relevant environmental contexts, such as time, location, operation state, or other environmental information. As in traditional RBAC,

access control policies are defined as a set of permissions to execute Web service operations. Service requestors are assigned to roles that in turn are associated with a set of permissions. The assignment of service requestor to roles is based on their identity and on the context's parameters. Also, an architecture similar to the one proposed in the XACML standard is presented.

- Emig et al. [98] present an access control model that is a combination of traditional hierarchical role-based (RBAC) and attribute-based (ABAC) access control models. From ABAC it inherits the way service requestors are authenticated: a requestor is identified by a set of attributes. From RBAC it adopts the definition of role hierarchy and of policies as a set of permissions. An access control policy is a combination of permissions combining an object (an operation or the whole Web service), and a set of attributes that the requestor has to provide, with constraints on the environmental state (like date, time or any other attribute that is not related to the service requestor or object). Unlike in RBAC, the permissions are not associated with a role but with a set of the service requestor's attributes. Moreover, a role identifies not a business role but a set of the service requestor's attributes. Emig et al. extend the model to composite Web services; the composite Web service enforces a policy that is the result of the conjunction of the policies protecting the operations that are invoked in the composition.

- Wonohoesodo et al. [285] propose two RBAC (Role-Based Access Control) models, SWS-RBAC, for single Web services, and CWS-RBAC, for composite Web services. Permissions are defined at both service and service parameter levels. A role is associated with a list of services that service requestors, assigned to that role, have permission to execute. Therefore, the proposed model enforces access control at both the service level and the parameter level to ensure that service requestors that have permission to call a service, also have appropriate access to its parameters to successfully execute it. In the CWS-RBAC model, the role to which a service requestor is assigned for accessing a composite service must be a global role, which is mapped onto local roles of the service providers of the component Web services.

- Srivatsa et al. [241] propose an RBAC access control model for Web service compositions. Access control rules express constraints like separation of duty constraints and constraints based on the past histories of service invocations. They can also be dependent on one or more parameters associated with a Web service invocation. A pure-past linear temporal logic language (PPLTL) is used to represent access control rules. Access control is enforced through role translation. Each organization involved in the composition defines these role translations in the form of a table that maps the roles in the organization to some roles in the other organizations. When an operation of the composite Web service is invoked by a user under a certain role, the enforcement system performs the role translation and creates a composite role. A composite role consists of a temporally ordered sequence of roles and services that are involved in the invocation. The decision to grant the invocation is a model-checking problem: if the composite role is a logical consequence of the access control rules applied to the request, the operation invocation is granted.

All the access control proposals are concerned with access control policy specification and enforcement. Gun et al. [237] propose attribute-based access control models, while Feng et al., Wonohoesodo et al., and Srivatsa et al. [103, 285, 241] propose role-based access control models. Emig et al. [98] propose a model that inherits features from both ABAC and RBAC access control models. Finally, the proposals of Gun et al. and Feng et al. [237, 103] are applied only to simple Web services, while the approaches by Wonohoesodo et al., Srivatsa et al., and Emig et al. [285, 241, 98] deal with both simple and composite Web services.

Other proposals about access control for Web services are related to Semantic Web services. The focus is on richer formalisms and specification languages for policies, based on specific ontologies for "security" [91], in order to be able to match service and service requestor requirements [146, 3] during the Web services discovery phase. Finally, another interesting proposal about access control policy specification and enforcement for Web services comes from the OASIS XACML Technical Committee which has proposed a Web Service Profile of XACML (WS-XACML) [14]. WS-XACML specifies how to use XACML in a Web services environment. WS-XACML introduces two new types of policy assertion to allow Web service providers and consumers to specify their authorization, access control, and privacy requirements and capabilities regarding Web service interactions. Moreover, WS-XACML proposes a way to verify whether a Web service consumer's capabilities and a Web SP's requirements match and viceversa. We provide an overview of XACML and WS-XACML in section 4.3.7 about access control policy standards.

All these proposals for access control for Web services assume that the interactions with a Web service are stateless. Moreover, the access control enforcement mechanism is not flexible; service requestors either unconditionally disclose their information, or do not get access to the service at all.

In this chapter, we focus on the description of an access control model for stateless Web services, referred to as WS-AC$_1$, characterized by a flexible access control enforcement approach based on a negotiation process and on the only access control model for stateful Web services.

6.2 WS-AC$_1$: An Adaptive Access Control Model for Stateless Web Services

WS-AC$_1$ is an implementation-independent, attribute-based access control model for Web services, providing mechanisms for negotiation of service parameters. In WS-AC$_1$, the service requestors are entities (human beings or software agents) the requests by which have to be evaluated and to which authorizations (permissions or denials) can be granted. Service requestors are identified by means of identity attributes qualifying them, such as name, birth date, credit card number, and passport number. Identity attributes are disclosed within access requests by invoking the desired service. Access requests to a Web service are evaluated with respect to access control policies. Note that, for the sake of simplicity, the model does not distinguish between the Web service and the different operations it provides; that is, a Web service provides a single operation. The proposed access model can be applied to the various operations provided by a Web service without any extension. Access control policies are defined in terms of the identity attributes of the service requestor and the set of allowed service parameter values. Both identity attributes and service parameters are further differentiated into mandatory and optional ones. For privacy and security purposes, access control policies are not published with the service description, but are internal to the WS-AC$_1$ system. WS-AC$_1$ also allows one to specify multiple policies at different levels of granularity. It is possible to associate fine-grained policies with a specific service as well with several services. To this end, it is possible to group different services in one or more classes and specify policies referring to a specific service class, thus reducing the number of policies that need to be specified by a policy administrator. A policy for a class of services is then applied to all the services of that class, unless policies associated with specific services are defined.

The following sections present the conditions under which services can be grouped into classes, and the criteria used by WS-AC$_1$ to select the policies to use upon a service request. Moreover, to adapt the provision of the service to dynamically changing conditions, the WS-AC$_1$ policy language allows one to specify constraints, dynamically evaluated, over a set of environmental variables, referred to as *context*, as well as over service parameters. The context is associated with a specific service implementation, and it might consist of monitored system variables, such as the system load.

As illustrated in Figure 6.1, the access control process of the WS-AC$_1$ system is organized into two main sequential phases. The first phase deals with identification of the subject requesting the service. The second phase, executed only if identification succeeds, verifies the service parameters specified by the service requestor against the authorized service parameters. The identification phase is adaptive, in that the access control system might eventually require the requestor to submit additional identity attributes in addition to those originally submitted. Such an approach allows the SP to adapt the service provisioning to dynamic situations. For example, after a security attack, the SP might require additional identity attributes from the service requestors. In addition, to enhance the flexibility of access control, the service parameter verification phase can trigger a negotiation process. The purpose of this process is to drive the requestors toward the specification of an access request compliant with the service specification and policies. The negotiation consists

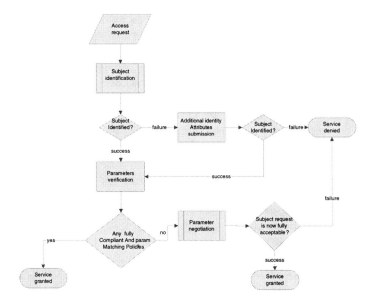

Fig. 6.1. Conceptual Organization of access control in WS-AC$_1$

in an exchange of messages between the two negotiating entities to limit, fix or propose the authorized parameters the service requestor may use. The negotiation of service parameters allows the SP to tailor the service provisioning to the service requestor preferences or, at the opposite, to "enforce" its own preferred service provisioning conditions.

6.2.1 The WS-AC$_1$ Model

This section introduces the main notions underlying the WS-AC$_1$ access control model. A Web service, called *BookStore*, supplying books and magazines to general customers and to supermarkets is used as running example. First the notion of *service description* is presented; it specifies the information necessary to invoke a service. Then, the notion of Web service *context, access request* and *access control policy* are introduced.

A service description serves the following main purposes:

1. It allows the potential service requestors to obtain the description of both the identity attributes (*AuthAttrs*) and the service parameters (*Parameters*) needed to submit a request to the service. Identity attributes are properties, such as name, birth date, credit card and passport, qualifying a service requestor. Service parameters represent information the service requestor has to provide to activate the operation supported by the service, and also information related to the level of quality of service required by the service requestor.

2. It conveys to potential service requestors which identity attributes are mandatory and optional and which service parameters are mandatory and optional.

A service description of a Web service s is formally represented as a tuple of the form $Serv\text{-}descr = <s;\ Parameters;\ AuthAttrs>$. $Parameters = [Pspec_1,..,Pspec_n]$ is the set of the Web service's parameter. $Pspec_i$, $i = 1,..,n$, is a triple of the form $(P_i, Domain_{P_i}, ParamType_{P_i})$ where P_i is a parameter name; $Domain_{P_i}$ denotes the set of values the parameter can assume; $ParamType_{P_i} \in \{mand, opt\}$ specifies whether the parameter is mandatory or optional. $AuthAttrs = [(A_1, AttrType_{A_1}), (A_2, AttrType_{A_2}),...,(A_k, AttrType_{A_k})]$ is the set of identity attributes. $(A_i, AttrType_{A_i})$, $i = 1,..,k$, represents an identity attribute where A_i is the name of the attribute, and $AttrType_{A_i}$ indicates whether the attribute is mandatory or optional.

Given a description of a service s, in the following $MandAtt$ represents the set of mandatory attributes in $AuthAttrs$, and $MandPar$ represents the set of mandatory parameters in $Parameters$. Further, PN is the set of parameter names in $Serv\text{-}descr$.

While mandatory identity attributes and service parameters must be assigned a value by the service requestor as part of the initial request for the service, the optional ones do not have such a requirement. However, depending on their values, submission of the mandatory attributes by the service requestor may not be enough for gaining access to the service. As such, values for the optional identity attributes may be required by the SP during the subsequent negotiation process. The following section further elaborates on service requestor authentication. Accesses in WS-AC₁ are either granted or denied on the basis of access conditions referring to the identity attributes of the service requestor and in terms of the parameters characterizing the service.

Example 6.1. Consider the *BookStore* service. Such a service is described by the tuple $< BookStore;\ ((Title,$ string, mand$)\ (Authors,$ string, opt$),\ (Price,$ Lowest, Medium, High, mand$),\ (Quantity, \{\},$ mand$));\ (CustomerId,$ mand$) >$ where:

- *BookStore* is the service identifier.
- *Title, Authors, Price*, and *Quantity* are the service parameters necessary to invoke the *BookStore* service. *Title* is a mandatory parameter and indicates the title of the book or magazine the customer wants to order. *Authors* specifies the author names of the book or magazine the customer wants to purchase, *Price* represents customer preference about the book or magazine *Price*, and *Quantity* is the number of the book or magazine items required by the customer.
- *CustomerId* is the attribute used by the WS-AC₁ system to identify the service requester. *CustomerId* can be the name of a final user or the name of a supermarket chain's dealer.

The WS-AC$_1$ system associates with a service a *context*, composed of a set of variables that can influence service provisioning. The context is evaluated by the WS-AC$_1$ system to enforce access control to the service as explained later in this section. The WS-AC$_1$ system updates the context variables each time an access request is received or the context changes. In what follows, the set of context variable names for a service s is abbreviated with CVN.

Example 6.2. An example of context that can be associated with the *BookStore* service is

$$serv\_context_{BookStore} = [UsersConnected : 1000]$$

where $UsersConnected$ records the number of users connected to the service during a given time period.

The invocation of a service is formalized as an *access request* in which the service requestor has to provide the information specified in the service description, that is, its qualifying attributes, the parameters of the Web service and the Web service identifier. An access request for a Web service s can be represented as a tuple $(\underline{a}, s, \underline{p})$ where $\underline{a} = [A_1 : a_1, A_2 : a_2, ..., A_m : a_m]$ represents the service requestor identity's attributes where A_i is an identity attribute name and a_i is the associated value, $i = 1, ..., m$; s is a service identifier; and $\underline{p} = [P_1 : p_1, P_2 : p_2, ..., P_k : p_k]$ is the set of service parameters where P_i is a parameter name and p_i is the associated value, $i = 1, ..., k$.

Example 6.3. Referring to the service description introduced in Example 6.1, the access request must contain the identity attribute $CustomerId$ and the service parameters $Title$, $Price$, and $Quantity$. An example of such an access request is ([$CustomerId$: Wallmart of New York]; $BookStore$; [$Title$: Cosmopolitan, $Price$:Medium; $Quantity$:20000]).

The WS-AC$_1$ system evaluates access requests with respect to the access control policies protecting the required service. The same service may be protected by several access control policies. Informally, an access control policy is expressed by means of three components: a component to denote the requester, a component for specifying the parameters to which the policy applies, and a component for specifying the parameter values allowed by the service. Subjects are denoted in policies by attribute conditions specifying the conditions that each identity attribute of the service requestor has to satisfy in order to access the service. To enhance flexibility, the model allows one to specify for each service the set of legal parameter values that the service parameters can be assigned. Legal parameter values are defined by ad hoc rules, referred to as *constraints*, defined over the set of the service parameters and/or the set of the service context variables. A constraint is represented by a logic rule of the form $H \leftarrow L_1, L_2, ..., L_n, notF_1, notF_2, ...notF_m$. H is the *head* of the rule and is an expression of the form $ArgName\ op\ Values$ where $ArgName$ is an element of PN, op is a comparison operator or the $\in$ operator, and $Values$ is either a set of values defined through enumeration or a range expression

$[v_{begin}, v_{end}]$, or a single value. $L_1, L_2, .., L_n, notF_1, notF_2, ..., notF_m$ is the *body* of the rule; each L_i, $i = 1, .., n$, or F_k, $k = 1, .., m$, in the body of the rule can be an expression of the form *ArgName op Values*, where *ArgName* is an element of either *PN* or *CVN*. The body of a rule is empty to denote always true rules. Constraints are evaluated dynamically. It is thus possible to adapt the access control policies to dynamically varying conditions.

A constraint restricts the set of values associated with a parameter on the basis of the current values of the context variables and/or the values assumed by other services' parameters. In the following, given a constraint $Constr_k$, $Legal\_Values_{Constr_k}(P_i)$ denotes the set of values assigned to the parameter P_i in the head of $Constr_k$, and $Target_{Constr_k}$ denotes the service parameter name P_i in H.

Example 6.4. With respect to the Web service presented in Example 6.1, the following constraints can be specified:

- $Quantity = 10 \leftarrow Title =$ The Times; $Price =$ Low
- $Price =$ High $\leftarrow StockLevel < 100, Title =$ Glamour

The first constraint states that if the service requestor wants to purchase "The Times" magazine, it can order only ten items. The second constraint specifies that when the stock level of the requested magazine is less than 100, and the user wants to order "Glamour" magazine, she can only place the order by paying a high $Price$ for it.

As already mentioned, access control policies in WS-AC$_1$ can be specified at different granularity levels. A policy can govern access to either a single service (corresponding to a Web service description) or a class of services. Services can be clustered in *classes* and be referred to as a whole in a policy. In the following, a class of services is represented as a set of service identifiers $WSClass = s_1, .., s_k$, where s_i, $i = 1, .., k$, denotes a service identifier.

Example 6.5. The *BookStore* service introduced in Example 6.1 is an element of the WSClass *BuyOnline*. *BuyOnline* is composed of three Web services: *BookStore*, *FoodStore*, and *OnlineStore*. *FoodStore* is a Web service allowing one to buy food online. *OnlineStore* is a Web service that allows one to buy different kinds of products belonging to different categories, like Music and Electronics. *BookStore*, *FoodStore*, and *OnlineStore* are characterized by the same mandatory identity attribute *CustomerId* and by the mandatory parameters *Price* and *Quantity*.

A *service access control policy* for a Web service s is defined as a tuple $<$ $st; C; ParamConstr; ParamSet>$. C is a list of the form $CA_1, CA_2, .., CA_n$, $n \geq 1$, where CA_i, $i = 1, .., n$, is either an attribute condition or an attribute name; $ParamConstr = \{Constr_1, Constr_2, .., Constr_k\}$, $k \geq 1$, is a (possibly) empty set of constraints defined over parameters in $ParamSet$ such that for each $Constr_i$, $Constr_j$, $i \neq j$, $Target_{constr_i} \neq Target_{constr_j}$; and $ParamSet$ is a set of parameter names referring to the description of s, such that $ParamSet \subseteq Parameters$. The above definition shows that the proposed access control model allows one to specify fine-grained access control policies in that one can associate a policy with a single service and even specify with which input parameters the service has to be invoked under a given policy. However, to simplify access control administration as much as possible, it is also important to support access control policies with coarse granularities. Such a requirement is addressed in the model by associating access control policies with classes of services. In other words, a single policy can be specified for all services belonging to a given class of services. However, to be regulated by a single policy, a service class has to include Web services satisfying the condition that the set of mandatory parameters and the set of mandatory attributes for all the services in the class be the same. In the following, the dot notation is used to refer to a component of a tuple, that is, $R.a$ denotes the component a of tuple R.

Given a class of services $WSClass = s_1,..,s_k$ where each s_i, $i = 1,..,k$, is a service identifier in $WSClass$ and $serv\text{-}descr_i = <s_i$; $Parameters$; $AuthAttrs>$ is the service description of s_i, a *class access control policy* specified for $WSClass$ is defined as a tuple $< WSClass$; C; $ParamConstr$; $ParamSet >$. C is a list of the form $CA_1,..,CA_n$, and each CA_i, $i = 1,..,n$, is either an attribute condition or an attribute name. Each attribute name is a mandatory attribute for every service $s_i \in WSClass$; $Paramset$ is a set of parameter names. For each s_i in $WSClass$ and for each p in $Paramset$, $p \in s_i.Parameters$ and $s_i.p.ParamType = mand$; $ParamConstr = Constr_1, Constr_2,.., Constr_k$ is a (possibly) empty set of constraints defined over parameters in $ParamSet$ such that for each $Constr_i$, $Constr_j$, $i \neq j$, $Target_{constr_i} \neq Target_{constr_j}$.

Policies specified at the class level apply to any service in the class. The advantage of supporting class policies for service providers managing a large number of services is obvious. Service providers have the ability of clustering as many services as they wish and specifying a unique policy while being able to refine policies for particular services, if required.

Example 6.6. With reference to the *BookStore* Web service introduced in Example 6.1, consider the following access control policies:

- $pol_1 = < BookStore$; $\{CustomerId \in \{$Ann Meeker, John Smith$\}$, *Target-CustomerCardId* $\in \{$AS128456, AX3455643$\}$; $\{Title, PriceFare, Quantity \}$; $Quantity = 10 \leftarrow Title = $ The Times; $Price = $ Low $>$
- $pol_2 = < BookStore$; $\{CustomerId = $ Wallmart of New York, Wallmart-DealerId $= 123451\}$; $\{$ Title, *Price*, *Quantity* $\}$; $\{\ \} >$
- $pol_3 = < BookStore$; $\{CustomerId = $ Wallmart of New York$\}$; $\{$ *Title*, *Price*$\}$; $Price = $ High $\leftarrow StockLevel < 100$, $Title = $ Glamour $>$.

Policy pol_1 states that users Ann Meeker and John Smith having a *Target CustomerCardId* equal to either AS128456 or AX3455643 can invoke the service. Specifically, the policy constraints limit the *Quantity* that can be ordered to ten items. Policy pol_2 states that the Wallmart's dealer "123451" of New York can access the service. The policy does not impose any restriction on the values the service parameters can assume. Finally, policy pol_3 requires that any Wallmart supermarket of New York only can get "Glamour" magazines at a high *Price* if the user has submitted the request when the stock level of the magazine is less than ten.

6.2.2 WS-AC$_1$ Identity Attribute Negotiation

WS-AC$_1$ evaluates access requests with respect to the access control policies protecting the corresponding services or if no ad-hoc policies are specified for the required services, the service classes. Each access request is first evaluated with respect to the submitted identifying attributes. An access request in WS-AC$_1$ can be either *totally* or *partially compliant* with a (single or class) access control policy. An access request is *totally compliant* with an access control policy if all the attribute conditions specified in the policy are evaluated to true according to the attribute values specified in the access request. If no access control policy exists for which the access request is totally compliant, the request is not rejected. WS-AC$_1$ gives the requester the ability of providing additional attributes to fully comply with an access control policy. To this end, the concept of partial compliance of an access request is introduced. An access request for a specified service is said to be *partially compliant* with an access control policy if a subset of the attribute names of the policy appears in the access request, or if some attribute of the access request appears in some condition of the policy and the condition evaluates to true according to the attribute s submitted in the access request. In the case of partial compliance of the attributes, WS-AC$_1$ asks the service requestor to disclose the attributes not provided in the submitted request, but specified in the access control policies the access request partially complies with.

Moreover, an access request may be totally compliant with respect to a policy, but may specify parameter values not allowed by the service. In this case also, the access request cannot be accepted as it is. Therefore, it is necessary to introduce another form of partial compliance with respect to a policy. An access request is *parameter matching* if each parameter value requested is acceptable; that is, it either satisfies a policy constraint (if applicable) or falls in the corresponding parameter domain. In the end, access to a Web service can only be granted if an access request fully satisfies an access control policy. This requires both the successful identification of the service requestor and an agreement on the parameter values for invoking the service. The next section details the service requestor identification process through attribute negotiation.

Example 6.7. Consider the access request introduced in Example 6.3 and the access control policies specified in Example 6.5. *Acc* totally complies with pol_3, and partially complies with pol_2. In fact, the attribute condition *CustomerId* = Wallmart of New York is evaluated to true according the *CustomerId* attribute value specified in the access request. Hence, the WS-AC$_1$ system asks the service requester for attribute $rfa = WallmartDealerId$ where $WallmartDealerId$ is the attribute name specified in pol_2, not provided in the access request.

The Negotiation Process

As mentioned in the previous discussion, upon receiving an access request, the system determines whether any access control policy exists for the required service or for the class the service belongs to with which the access request is totally compliant for the identity attributes. If such a policy is found, the pending request is further evaluated for parameter matching, to check if the access can be granted. If no policy with which the access request is totally compliant is found, instead of rejecting the request, the WS-AC$_1$ system checks if the access request is partially compliant with any of the enforced policies. If this is the case, the system asks the service requestor to provide additional attributes. In particular, the service requestor has to submit the attributes not provided in the request but specified in the access control policies the access request partially complies with. Such attributes are requested by the server from the service requestor with an ad hoc message, referred to as *request for attributes* or *rfa*. Given an access request $acc = (\underline{a}, s, \underline{p})$ and $PartialCompliantPolSet = (pol_1, .., pol_k)$, the set of access control policies acc partially complies with rfa is a disjunction of attribute sets $rfa = AttrSet_1 \vee AttrSet_2 \vee .... \vee AttrSet_k$, where each $AttrSet_i = (A_1, A_2, .., A_m)$, $i = 1, .., k$, is the set of attribute names specified in $pol_i.C$ but not contained in $acc.\underline{a}$.

If more than one access control policy is found, WS-AC$_1$ selects from these policies the ones the access request parameter matches with. If the result of the selection is not empty, the *rfa* contains an attribute set for each selected access control policy. Otherwise, *rfa* contains an attribute set for each access control policy the access request partially complies with. The service requestor, thus, has the freedom to decide which set of attributes to reveal. The message used by the service requestor to reply to an *rfa* sent by the server is referred to as *response for attributes* or *rsfa*. Given a request for attributes $rfa = AttrSet_1 \vee AttrSet_2 \vee .... \vee AttrSet_k$, a response for attributes is a tuple $rsfa = [Attr_1 : a_1, Attr_2 : a_2, ..., Attr_m : a_m]$ where each $Attr_i \in AttrSet_i$, $i = 1, ..., n$, is one of the attributes specified in the corresponding *rfa*, and a_i is the associated value.

After receiving the *rsfa* message, the WS-AC$_1$ system verifies if the access request updated with the attributes just submitted is now totally compliant with one of the access control policies the original access request was partially compliant with. If the access request now provides all attributes required by one of the access control policies, the system evaluates whether the service requestor can access the service on the basis of the parameters values specified. It is important to note that the identification process is not iterative: it lasts two rounds in the worst case, one round for sending the attribute request and another for the reply. In case no fully compliant policy can be found, the request is rejected without possibility of further negotiation.

Algorithm 2: Identity Attribute Negotiation

Input:
acc: access request$\underline{a}$, s, $\underline{p}$)$\vee$
rfsa: response for attribute $[Attr_1 : a_1, Attr_2 : a_2, ..., Attr_m : a_m]$

Output: rfa: request for attribute $AttrSet_1 \vee AttrSet_2 \vee .... \vee AttrSet_k \vee$

(1)   var $PartialCompliantPolSet$: SetOfAccessControlPolicy;
(2)   var $SelectedPolSet$: SetOfAccessControlPolicy;
(3)   var msg_Type: Boolean;
(4)   **if** input msg is an acc
(5) $msg\_Type:=false$;
(6)   **else**
(7)   **if** input msg is an rfa
(8) $acc:=Update\text{-}acc(acc, rsfa)$;
(9) $msg\_Type:=true$;
(10) $TotalCompliantPolSet:=\{$Set of Access Control Policies, acc totally complies with$\}$;
(11)   **if** $TotalCompliantPolSet == \emptyset$
(12)   **if** $msg\_Type==false$
(13) $PartialCompliantPolSet:=\{$Set of Access Control Policies, acc partially complies with$\}$;
(14)   **if** $PartialCompliantPolSet == \emptyset$
(15) $AccessDenied:=$true;
(16)   **return** $AccessDenied$;
(17)   **else**
(18)   **foreach** $pol_i \in PartialCompliantPolSet$
(19)   **if** acc is parameter matching with pol_i
(20) $SelectedPolSet:=SelectedPolSet \cup pol_i$;
(21)   **if** $SelectedPolSet \neq \emptyset$
(22) $rfa:=Generate\text{-}RFA(SelectedPolSet, acc)$;
(23)   **else**
(24) $rfa:=Generate\text{-}RFA(PartialCompliantPolSet, acc)$;
(25)   **return** rfa;
(26)   **else**
(27) $AccessDenied:=$true;
(28)   **return** $AccessDenied$;
(29)   **else**
(30)   **return** $TotalCompliantPolSet$;

Algorithm 1 describes the negotiation process for identity attributes submitted by a service requestor. The algorithm accepts as input two different types of messages: an access request *acc* and a response for attributes *rsfa*. If the input message is an access request, the algorithm builds *TotalCompliant-PolSet*, that is, the set of access control policies the request *acc* totally complies with (line 10). If the set is empty, the algorithm builds a so-called *PartialCompliantPolSet*, that is, the set of access control policies the request *acc* partially complies with (line 13). If there are no policies, the access to the service is denied to the user (lines 15 and 16). Otherwise, the request for attribute message *rfa* is created by invoking function *Generate-RFA()* (lines 17 through 25).

To generate the request for an attribute message, the algorithm can adopt two strategies. First, it checks whether acc is parameter matching with some of the policies in the set $PartialCompliantPolSet$. If this is the case, the algorithm builds the set $SelectedPol$, a subset of $PartialCompliantPolSet$ containing the policies with which acc is parameter matching (lines 18 through 20). If $SelectedPol$ is not an empty set, the function $Generate\text{-}RFA()$ is activated and generates a response for an attribute message containing an attributes set for each policy in $SelectedPol$: the set of attributes specified in rfa contains the attributes specified in the policy, not provided by the user in acc (lines 21 and 22). Instead, if $SelectedPol$ is empty, $Generate\text{-}RFA()$ is activated and generates a request for attribute message containing an attribute set for each policy in $PartialCompliantPolSet$ (line 25). If set $TotalCompliantPolSet$ is not empty, the algorithm returns this set, as it represents the input for the service parameter negotiation process (line 30). If the input message is a response for attributes, the algorithm first updates the access request acc previously received, invoking $Update\text{-}acc()$. $Update\text{-}acc()$ adds to acc the attributes the service requester has specified in the request for attributes. Then, it builds the set of access control policies the updated acc totally complies with (line 10), referred to as $TotalCompliantPolSet$. If such a set is empty, the algorithm ends by denying the service access (lines 26 through 28).

6.2.3 WS-AC$_1$ Parameter Negotiation

The other relevant negotiation process of WS-AC$_1$ is the parameter negotiation. In what follows, we first present the formal definition of request acceptance. Then, the conditions triggering a negotiation process and formalizing the type of messages and the protocol to follow are described.

Access Request Acceptance

Given a set of policies totally compliant with the service requestor's request, the WS-AC$_1$ system checks whether an access control policy exists that makes the access request fully acceptable. An access request is *fully acceptable* if it is totally compliant and parameter matching. If the access request is fully acceptable, the SP grants the service requestor access to the service. An access request is not fully acceptable and can be negotiated if it is totally compliant with a policy but is not parameter matching. Precisely, one of the following conditions occurs:

- The access request is specified using all the parameters appearing in one or more access control policies, and contains parameter values that are not legal under these policies.
- The access request is specified using a subset of the parameters provided by the policies enforced for the required service. Therefore, the service requestor has to provide the missing parameters.

The service requestor, thus, is given the possibility of negotiating the incorrect parameters.

Example 6.8. With respect to the running example, consider the following policies:

- $pol_1 = < BookStore; \{CustomerId =$ Wallmart of New York, Wallmart-DealerId$\}; \{Quantity\}; \{Quantity \in [1, 5000] \leftarrow\} >$
- $pol_2 = < BookStore; \{CustomerId =$ Wallmart of New York$\}; \{Quantity\}; \{Quantity \in [1, 1000] \leftarrow\} >$

Consider now the access request ($[CustomerId$: Wallmart of New York]; $BookStore$; $[Title$: Cosmopolitan, $Price$:High; $Quantity$:2500]). The access request is partially compliant and parameter matching with policy pol_1 and totally compliant with policy pol_2. The service requestor can then opt for negotiating parameters and purchase the drugs in the $Quantity$ allowed, or it can also disclose its $WallmartDealerId$ and obtain authorization to buy up to 2,500 items.

The Negotiation Process for Parameters

The process of parameter negotiation consists of message exchanges between the two parties. The SP starts the negotiation by sending to the service requestor a message denoted *negotiation access proposal* (NAP). The NAP contains a combination of admitted values for the parameters. Given a totally compliant access request acc and an access control policy, a NAP is a tuple of the form $nap = < NegId; ap, end >$ where:

- $NegId$ is the negotiation identifier denoting the current negotiation.
- $ap = P_1 : p_1, ..., P_n : p_n$ is a list of pairs where P_i is a parameter name belonging to $ParamSet$ and p_i is the corresponding value, $i = 1, ..., n$.
- $end \in \{yes, no\}$ is a flag denoting whether or not the NAP is the last one in the negotiation process.

The parameters included in a NAP depend on the misplaced values in the submitted access request. If the access request is specified using non-admitted parameter values, the generated NAP will suggest legal values for the incorrect parameter values. The current version of WS-AC$_1$ does not provide any inference engine for checking conflicts among the enforced access control policies. Therefore, policies may overlap or subsume one another. Hence, the same access request may be negotiated against several policies. If this is the case, the requestor will receive as many NAPs as there policies, with all the parameter name p appearing in both $ParamSet$ and the p component of the access request. Of course, although this approach maximizes the chances of success of the negotiation process, it has the drawback that in the case of a large number of fully compliant policies, the service requestor will be flooded by alternative NAPs. If the required service parameters are not specified at all in the access request, the policies to be considered are the access control policies having at least one parameter name in common with the received access request. Here, the NAP will be composed by the parameter values chosen by the requesting agent whenever possible, and the parameter values set by the system for the remaining parameters.

Algorithm 3: Parameter Negotiation

Input:
Output: acc: access request$(\underline{a},s,\underline{p})$ $\vee$
nap: negotiation access proposal $\overline{nap}$ = $< NegId;\ ap,\ end >$

$NapList$: NapList$\{nap_1,\ \ldots,nap_2\}$ $\vee$
$AccessDenied$: Boolean

(1)   var s: WebServiceIdentifier;
(2)   var $WSClass$: WebServiceClass;
(3)   var $PolSet$: SetOfAccessControlPolicy;
(4)   var msg_Type: Boolean;
(5)   if input msg is an acc
(6)   if $\neg\exists pols.tacc.s == pol.s$
(7) $WSClass$:= class service s belongs to;
(8) $PolSet$:=$\{pol_1,..,pol_k$ class policies of $WSClass\}$;
(9)   else
(10) $PolSet$:=$\{pol_1,..,pol_k$ policies such that $acc.s == pol.s\}$;
(11) $accPNames$:=$\{$set of parameter names in $acc.p\}$;
(12)   **foreach** $pol_i \in PolSet$ s.t. $pol_i.ParName==accPNames$
(13) $Case_1$:=$Case_1 \cup pol_i$;
(14) i:=1;
(15)   **repeat**
(16)   **if** $acc.p.p_i \in pol_i.ParName$ s.t $acc.p.p_i \notin$ $Legal\_values(p_z)$
(17) $Case_1$:=$Case_1 - pol_i$;
(18) $Case_2$:=$Case_2 \cup pol_i$;
(19) $exit$:=$true$;
(20)   **else**
(21) i:=$i + 1$;
(22)   **until** $i==|accPNames| \vee exit==true$
(23)
(24)   if $Case_1 \neq \emptyset$
(25) pol_k:= randomly chosen policy $\in Case_1$;
(26) $AccessDenied$:=$alse$;
(27)   **return** $AccessDenied$;
(28)   else
(29)   if $Case_2 \neq \emptyset$
(30) $CreateProposal(PolSet, acc)$;
(31)   **foreach** $pol_i \in PolSet$ s.t. $pol_i.ParName \cap accPNames \neq \emptyset$
(32)   **if** $\exists acc.p.p_i \in Legal\_values(p_z)$
(33) $Case_3$:=$Case_3 \cup pol_i$;
(34) $CreateProposal()$;
(35)   if $Case_3 \neq \emptyset$
(36) $AccessDenied$:=$alse$;
(37)   **return** $AccessDenied$;

Type of *acc* Compliance to pol	Num pol	Action
acc is TC with *pol*	0	Verify if exists some *pol* s.t. *acc* PC *pol* holds
	≥ 1	For each *pol*, verify if *acc* PM *pol* holds
acc is PC with *pol*	0	Deny access
	≥ 1	Request missing attributes for all PC *pols*; then verify if *acc* PM *pol* holds
acc is PM with *pol*	0	Negotiate parameters
	1	Grant access, if *acc* is TC too
	> 1	Negotiate by sending NAPS for each of the parameters matching policies
acc is FA by *pol*	0	Deny access
	1	Grant access
	≥ 1	Grant access randomly selecting a policy

Fig. 6.2. Action to be taken to enforce access control

As in the previous case, only policies having a parameter p appearing in both *ParamSet* and the component of the access requests are selected. Note that the criteria adopted for defining parameter values in an NAP are based on a "user-oriented" criterion. Therefore, given an access request which is not fully acceptable, the fewest number of modifications necessary on the original access request are applied. In other words, all the acceptable parameter values are kept, while the non-acceptable ones are replaced with legal values. The replacement might be executed according to different approaches. A straight-forward solution consists of specifying constant default parameter values to be used for filling the missing or wrong ones. A more sophisticated approach is to determine such values on the fly while the proposal is generated. A possible solution in this sense is to make use of scripts, as proposed by Bertino et al. [40]. Basically, the idea is to represent parameter values and context variables in a relational form and query them with ad hoc scripts. Scripts, in turn, may or may not be parametric. Parameters might also be dynamically determined by invoking ad hoc procedures having names as input parameter and returning legal values for those names. How these procedures are actually encoded depends, however, on the specific Web service implementation. The negotiation algorithm is reported in Algorithm 4. The process is iterative and the NAP exchanges are carried on until the service requestor, based on the received NAP, submits a fully acceptable request or the process is interrupted by one of the parties. The wish to end the negotiation is explicitly notified to the counterpart, and it is represented in the algorithm by setting the flag *end* in the NAP message to *yes*.

6.3 An Access Control Framework for Conversation-Based Web services

This section presents the only approach [175] that investigates the problem of how to enforce access control for conversational Web services. While many approaches consider Web services as a set of independent single operations, in many applications interactions with a Web service often require a *sequence* of invocations of several of its operations, referred to as *conversation*. A simple example is a travel agent Web service; booking a trip involves generally searching for the trip, browsing the details and rules about possible options for this trip, booking a specific trip, checking out, paying, and so forth. Thus, service requestors interact with Web services through a conversation process where each step consists of invoking a specific operation offered by the Web service. The potential operations that can be invoked depend on the state of the current conversation between the callee and the Web service.

Conversations allow one to capture an important aspect of Web services, namely their "behavioral semantics". In most cases, the representation of the potential conversations that can take place between the Web service and its service requestors is based on the use of transition systems.

It is important to observe that Web service operations represent a coarse-grained process that takes place in the application supporting the Web service and usually involves the consumption of several resources. Therefore, it is important for the Web service to maximize the chance that a service requestor reaches a final state in order to avoid wasting resources. However, this should be balanced with the need to retain some control on the disclosure of access policies.

The access control model for conversation-based Web services, which is described in this section, enables service providers to retain some control on the disclosure of their access control policies while giving service requestors some guarantees on the termination of their interactions, that is, on their reaching some final state. First, in line with current approaches, all possible conversations are modeled as finite transition systems (aka finite state machines) [245, 28], in which final states represent those in which the interaction with the service requestor can be, but is not necessarily, ended. Furthermore, this access control model attempts to maximize the *likelihood* that a service requestor reaches a final state without necessarily having to be made aware of all access control policies. The model is based on the novel concept of *k-trustworthiness* (*k-trust* in the following for simplicity) where *k* can be seen as the *level of trust* that a Web service has with a service requestor at any point during their interaction. The greater the level of trust associated with a service requestor, the greater the amount of information about access control policies that can be disclosed to it. A level of trust *k* represents the *length* of a conversation such that from the current state of the interactions leads to a final state and a service requestor is requested to provide the credentials to invoke any operation composing the conversation. Thus, the service requestor is assured that its conversation can eventually terminate. Based on this simple notion of k-trust, this access control model is a flexible model with limited policy disclosure for conversation-based Web services.

6.3.1 Conversation-Based Access Control

This section introduces the basic concepts for Web service conversations, access control, and credentials.

Conversation Model for Web Services

The *behavioral semantics* of a Web service is represented as the set of operations it exports and constraints on the possible conversations it can execute. For a large class of Web service, as discussed by Benatallah et al. [27], all such aspects can be compactly represented as a finite transition system (the WSMO choreography concept). This semantics is usually expressed according to a given OWL, OWL-S, WSMO ontology. Thus, a service is generally characterized by two facets: *(i) static* semantics, dealing with messages, operations, and parameters exchanged and their types, and *(ii) dynamic* semantics, dealing with the correct sequencing of operations that represents the external workflow offered by the service.

The *transition system* of a Web service $\mathcal{WS}$ is represented as a tuple $\mathcal{TS} = (\Sigma, S, s_0, \delta, F)$ where Σ is the alphabet of operations offered by the service, S is a finite set of states, $s_0 \in S$ is the single initial state, $\delta : S \times \Sigma \to S$ is the transition function, and $F \subseteq S$ is the set of final states. These are states in which a conversation may end, but does not necessarily have to.

The relation $\delta(s_i, a) = s_j$ is represented as $s_i \xrightarrow{a} s_j$, and where a is the *label of the transition*. The transition function can be extended to finite length sequences of operations or conversations, defined as traces by Stirling et al. [245]. Given a conversation $conv : a_1 \cdot a_2 \cdot \ldots a_n$ and two states s_0 and s_n, $s_0 \xRightarrow{conv} s_n$ iff $\exists\, s'$ such that $s_0 \xrightarrow{a_1} s'$ and $s' \xRightarrow{a_2 \cdot \ldots a_n} s_n$.

Example 6.9. Figure 6.3 represents the transition system of a simple online travel agent Web service eTravel. The different labels represent the operations that a service requestor can invoke from any given state and are self-explanatory. Final states are represented by gray circles. A service requestor can be involved in different conversations with the service. The service requestor can search for trips (searchTrips), refine the search results several times (refineResults), and then select a specific trip (selectTrip). After this operation, the service requestor can decide to either book the trip and complete the booking (bookTrip and completeBooking operations) or hold the selected trip (holdReservation) and end the interaction.

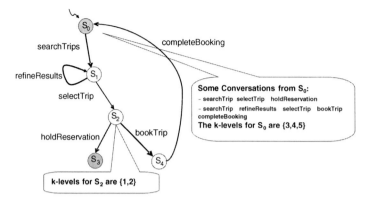

Fig. 6.3. eTravel service's transition system

6.3.2 Access Control and Credentials

Access control is enforced through the use of credentials. *Credentials* are the means to establish trust between a service requestor and the SP. They are assertions about a given service requestor, referred to as the owner, issued by trusted third parties called Certification Authorities (CAs). They are digitally signed using the private key of the issuer CA and can be verified using the issuer's public key. Credentials are usually implemented through the use of X.509 certificates [279] or SAML assertions [61]. Each credential contains a set of attributes characterizing the owner specified by means of (name, value) pairs. Conditions on credential attributes specify the security requirements of the SP. An *operation access control policy* specifies such conditions for a given operation, i.e., iff a client has credentials satisfying such conditions, it can then execute the operation [146].

A *conversation access control policy* represents all access control policies of a given conversation. For a conversation $conv = a_1 \cdot \ldots a_k$ where $a_1, \ldots a_k$ are operations of the Web service and each operation a_i has its corresponding operation access control policy pol_i, the *conversation access control policy* for $conv$ is the conjunction of $pol_1, \ldots, pol_k$. This formalization captures the intuition that a service requestor, owning credentials satisfying a conversation access control policy, is granted access to all the operations in the conversation. If the conversation is such that it reaches a final state, then the satisfaction of the policy assures that the service requestor will be authorized up to reaching its own goal. The SP will not be forced to deny access to some operations in the middle of the conversation due to lack of authorization.

Example 6.10. 6.9 Examples of access control policies for operations selectTrip and holdReservation are respectively:

$pol_1 : \text{selectTrip} \leftarrow CreditCard\_Holder(Type = MasterCard \text{ or } Visa)$

$$pol_2 : \texttt{holdReservation} \leftarrow Gold\_Member$$

Policy pol_1 states that only the service requestors having a MasterCard or Visa credit card can perform operation $\texttt{selectTrip}$, while policy pol_2 authorizes the gold member service requestors to execute $\texttt{holdReservation}$. The conversation access control policy for the conversation $conv$: $\texttt{selectTrip} \cdot \texttt{holdReservation}$ is:

$$conv \leftarrow CreditCard\_Holder(Type = MasterCard\ or\ Visa), Gold\_Member.$$

6.3.3 k-Trust Levels and Policies

The main idea of this approach is that service requestors, as they interact with the Web service, will be assigned to k-trust level. Such level represents how much trust the Web service has of the service requestor. A *trustworthiness level* is defined as the length of a conversation that from a given state s in the transition system leads to a final state. More than one trustworthiness level can be associated with a state s because there might be different conversations of different lengths that lead from s to a final state. To assign one of these k-trust levels to a service requestor, the concept of k-trust policy has been introduced. A *k-trust policy* specifies the conditions on the credentials of a service requestor that must hold in order for it to be assigned a trustworthiness level k_s in state s.

The concept of trustworthiness level (k-trust in the following for simplicity) is also used to limit the disclosure of a service provider's access control policies. Therefore, when a service requestor is assigned the level k on the basis of an appropriate k-trust policy, the enforcement system asks only for the credentials needed to satisfy all the conversation access control policies associated with the conversations from the current state to the final states and having length less than or equal to k. The actual value of k does not have to be known by the service requestor. The service requestor is more interested in knowing which credentials to provide.

Example 6.11. 6.9 Consider the start state (labeled with S_0) in Figure 6.3. The potential conversations that lead to a final state and that must be considered in order to compute the k-trust levels are

(1) $\texttt{searchTrips} \cdot \texttt{selectTrip} \cdot \texttt{holdReservation}$;
(2) $\texttt{searchTrips} \cdot \texttt{refineResults} \cdot \texttt{selectTrip} \cdot \texttt{hold-Reservation}$;
(3) $\texttt{searchTrips} \cdot \texttt{selectTrip} \cdot \texttt{bookTrip} \cdot \texttt{completeBooking}$;
(4) $\texttt{searchTrips} \cdot \texttt{refineResults} \cdot \texttt{selectTrip} \cdot \texttt{bookTrip} \cdot \texttt{completeBooking}$.

Adding more conversations will be useless from the access control perspective since the same conversations will be repeated. Although there are four different conversations, they imply only three different k-trust levels: $\{3, 4, 5\}$. For instance, the $\{k_{s_0} = 3\}$-trust policy to assign a service requestor to trustworthiness level 3 is of the form $\{k_{s_0} = 3\} \leftarrow PictureID(Age > 18)$; it means that service requestors older than eighteen are entrusted with trustworthiness level 3. Such a service requestor has to fulfill the access control policies associated with the conversations having length less than or equal to 3. These conversations include the following operations: searchTrips, selectTrip, and holdReservation.

6.3.4 Access Control Enforcement

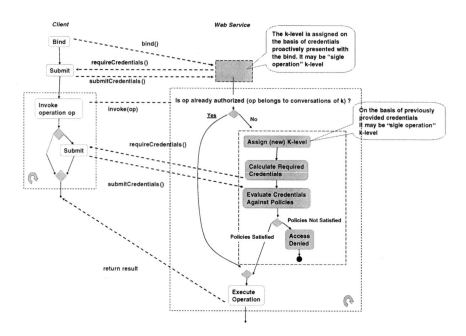

Fig. 6.4. Access control enforcement process

This section describes how a specific k-trust level is assigned to a service requestor in a given state of the interaction with the Web service and how access control is enforced on the basis of the assigned k-trust level for both simple and composite Web services.

Enforcement Process

The access control enforcement process has two phases. The first phase associates with the service requestor a k-trust level that determines the conversations the service requestor can have with the Web service. The second phase verifies whether the service requestor owns the credentials to be authorized to execute any of the conversations corresponding to the specific k-trust level assigned to it.

The enforcement process is represented in Figure 6.4. It starts when a service requestor contacts the Web service for the first time and submits an initial set of credentials, e.g., with the IP address of the service requestor's machine (line 1). The enforcement system assigns an initial k-trust level k_0, from amongst the possible ones in the initial state, based on the credentials provided by the service requestor and the Web service's k-trust policies. If the initial credentials are not compliant with the policies, the service requestor is assigned a default value $\perp$ corresponding to "single operation" access control enforcement. Once the service requestor is assigned a trustworthiness level k_0, the access control enforcement system determines the access control policies protecting the operations of the conversations associated with k_0. These are all the conversations that from the current state lead to a final state and have length less than or equal to k_0. Then, the service requestor is requested to provide all the credentials specified in the operation access control policies. If the service requestor can provide all the required credentials, the service requestor is authorized to invoke all operations of the conversations associated with k_0. If the k_0 assigned is $\perp$, this request for credentials is skipped and will take place when an operation is effectively invoked.

Whenever the service requestor requests an operation, the enforcement system first checks if the operation is included in the set of authorized conversations. If this is the case, the operation is executed and the result is sent to the service requestor. Otherwise, the enforcement system associates with the service requestor a new k-trust level which on the basis of the credentials submitted so far (again may be $\perp$). Then the enforcement system requests from the service requestor all the credentials specified in the operation access control policies of those conversations. If k assigned is $\perp$, then only the credentials corresponding to the single operation just invoked are requested. If the service requestor can provide all the requested credentials, the service requestor is authorized to invoke all operations of the conversations associated with the new k. If during the service requestor-Web service interaction some of the service requestor's previously submitted credentials are no longer valid, the access control enforcement system requests them again from the service requestor. In Figure 6.4 the initial binding of the service requestor to the Web service is represented, along with the generic operation invocation. The invocation of an operation by the service requestor is continuously repeated until the service requestor reaches its own goal; and it is graphically represented by surrounding all the steps with a dashed box and marking such a box with a loop symbol.

6.3.5 K-Trustworthiness Levels Computation

To support k-trust-based access control, it is necessary to determine at each
state of the transition system all the possible trustworthiness levels that can
be assigned to the service requestor on the basis of the k-trust policies. The
k-trust levels determine the set of conversations service requestors can have
with a Web service; service requestors can execute only the conversations
having length less than or equal to k if the credentials they provide satisfy
the conversation access control policies.

This section shows how such a computation can be executed off-line, that
is, before initiating the interaction with the service requestors. The computation is straightforward if Web service transition systems are acyclic, but
becomes tricky if, as may often happen, the transition systems have loops.

Preliminary Observations

Before presenting the different algorithms, it is useful to make the following
observations:

1. For an acyclic transition system, the set of potential paths leading from
   any state to any final state is finite. This set can be easily calculated by
   a simple traversal of the transition system.
2. If from a given state a conversation involves a cycle, there is an infinite
   number of paths reaching a final state.
3. If the access control policy of an operation a has been checked against
   a service requestor, it is not necessary to check it again if the service
   requestor invokes the operation a more than once.

The main difficulties in traversing the transition system and determining
the potential conversations arise because of cycles.

Strongly Connected Components

The algorithm proposed to compute all the possible k-levels for each state of
a Web service transition system is based on the concept of *strongly connected
component* (SCC for short). A strongly connected component is the maximal
subgraph of a directed graph such that for every pair of vertices (u, v) in the
subgraph, there is a directed path from u to v and a directed path from v to
u [252]. The transition system of a Web service can be regarded as a directed
graph where a transition between two states is a directed edge without the
labeling.

Based on the above concept, a new acyclic graph can be generated in
which nodes represent the different strongly connected components of the initial graph. This graph is called the *directed graph of the strongly connected
components* and is denoted by $\mathcal{G}^{scc}$. More formally, given a transition system

$TS = (\Sigma, S, s_0, \delta, F)$, the directed graph of the strongly connected components $\mathcal{G}^{scc} = \langle N^{scc}, E^{scc} \rangle$ is the graph with nodes N^{scc} and oriented edges E^{scc} in which (i) $N^{scc} = \{c \mid c$ is a strongly connected component in $TS\}$, and (ii) $E^{scc} = \{\langle c_1, c_2 \rangle \mid c_1 \neq c_2$ and $\exists a \in \delta, s_1 \in c_1, s_2 \in c_2 \mid s_1 \xrightarrow{a} s_2\}$.

Given a state $s \in TS$, the node of $\mathcal{G}^{scc}$ represents the strongly connected component to which s belongs as $c(s)$; $c(s)$ is the *image* of s. $\mathcal{G}^{scc}$ can be efficiently computed through the classical Tarjan's algorithm [252] or more recent optimizations [206].

This new graph has some interesting properties: (i) if the initial Web service transition system TS is acyclic then $\mathcal{G}^{scc} = \langle N^{scc}, E^{scc} \rangle$ is the graph with nodes N^{scc} and oriented edges E^{scc} in which (a) $N^{scc} = \{c \mid c$ is a state $\in S \cup F \cup s_0$ in $TS\}$, and (b) $E^{scc} = \{\langle c_1, c_2 \rangle \mid c_1 \neq c_2$ and $\exists a \in \delta, s_1 \equiv c_1,$ $s_2 \equiv c_2$ such that $s_1 \xrightarrow{a} s_2\}$ [94]; (ii) the nodes that are not involved in cycles will remain unchanged in the new graph; and (iii) cycles are "collapsed" into strongly connected components and need to be dealt with in an appropriate way (according to the specific aim $\mathcal{G}^{scc}$ is considered for).

Special nodes

Given an SCC, an *in-going* node is any node with an edge/transition coming from outside the SCC, and an *out-going* node is any node with an edge/transition going outside the SCC.

Cardinality

For each node/SCC of $\mathcal{G}^{scc}$, the number of different operations that label the transitions between the corresponding states of TS is known. More specifically, for each SCC c, the set $\mathcal{O}_c = \{a \mid s_1 \xrightarrow{a} s_2$ and $c(s_1) = c(s_2) = c \}$ can be easily determined. The *cardinality* of $\mathcal{O}_c$ is referred to as $card(c)$. If the connected component c is the image of a single state of TS, then $card(c) = 0$.

Coverage

For each node/SCC of $\mathcal{G}^{scc}$, the shortest path is considered that (i) starts from an in-going node finishes in an out-going node, and (ii) comprises all the different operations in $\mathcal{O}_c$. More specifically, for each SCC c, a sequence of operations str is said to be *covering* iff str goes from the in-going node e to the out-going node o of c ($c(e) = c(o) = c$) AND $str.\text{set}()^1 = \mathcal{O}_c$. The notation $\widetilde{str}$ refers to a traversing sequence of operations [2]. For each SCC c, a set $\mathcal{C}_c$ is defined: $\mathcal{C}_c = \{\ \widetilde{str_i} \mid (\widetilde{str_i}.\text{length}()) \neq 0)$ AND $(\forall \widetilde{str_k}$ with $o_i = o_k$, $\widetilde{str_k}.\text{length}() \geq \widetilde{str_i}.\text{length}())\ \}$. *coverage(c)* is the length of $\min(\widetilde{str_i} \in \mathcal{C}_c)$.

---

[1] $str.\text{set}()$ denotes the set of the operations in str

[2] A traversing sequence is not necessarily an Eulerian path of c, whereas each Eulerian path, if it exists, is a traversing sequence.

The coverage of an SCC can be computed by enumerating all the paths from any in-going node to an out-going one. A global array of boolean variables, with dimension equal to the number of distinct out-going nodes, is used to record whether the out-going node has been reached, and another global array of integer variables maintains the length of the path that evolves from the in-going node to the out-going one. As soon as all the boolean variables in the first vector are set to true, meaning that all the paths from any in-going node to any outgoing one have been found, the minimum among the values in the other array is determined.

Rank

For each node/SCC of $\mathcal{G}^{scc}$, the rank is defined as follows:

$$rank(c) = \begin{cases} coverage(c) & \text{if c is the root of } \mathcal{G}^{scc} \\ 1 + coverage(c) + max(rank(m)) & \text{where the } m \text{ are all the possible} \\ & \text{predecessors of } c \end{cases}$$

As $\mathcal{G}^{scc}$ is acyclic, the rank of each node can be computed in three steps (by using two stacks as auxiliary data structures):

(i) A preliminary depth-first search algorithm visits $\mathcal{G}^{scc}$ and pushes on a stack, for each visited node, a record containing the predecessor node; such a node is labeled with the given node. Note that during a depth-first search visit of the graph, each node has one predecessor node.

(ii) The stack is then traversed, and for each encountered record, all the records labeled with the same node are removed from the stack; during this step, the predecessor node of the removed one is recorded, and for each of these the formula for calculating the rank is pushed on a second different stack.

(iii) Finally, the second stack is traversed by calculating the rank for each removed record. Before executing step (iii), the formulas to compute the rank are pushed in the order in which they have to be calculated; each removed record gives the values to be used in the following records.

Table 6.1 reports all the notations used in the rest of this section.

Computing the k-trustworthiness Levels

The overall idea of the main algorithm that computes all potential k-trust levels for any state is as follows: for a given state, determine all subsequent strongly connected components, including the one to which the current state belongs; then traverse the transition system from that state and record all conversations leading to a final state. By computing all possible conversations of all strongly connected components, and based on observation (3) of Section 6.3.5, finite conversations are obtained even in the case of cycles.

Notation	Meaning	Available operators
Type	Used for indicating any object type	–
object	Used for indicating object instances	–
op(param list) → return type	Used for specifying an operator/method of an object type	–
SetOf<element>	Set of <element>, in which <element> can be any object type. The elements are without repetitions and without any order	• `=` → boolean (for comparing two homogeneous sets for equality) • `add(<element> e)` → void (for adding a new element) • `| |` → int (for calculating the number of elements)
OrderedSetOf<element>	Ordered set of <element>s	As above
Sequence	Sequence of symbols, used for representing sequences of operations (i.e., conversations)	• `length()` → int (returns the length of the sequence) • `set()` → SetOfOperation (returns the set of all the distinct operations) As an example, if $seq = acg$ is a sequence, and $seq' = acgcgcg$ is another sequence, then $seq.set() = \{a, c, g\} = seq'.set()$
GraphSCC	Represents a graph of strongly connected components	• `projection(Node c)` → GraphSCC (takes as input a node c and returns a new subgraph obtained by considering c and all nodes reachable by it, i.e., it is the subgraph obtained by visiting depth-first the graph starting from c) • `card(Node c)` → int (takes as input a node c and returns its *cardinality*) • `coverage(Node c)` → int (takes as input a node c and returns its *coverage*) • `rank(Node c)` → int (takes as input a node c and returns its *rank*)

Table 6.1. Notation used in the algorithms. A pseudo-programming language syntax is used, and the common programming languages' basic types are assumed

The computation of the possible k-trust levels and the corresponding conversations is achieved using Algorithms 1 through 4. These algorithms assume the following global variables that can be accessed by all instances of the recursion:

- the transition system $\mathcal{TS}$ of type TS, representing the behavior of the Web service;
- the $\mathcal{G}^{scc}$ of type GraphSCC, representing the graph of the strongly connected components obtained from $\mathcal{TS}$;
- the C_Bag of type SetOfSequence, representing the set of conversations defining the k-trust levels. It is built during the execution of the algorithms.

The main algorithm computeOverallConversations&KLevelsBags() builds, for each state s of the Web service transition system, the k-trust levels $K\_Bag[s]$ and the set of sets of corresponding conversations $C\_Bag[s]$.

The `buildConversations&KLevelsBags()` algorithm computes for the given state s of the transition system the set C_Bag of all possible conversations that reach a final state from s and the set K_Bag of corresponding k-trust levels, representing the lengths of the conversations in C_Bag.

Algorithm 4: `computeOverallConversations&KLevelsBags()`

Input: $\mathcal{TS}$: Transition System
Output:
  C_Bag_Set: Array of SetOfSequence; K_Bag_Set: Array of SetOfInteger

```
(1)     var C_Bag_Set: Array of SetOfSequence;
(2)     var K_Bag_Set: Array of SetOfInteger;
(3)
(4)     foreach s ∈ TS.S
(5)        {      C_Bag_Set[s],        K_Bag[s]      }      :=
           buildConversations&KLevelsBags(s);
```

Algorithm 5: `buildConversations&KLevelsBags()`

Input: s: State
Output: C_Bag: SetOfSequence; K_Bag: SetOfInteger

```
(1)     var C_Bag : SetOfSequence;
(2)     var K_Bag : SetOfInteger;
(3)     var K_Ord_Bag : OrderedSetOfInteger;
(4)     var Op_Set_1 : SetOfOperation;
(5)     var Op_Set_2 : SetOfOperation;
(6)     var K_Prune_Set : SetOfInteger;
(7)     var conv_set[] : Array of SetOfSequence;
(8)     C_Bag := ∅;
(9)     K_Bag := ∅;
(10)    build(s,ε);                          /* ε is the empty Sequence */
(11)    foreach str ∈ C_Bag
(12)        K_Bag.add(str.length());
(13)    K_Ord_Bag := (K_Bag, ≤);
(14)    foreach k ∈ K_Ord_Bag
(15)        conv_set[k] := {str ∈ C_Bag : str.length() ≤ k};
(16)    foreach h ∈ K_Ord_Bag
(17)        Op_Set_1  :=  ⋃ conv_set[kₜ].set() where kₜ ∈ {k' ∈
               K_Ord_Bag|k' ≤ h};
(18)        Op_Set_2  :=  ⋃ conv_set[k_z].set() where k_z ∈ {k' ∈
               K_Ord_Bag|k' ≤ h.next() };
(19)        if Op_Set_2 = Op_Set_1
(20)            K_Prune_Set.add(h.next());
(21)    K_Bag:= K_Bag \ K_Prune_Set;
(22)    return C_Bag, K_Bag;
```

First, `build()` (detailed in the following) returns C_Bag, the set containing all the conversations that from input state s lead to a final state (line 10). Then, K_Bag, the set of k-trust levels associated with s, is generated based on the length of the conversations in C_Bag (lines 11 and 12). For each k-trust level in K_Bag, the set of conversations in C_Bag having length less than or equal to k is computed (lines 13 and 14). After that, the set K_Ord_Bag is created, by ordering the k-trust levels in K_Bag from the minimum to the maximum (line 15). At this point, the k-trust levels that are redundant from an access control point of view are removed since the set of operations associated with them is equal to the one of the lower k-trust levels. To identify whether a k-trust level k_h has to be removed, two sets are created, Op_Set_1 and Op_Set_2 (lines 16 through 18): Op_Set_1 contains all the operations associated with k_h and the levels lower than k_h; Op_Set_2 contains all the operations associated with k_{h+1} and the levels lower than k_{h+1}. If the two sets contains the same operations, k_{h+1} level is redundant and can be safely removed from K_Bag (lines 19 through 21).

As an example, the lines 10-12 in the example in Figure 6.3 would add a k-level equal to 7 for the initial state, which is eliminated by the lines 13-21.

Algorithm 6: build()

```
Input:   s: State; str: Sequence
Output:  – (directly operates on the global variable C_Bag)
(1)         if s has no out-going transition (i.e., is a leaf)
(2)            if str.isNewString()
(3)               C_Bag.add(str);
(4)               return ();
(5)         else
(6)            if | str.length()| > G^{scc}.rank(c(s))
(7)               return ();
(8)            else
(9)               if s ∈ TS.F (i.e., s is final) AND str.isNewString()
(10)                  C_Bag.add(str);
(11)               foreach s --a--> t
(12)                  build(t, str · a);
```

The build() algorithm computes for the given state s of the transition system the set of all the possible conversations that from s lead to a final state. To avoid possible infinite recursion (due to the infinite paths in presence of loops), the concept of rank of a strongly connected component is used, as it characterizes the length of conversations over which it is not necessary (due to observation (3) of Section 6.3.5) to add more operations.

Algorithm 7: isNewString()

```
Input:   – (operates on the object on which it is invoked)
Output:  b: Boolean
(1)         foreach x ∈ C_Bag
(2)            if this.set() = x.set()
(3)               if this.length()>= x.length()
(4)                  return (false);
(5)         return (true);
```

The isNewString() algorithm checks whether the conversation on which it is invoked is already in C_Bag, the set of all the possible conversations that from the given state s reach a final state in the transition system.

The complexity of computing the k-trust levels is linear in time in the sum of the number of states and transitions of the Web service transition system; this stems from the computation of the strongly connected components, of the rank, and of the Algorithms 1 through 4 being linear as well. Moreover, the computation of the k-trust levels is conducted off-line with respect to the access control enforcement (during the deployment of the Web service); therefore its complexity is not critical.

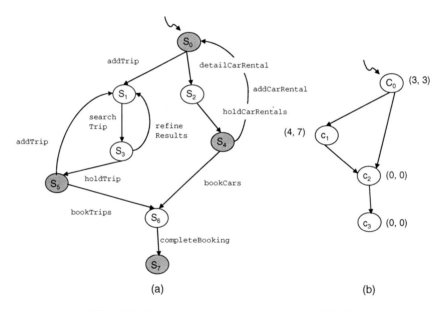

Fig. 6.5. A transition system (a) with its $\mathcal{G}^{scc}$ (b)

Example 6.12. Figure 6.5(a) represents the transition system of some Web service (which represents a more complex behavior than the one presented in Figure 6.3). This transition system can be reduced to the graph in Figure 6.5(b), containing four strongly connected components. The different states, representing each a strongly connected component, are labeled with pairs (x, y) representing the number of symbols (operations) and the coverage of that strongly connected component, respectively. These numbers are then used to calculate all the k-trust levels for all states in the transition system. For example, the k-trust levels assigned to S_1 are 2 (searchTrip · holdTrip), 4 (searchTrip · refineResults · searchTrip · holdTrip), 5 (searchTrip · holdTrip · addTrip · searchTrip · holdTrip), and 7 (by adding the operations `bookTrips` and `completeBooking` to the conversation representative of level 5).

6.3.6 Architecture of the Enforcement System

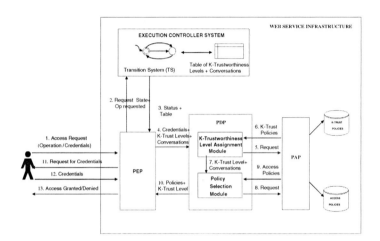

Fig. 6.6. System Architecture for a Simple Web service

This section describes how the proposed access control model for conversation-based Web services is implemented in a Web service environment. The system architecture for a simple Web service is shown in Figure 6.6. To be compliant with the XACML standard[188], the *access control enforcement system* is composed of a Policy Enforcement Point (PEP), a Policy Decision Point (PDP), and a Policy Administration Point (PAP). With respect to the XACML architecture, a component called Execution Controller System (ECS) has been added. The ECS maintains a copy of the transition system of conversations to keep track of the state of the interaction between the service requestor and the service. Further, before the enforcement process is executed, the ECS generates a data structure reporting for each state in the transition system all the possible k-trust levels that can be assigned to a service requestor and the associated conversations. Basically, ECS executes Algorithms 1 through 4 and returns the results in an appropriate data structure.

The PEP Module is the interface between the Web service's service requestors and the ECS. According to the enforcement process described in Section 6.3.4, when the service requestor contacts the Web service for the first time, it sends a message with a set of initial credentials. Once the PEP receives the information to update the state of the interaction, it forwards it to the ECS. The ECS returns to the PEP the current state of the interaction and the precomputed data structure containing all the possible k-trust levels and conversations (lines 2 and 3). Then, the PEP sends to the PDP the service requestor's credentials, all the possible k-trust levels that can be assigned to the service requestor in that state of the interaction, and the related set of conversations (line 4). The PDP's k-Trustworthiness Level Assignment (TLA) Module interacts with the PAP, which manages the policies, to retrieve the k-trust policies associated with the received k-trust levels (lines 5 and 6). It evaluates whether the service requestor's credentials satisfy the policies. If they do, the service requestor is assigned to the k-trust level k_i associated with the k_i-trust policy the service requestor is compliant with. The TLA sends k_i to the PDP's Policy Selection (PS) Module, together with the conversations of length less than or equal to k_i (line 7). The PS module asks the PAP for the access control policies related to the operations composing the conversations received from the TLA module (lines 8 and 9). The PS module combines the selected policies to obtain the corresponding conversation access control policy. It returns the policies to the PEP with k_i (line 10). At this point, the PEP asks the service requestor to provide the credentials required by the policies and evaluates them against the policies (lines 11 and 12). If the check is positive, the service requestor can perform any operation in the conversations related to k_i.

Bibliographic notes

The book of Matt Bishop [47] is recommended for the readers interested in access control.

For an interesting discussion about stateless and stateful Web services we refer the reader to [108, 83, 109].

7

Secure Publishing Techniques

Integrity is a key security requirement. It deals with assuring that information is not tampered with and is only modified by properly authorized subjects. In the Web service world, integrity is crucial from at least two different perspectives. The first is related to integrity of information transmitted across the network. Integrity in such context is assured by the use of digital signatures, for which an XML standard has been specified (see Chapter 4). The second, more important issue is related to the integrity of UDDI registries [139]. Because such registries provide structured and standard descriptions of Web services, as well as searching facilities for finding the service providers that better fit client requirements, their integrity is crucial. To address such issue, UDDI specifications include signatures for registry elements, according to the W3C XML Signature syntax.

A major issue, not covered by any standard, is the integrity and authenticity of UDDI registries managed in the context of third-party architectures. In such an architecture, the owner of the services, which we refer to as *service provider* (SP), is different from the parties, referred to as *discovery agencies* (DAs), which manage (a portion of) the UDDI registries related to the services and answer queries by *clients*, also referred to as *service requestors*. Such architectures are today becoming increasingly popular because of their scalability and ability of efficiently managing a large number of clients and large volumes of data. The main problem in such an architecture is how the SP can assure the integrity of data about its services when the data are managed by third parties, that is, the DAs. The first obvious solution is to require the DA to be trusted with respect to integrity. However, a major drawback of such a solution is that it is not feasible to verify large Web-based systems like DAs and, moreover, these systems can be easily penetrated. An alternative approach is based on the use of digital signature techniques. Such techniques, however, cannot be directly applied because service requestors typically require only selected portions of the UDDI registries through possibly fine-grained queries. Because the possible queries are not known in advance, the SP would have to sign elements at a very small granularity. Such an approach, however, would

E. Bertino et al., *Security for Web Services and Service-Oriented Architectures*,
DOI 10.1007/978-3-540-87742-4_7, © Springer-Verlag Berlin Heidelberg 2010

not make it possible to detect if the DA has on purpose removed some portion
of the reply. An alternative solution has been proposed by Bertino et al. [35]
based on the use of secure publishing techniques. Such techniques, based on
the well-known Merkle hash tree technique [179], had been initially developed
for addressing integrity in the context of XML data publishing in third-party
architectures [36] and were later extended to address the problem of UDDI
registry integrity [35].

In this chapter we first review basic notions of the Merkle Hash tree technique and discuss its application to the signature of XML documents. We
then discuss in detail its application to the problem of signing UDDI registries, based on the approach by Bertino et al. [35], and contrast its use with
that of conventional signature techniques.

7.1 The Merkle Signatures

The technique proposed by Ralph Merkle is a well-known mechanism for authenticating hierarchical data structures such as trees. It has been widely
applied in a number of different contexts, such as for the authentication of
data structures recording information about the validity of certificates [198];
for micropayments, in order to minimize the number of public key signatures
needed in issuing or authenticating a sequence of certificates for payments [66];
and for completeness and authenticity of queries in relational databases [92].
Bertino et al. have also used the Merkle hash tree for enforcing integrity and
authenticity of queries against XML documents in the context of third-party
publishing [36]. In what follows we first introduce the notion of the Merkle
tree and describe its application to XML documents.

7.1.1 Merkle Signatures for Trees

Merkle initially proposed the use of binary trees to address the problem of
authenticating a large number of public keys with a single value, that is, the
root of the tree. In such a binary tree each node is associated with a hash value,
referred to as the *Merkle hash* of the node. In particular, the Merkle hash for
a leaf node is computed by applying a hash function h to the content of the
node. The Merkle hash for an interior node is computed by applying h to the
concatenation of the Merkle hash of its left child node and the Merkle hash of
its right child node. More specifically, let h be a one-way hash function. Let
T be a tree and n be a node in T; the Merkle hash of n, denoted as $MH(n)$,
is defined as follows:

- $MH(n) = h(n)$ if n is a leaf node;
- $MH(n) = h(MH(n_l)) \parallel MH(n_r))$ if n is an interior node; in this expression, $\parallel$ denotes the concatenation operation, and n_l and n_r denote the left
  and right chilren of n, respectively.

The Merkle hashes are computed for all the nodes in the tree, starting from the leaf nodes. The Merkle hash of the root computed according to the above definition is the Merkle hash of the entire tree. The Merkle hash of the root is then signed. Such a signature is thus the signature of the entire tree. Note that such an approach is very efficient since signing a tree requires signing a single hash value. The verification of the tree signature requires the hash value of the tree to be recomputed according to the same procedure as that followed for the generation of such a value.

The Merkle hash technique can be easily extended to the case of non-binary trees, as we show in the following subsection, by considering the case of XML documents that are typically organized as non binary trees.

7.1.2 Merkle Signatures for XML Documents

Because the organization of an XML document is in essence based on the tree structure, the Merkle signature for trees can be directly applied to the signature of XML documents. The application of such a technique allows one to generate a unique digital signature for an entire XML document, to assure the integrity of an entire document as well as of any portion of it, that is, of one or more elements and attributes.

Before describing the approach for computing the Merkle hash values for XML documents, we need to introduce some notation. Let e be an XML element; then, $e.contents$ and $e.tagname$ denote the data contents and tagname of e, respectively. Let a be an XML attribute; then $a.value$ and $a.name$ denote the value and name of a, respectively. We use the term node to refer to an attribute or an element.

Let d be an XML document, and let n be a node of d. The Merkle hash value associated with d, denoted as $MH_d(n)$, is computed as follows:

- $MH_d(n) = h(h(n.value)) \parallel h(n.name))$ if n is an attribute;
- $MH_d(n) = h(h(n.contents \parallel h(n.tagname) \parallel MH_d(child(1,n) \parallel \ldots \parallel MH_d (child(Nc_n, n)))$ if n is an element.

In the above expressions, $\parallel$ denotes the concatenation operator; function $child(i,n)$ returns the i-th child of node n; and Nc_n denotes the number of children nodes of node n.

According to the above expressions, the Merkle hash value of an attribute is the value returned by the application of the hash function to the concatenation of the hashed attribute value and the hashed attribute name. The Merkle hash value of an element is obtained by applying the hash function to the concatenation of the hashed element content, the hashed element tagname, and the Merkle hash values associated with its children nodes, both attributes and elements. As with binary trees, the Merkle hash value of the tree is the hash value of the root node computed by recursively applying the above expressions. The Merkle hash value is then signed; the resulting signature is referred to as the Merkle signature of the document.

A relevant property of such an approach is that if the correct Merkle hash value of a node n is known to a client, a malicious party cannot forge the values of the children of n or the contents and tagname of n. A malicious party can neither remove nor modify any element or attribute from the document. Thus, a client only needs to have available the Merkle hash value of the root node of a document in order to be able to verify the entire tree. The verification process follows the same approach as that we outlined for the verification of binary trees.

7.1.3 Merkle Hash Verification for Documents with Partially Hidden Contents

An important requirement to address when dealing with third-party publishing is the support of integrity verification in the case in which portions of an XML document are pruned by the publishing party before being sent to the requiring party. Portions of the document may be pruned as a result of the query issued by the client or for confidentiality reasons. Confidentiality has to be assured whenever the receiving party is not authorized to see the entire document content. Whenever the document is pruned, a traditional approach to digital signatures is not applicable, since its correctness is based on the assumption that the signing and verification processes are performed on exactly the same bits. In contrast, if the Merkle signature is applied, the client is still able to validate the signature provided that it receives from the third party a set of additional hash values, referring to the missing document portions. Such an approach makes the client able to locally perform the computation of the summary signature and compare it with the received one. Such additional information, referred to as the *Merkle hash path*, consists of the hash values of those nodes pruned away and needed by the client for computing the Merkle hash value of the document.

Let d be an XML document, and let n and m be nodes in d such that $n \in Path(m)$, where $Path(m)$ denotes the set of nodes connecting m to the root of d. The Merkle hash path between m and n, denoted as $MhPath(m,n)$, is the set of hash values, having the Merkle hash value of m, needed to compute the Merkle hash value of n. Thus, the Merkle hash path between m and n consists of the hash values of the tagnames and the contents of all nodes in the path from m to n (apart from m) and of all the Merkle hash values of the siblings of the nodes belonging to the path from m to n (apart from n).

Figure 7.1 shows various examples of Merkle hash paths. In the graphical representation, the triangle denotes the document portion returned to the client, whereas black circles represent the nodes for which the Merkle hash values are returned together with the document portion, that is, the Merkle hash paths.

Consider the first example from the left reported in Figure 7.1. The Merkle hash path between nodes 4 and 1 consists of the Merkle hash values of nodes 5 and 3, plus the hash values of the tagnames and contents of nodes 2 and

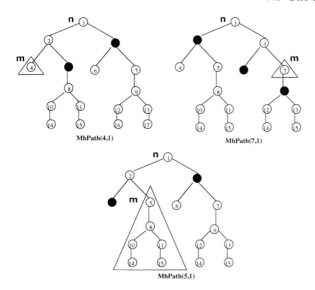

Fig. 7.1. Examples of Markle hash paths

1. By using node m, the Merkle hash value of node 5, and the hash value of the tagname and contents of node 2, the Merkle hash value of node 2 can be computed. Then, by using the Merkle hash values of nodes 2 and 3, and the hash values of the tagname and contents of node 1, the Merkle hash value of node 1 can be computed. Consider now the second example in Figure 7.1; the returned document portion consists of a non-leaf node. In such a case, MhPath(7, 1) contains also the Merkle hash value of the child of node 7, that is, node 9. Thus, by using the Merkle hash values of nodes 9 and 7, the Merkle hash value of node 7 can be computed. Then, by using this value, the Merkle hash value of node 6 and the hash values of the tagname and content of node 3, the Merkle hash value of node 3 can be obtained. Finally, by using the Merkle hash values of nodes 3 and 2, and the hash values of the tagname and contents of node 1, the Merkle hash value of node 1 can be generated. In contrast, in the third example the returned document portion consists of the entire subtree rooted at node 5. In such a case, MhPath(5, 1) does not contain the hash values of the children of node 5. Since the entire subtree rooted at 5 is available, it is possible to compute the Merkle hash value of node 5 without the need for further information. Then, as in the previous examples, by using the Merkle hash values of nodes 5 and 4, and the hash values of the tagname and contents of node 2 supplied by MhPath(5, 1), the Merkle hash value of node 2 can be computed. Finally, by using the Merkle hash values of nodes 2 and 3, and the hash values of the tagname and contents of node 1, the Merkle hash value of node 1 can be computed. Note that if the returned document portion consists of an entire subtree, the only necessary Merkle hash values are those

associated with the siblings of the nodes belonging to the path connecting the subtree root to the document root.

7.2 Application of the Merkle Signature to UDDI Registries

The use of Merkle signature techniques in the context of security for UDDI registries is important when the integrity of UDDI has to be verified by the clients that do not have access to entire contents of the registries. Under the approach by Bertino et al. [35], the SP first generates the Merkle signature of the businessEntity element, and then publishes it, together with the related data structures, in the UDDI registry. Then, when a client queries the UDDI, the Merkle signature and the set of needed hash values (i.e., the Merkle hash paths) are returned by the UDDI publisher to the client together with the results of the query.

Such an approach requires us to determine how to include the Merkle signature and the Merkle hash paths in the businessEntity element and the query result, respectively. To address such an issue, the solution by Bertino et al. [35] makes use of the dsig:Signature element introduced in version 3 of the UDDI specification [72]. The specification includes an additional option element, referred to as dsig:Signature, that allows an SP to sign the UDDI entry related to the service. The element can be included in any of the following UDDI registry elements: businessEntity, businessService, bindingTemplate, publisherAssertion, and tModel. Thus, according to the XML Signature syntax, an SP can sign the entire element to which the signature element refers, as well as can exclude selected portions from the signature. Such a solution is thus compliant with current standards. In what follows we provide more details on how the elements of the solution are represented in XML.

7.2.1 Merkle Signature Representation

A first required extension is to include the information that the signature of the signed XML document has been computed on the Merkle hash value of the document, which, as discussed in the previous section, is the Merkle hash value of the root node of the document. This information can be directly included by using the Transform Algorithm element, which is part of the XML Signature standard. The element specifies which transformations have to be executed on the document before signing it. Multiple transformations can be applied, each specified by a corresponding Transform Algorithm element. The order in which they are applied is given by the order in which the corresponding elements are given in the signature. As such, in the approach by Bertino et al. [35], the XML signature standard has been extended by adding the value "Merkle" to the set of possible values for the Transform

Algorithm element. Figure 7.2 shows a `dsig:Signature` element that includes the Merkle signature. Note that the URI attribute of the `Reference`
element is empty, denoting that the signed XML document is the one that
contains the `Signature`, that is, the `businessEntity` element. In addition to
the required enveloped signature and scheme-centric canonicalization transformations, the `dsig:Signature` element specifies also a Merkle transformation through a `Transform` element whose `Algorithm` attribute is equal to
"Merkle". Such a transformation indicates to the client and UDDI registries
that the SP has computed the Merkle signature on the `businessEntity` element.

```
<dsig:Signature>
  <SignedInfo>
    <CanonicalizationMethod
        Algorithm="http://www.w3.org/TR/2001/REC-xnl-c14n-20010315"/>
      <SignatureMethod
        Algorithm="http://www.w3.org/2000/09/xmldsig#dsa-sha1"/>
        <Reference  URI="">
          <Transforms>
            <Transform
              Algorithm="http://www.w3.org/2000/09/xmldsig#enveloped-
                                                        signature"/>
            <Transform
              Algorithm="urn:uddi-org:schemaCentricC14N:2002-07-10"/>
            <Transform Algorithm="Merkle"/>
          </Transforms>
          <DigestMethod
              Algorithm="http://www.w3.org/2000/09/xmldsig#sha1"/>
          <DigestValue>1fR07/Z/XFW375JG22bNGmFblMY=</DigestValue>
        </Reference>
  </SignedInfo>
  <SignatureValue>
    WOuO9b47TqmlpunAwmF4ubn1mdsb4HYR17c+3ULmLL2BxslwSsl6kQ
  </SignatureValue>
</ dsig:Signature>
```

Fig. 7.2. An example of a Signature element storing the Merkle signature

7.2.2 Merkle Hash Path Representation

In order to make it possible for the client to verify integrity when only a
portion of the UDDI registries is returned, the `dsig:Signature` element, returned with the inquiry answer, has to include the Merkle hash paths. A
subelement of such an element in which the paths can be recorded is the

dsig:SignatureProperties element, which records additional information useful for the signature validation process. Figure 7.3 shows an example of the dsig:Signature element containing the dsig:SignatureProperties element, which is inserted as a direct child of an Object element. It is important to note that, according to the XML Signature generation process, the only portion of the dsig:Signature element that is digitally signed is the SignedInfo element. Thus, by inserting the Object element outside the SignedInfo element, the UDDI registry does not invalidate the signature. Such an organization allows the UDDI to complement the dsig:Signature element representing the Merkle signature of the businessEntity element with the dsig:SignatureProperties element containing the appropriate Merkle hash paths, and then to insert the former element into the inquiry answer. More precisely, during the Merkle signature validation, the client must be able to recompute the Merkle hash value of the businessEntity element, and to compare it with the Merkle signature. In order to do that, the client must know the Merkle hash value of each subelement of the businessEntity element not included into the inquiry answer (that is, the Merkle hash path). To make the validation simpler, the Merkle hash paths are organized into an empty businessEntity element (see Figure 7.3), whose children contain a particular attribute, called hash, storing the Merkle hash value of the corresponding element. The businessEntity element is inserted into the dsig:SignatureProperties element.

7.2.3 A Comparison of Merkle Signatures with XML Signatures

Before discussing the differences between the approach based on the Merkle signature and the approach based on the XML signature standard, it is important to note that the latter approach, like the former one, allows one to generate a different hash value for each different node in the XML document, and then to generate a unique signature of all these values. To support such a feature, the XML Signature standard provides the Manifest element. This element consists of a list of Reference elements, one for each hashed node. However, the approach does not take into account the structure of the XML document, and therefore it is not able to assure the integrity of the relationships among document nodes. In contrast, the approach based on the Merkle signature is able to assure the integrity of node relationships. In what follows, we discuss the possible UDDI enquiries that a client can submit and discuss how integrity is assured.

- get_xxx **inquiries.** Such an enquiry allows one to retrieve up-to-date and complete registered details when actual keys to instances of specific structures (for example, businessEntity, businessService, bindingTemplate, and tModel) are known. According to the UDDI specification, the SP can complement all the data structures returned by a get_xxx API call with a dsig:Signature element. However, to ensure the integrity of all the

```
<dsig:Signature>
 <SignedInfo>
   <CanonicalizationMethod
       Algorithm="http://www.w3.org/TR/2001/REC-xnl-c14n-20010315"/>
   <SignatureMethod
       Algorithm="http://www.w3.org/2000/09/xmldsig#dsa-sha1"/>
   <Reference URI="">
    <Transforms>
     <Transform
      Algorithm="http://www.w3.org/2000/09/xmldsig#enveloped-signature"/>
     <Transform
         Algorithm="urn:uddi-org:schemaCentricC14N:2002-07-10"/>
      <Transform Algorithm="Merkle"/>
    </Transforms>
    <DigestMethod
          Algorithm="http://www.w3.org/2000/09/xmldsig#sha1"/>
     <DigestValue>
       1fRO7/Z/XFW375JG22bNGmFblMY=
     </DigestValue>
   </Reference>
 </SignedInfo>
 <SignatureValue>
   WOuO9b47TqmlpunAwmF4ubn1mdsb4HYR17c+3ULmLL2BxslwSsl6kQ
 </SignatureValue>
 <Object>
   <SignatureProperties>
     <SignatureProperty Target="MerkleHashPath">
       <businessEntity
           autorizhedName="value"
           operator="juddi.org"
           hash="sldghoghor....">
        <discoveryURLs hash="fdsgbdsl...." />
        <identifierBag hash="57438tgfkv...." />
        <categoryBag hash="57438tgfkv...." />
       <businessServices>
        <businessService>
          <description hash="gherogh..." />
          <bindingTemplates hash="hgkvdlsfv...." />
          <categoryBag hash="hdsbghfdlb..." />
        </businessService>
        <businessService>
          <description hash="gherogh..." />
          <bindingTemplates hash="hgkvdlsfv...." />
          <categoryBag hash="hdsbghfdlb..." />
        </businessService>
       </businessServices>
      </businessEntity>
     </SignatureProperty>
   </SignatureProperties>
 </Object>
</dsig:Signature>
```

Fig. 7.3. An example of a Signature element storing the Merkle signature

data structures the SP must compute five different XML signatures (one for each element). In contrast, by using the Merkle signature approach the SP generates only one signature, that is, the Merkle signature of the `businessEntity` element. Thus, the first benefit of the Merkle signature approach is that by its generating only a unique signature it is possible to ensure the integrity of all the data structures. When a client submits a `get_xxx` inquiry, the UDDI returns to it the entire requested data structure, where the enclosed `dsig:Signature` element contains the Merkle signature generated by the SP, together with the Merkle hash path between the root of the returned data structure and the `businessEntity` element.

- `find_xxx` **inquiries.** Such an enquiry returns overview information about the registered data. Consider, for instance, the inquiry API `find_business` that returns a structure containing information about each matching business, including a summary of its business services. This information is a subset of the information contained in the `businessEntity` and the `businessService` elements. For these kinds of inquiries, the UDDI specification states that if a client wants to verify the integrity of the information contained in the returned data structure, the client must retrieve the corresponding `dsig:Signature` element by using the `get_xxx` API call. This means that if a client wishes to verify the answer of a `find_business` inquiry, the client must retrieve the whole `businessEntity` element, together with the corresponding `dsig:Signature` element, as well as each `businessService` element, together with its `dsig:Signature` element.

In contrast, if the same API call is performed by using the Merkle signature approach, to make the client able to verify the integrity of the inquiry result it is not necessary to return to the client the whole `businessEntity` element and the `businessService` elements, together with their signatures. Only the Merkle hash values of the missing portions are required, that is, of the portions not returned by the inquiry. These Merkle hash values can be easily stored by the UDDI in the `dsig:Signature` element (more specifically in the `dsig:SignatureProperties` subelement) of the `businessEntity` element.

The main issue in applying the Merkle signature to the `find_xxx` inquiries is that the expected answers, defined by the UDDI specification, do not include the `dsig:Signature` element. Thus, in order to support the use of the Merkle signature for supporting the integrity verification of the replies to the `find_xxx` inquiries, the data structure returned by the UDDI must be modified by inserting one or more `dsig:Signature` elements. One possible approach to address this issue is to add one such element to each of the elements in the `xxxList` element. `xxxList` is the list of results returned by the enquiry. An algorithm specifying how to complement the reply to a `find_xxx` inquiry with the Merkle signature, and a prototype supporting such enhanced UDDI registries, has been developed by Bertino et al., and we refer the reader to [35] for additional details.

7.3 Bibliographic Notes

The approach by Bertino et al. [36] for integrity verification of XML documents in third-party publishing environments has been further extended by other researchers. Some notable extensions include support for dynamic data [163] and confidentiality [64]. The latter extension is particularly significant in that it has resulted in a technique supporting both integrity and confidentiality through encryption; as such the third party does not even have to have access to data in clear. To date, this approach is the only one supporting both confidentiality and integrity in third-party publishing. The Merkle hash signature technique has also been applied to the integrity verification of many different types of data structures, such as indexes [172] and directories [117], and to streaming data [164]. Recently, however, Kundu and Bertino [156], have shown that Merkle hash signatures suffer from information leakage. As such they are not suitable for applications requiring both integrity and confidentiality. To address this problem, Kundu and Bertino have proposed another approach to integrity verification for tree-structured data based on randomized postordering, preordering and in-order tree traversal; this approach does not suffer from information leakage and is more efficient than the Merkle hash signature approach with respect to the operation of signature verification. Third-party publishing architectures have also been widely investigated in the context of data management outsourcing. In this context, in addition to data integrity, data confidentiality is crucial and thus approaches have been proposed supporting query processing, including complex operations like joins, on top of encrypted data data [142]. Secure data management outsourcing is crucial in Web services and SOA when services deal with data management and information dissemination. Approaches developed to deal with these specialized services are based on the same architectural approach proposed by Bertino et al. [36]; their focus is mainly on the assurance of query reply correctness [290] through the use of authentication data structures, often defined as extension of the Merkle Hash Tree.

8

Access Control for Business Processes

Todays business environment is undergoing dramatic change. Competitive pressure from traditional and non-traditional sources, the rapid emergence and growth of new channels, increasing pressure to outsource selected business processes, and demands for compliance with a plethora of new regulatory and legal requirements are all contributing to an ever growing demand for change. Traditionally, many organizations have struggled to manage change. In order to survive and prosper in the coming years, these organizations will need to develop a capability to sustain a state of change and evolution. The ability of an organizations IT systems to cope with this level of change will be a significant factor in the organizations success in adapting to this increasingly dynamic business environment. Organizations are addressing this by adopting service-oriented architecture (SOA) principles. Service orientation (and SOA in general) is increasingly being viewed as a means to better align business and IT objectives and to better support the levels of flexibility and change required by the business. Business processes or workflows can be built by combining Web services through the use of a process specification language. Such languages basically allow one to specify which tasks have to be executed and the order in which they should be executed. Because of their importance, process specification languages have been widely investigated and a number of languages have been developed. One such language is WS-BPEL (Web services Business Process Execution Language), which has became the de facto standard to implement business processes based on Web services [10]. WS-BPEL resulted from the combination of two different workflow languages, WSFL [162] and XLANG [253], and adopts the best features of these language. WS-BPEL is layered on top of several XML standards, including WSDL 1.1[67], XML Schema 1.0 [258], and XPath 1.0 [71], but of these, WSDL has had the most influence on WS-BPEL. Despite significant progress toward the development of an expressive language for business processes, significant challenges still need to be addressed before business processes management systems can be widely used in distributed computer systems and Web services. Even if WS-BPEL has been developed to specify automated business processes that

E. Bertino et al., *Security for Web Services and Service-Oriented Architectures*, DOI 10.1007/978-3-540-87742-4_8, © Springer-Verlag Berlin Heidelberg 2010

orchestrate activities of multiple Web services, there are cases in which people must be considered as additional participants who can influence the execution of a process. Recently, a WS-BPEL extension to handle person-to-person processes has been proposed called BPEL4People [5]. In BPEL4People, users who have to perform the activities of a WS-BPEL business process are directly specified in the process by user identifiers or by groups of people names. No assumption is made on how the assignment is done or on how it is possible to enforce constraints like separation of duties.

WS-BPEL does not provide any support for the specification of authorization policies or of authorization constraints on the execution of activities composing a business process. We believe, however, that it is important to extend WS-BPEL to include the specification of human activities and an access control model able to support the specification and enforcement of authorizations to users for the execution of human tasks within a business process while enforcing constraints, such as separation of duty, on the execution of those tasks [43, 81, 65, 270].

This chapter presents RBAC-WS-BPEL [216], an authorization model for WS-BPEL business processes that also supports the specification of a large number of different types of constraints. Role-based access control (RBAC) (see Appendix A) is a natural paradigm for the specification and enforcement of authorization in workflow systems because of the correspondence between tasks and permissions. In recent years, several extensions to RBAC have been proposed with the goal of supporting access control for workflow systems [7, 43, 270]. However, a role-based model alone is not sufficient to meet all the authorization requirements of workflow systems, such as separation of duty constraints, and binding of duty constraints. Separation of duty exists to prevent conflicts of interest and to make fraudulent acts more difficult to commit. A simple example of a separation of duty constraint is to require two different signatures on a check. Binding of duty constraints require that if a certain user executes a particular task, then this user must also execute a second task in the workflow. This chapter introduces BPCL (Business Process Constraint Language), which can be used to specify authorization constraints for business processes.

The chapter is organized as follow. The next section presents the main proposals about access control for workflow and business process systems. Then, Section 8.2 introduces WS-BPEL and a loan approval business process that will be used throughout the chapter to illustrate the discussion. Section 8.3 defines the components of RBAC-WS-BPEL, including authorization policies and authorization constraints. Section 8.4 discusses how authorization information can be represented in RBAC-XACML. Section 8.5 describes the BPCL language and how it implements the authorization constraints described in Section 8.3. Section 8.6 describes how WS-BPEL can be extended to support the specification of human activities and authorizations and authorization constraints. Section 8.7 introduces an algorithm to evaluate whether a request by a user to execute an activity in a WS-BPEL process can be granted.

Section 8.8 overviews RBAC-WS-BPEL system architecture. Section 8.9 describes a prototypal implementation of RBAC-WS-BPEL architecture on top of an existing WS-BPEL engine.

8.1 Access Control for Workflows and Business Processes

The problem of associating an authorization model with a workflow has been widely investigated. Atluri et al. [23] have proposed a workflow authorization model (WTA) that supports the specification of authorizations in such a way that subjects gain access to required objects only during the execution of a task, thus synchronizing the authorization flow with the workflow. To achieve such synchronization, their approach associates an authorization template (AT) with each task in the workflow, which allows appropriate authorizations to be granted only when the task starts and to be revoked when the task finishes. They have proposed an implementation of WAT using Petri nets in order to be able to perform a safety analysis because the safety problem in WAT is equivalent to the reachability problem in Petri nets.

Arguably, the most sophisticated approach to the problem of authorizing users to execute tasks within a workflow while enforcing constraints is the one by Bertino et al. [43]. According to this approach a workflow is a list of task-role specifications. A task-role specification identifies a task and specifies the roles authorized to perform the task and the maximum number of activations of the task permitted in an instance of the workflow. The model, however, supports only sequential task execution. As part of such an approach, a language has been developed for defining constraints on role assignment and user assignment to tasks in a workflow. The constraint language supports, among other functions, both static and dynamic separation of duty constraints. The authors also have shown how such constraints can be formally expressed as clauses in a logic program; such a reduction makes it possible to exploit results from logic programming and deductive databases. A further contribution of this approach is the development of algorithms for planning role and user assignments to the various tasks. The goal of these algorithms is to pre compute all the possible role-task and user-task assignments, so that all constraints stated as part of the authorization specification are satisfied. A drawback of this approach is that the algorithms for role and user assignments to tasks run in time exponential in the number of tasks in the workflow.

Another interesting approach is by Crampton [81]. He has proposed an expressive method for specifying authorization constraints in workflow systems. In particular, his model allows one to specify separation of duty constraints, weak separation of duty constraints, binding of duty constraints, constraints on the relative seniority of users who perform different tasks, and constraints determined by contextual user-based information. All the constraints are expressed as binary relations on the set of users. The model has the advantage of being independent from any computational model or access control mechanism. As part of such an approach, an algorithm has been proposed for the assignment of authorized users to tasks in a workflow that guarantees that the workflow instance completes. The algorithm runs in a time polynomial in the number of users and tasks, unlike the equivalent procedure in the model by Bertino et al.

Casati et al. [65] have proposed an authorization framework for the assignment of tasks to roles, organizational levels, and agents. Roles and organizational levels are structured into hierarchies to facilitate the assignment of tasks to agents. Authorizations for agents to play roles and levels and for roles and levels to execute tasks can be specified for all instances of a given workflow process, independently of time and workflow execution history. Then, the framework enables the definition of instance-dependent, time-dependent, and history-dependent authorizations in the form of constraints: authorizations can be modified depending on the state or history of a workflow instance, on the time, or on the content of process data. Authorization constraints are enforced as Event-Condition-Action (ECA) rules, where the event part denotes when an authorization may need to be modified, the condition part verifies that the occurred event actually requires modifications of authorizations, and determines the involved agents, roles, tasks, and processes, and the action part enforces authorizations and prohibitions. Active rules are also exploited for managing authorization inheritance along the role and level hierarchies of the framework. Active database technology has been adopted for the implementation of the framework; it has been used, in particular, to support the definition and execution of ECA rules. Finally, Casati et al. have implemented the authorization framework within the WIDE workflow management system.

With the widespread adoption of Web services to implement complex business processes and of WS-BPEL as the standard language to specify business processes based on Web services, the problem of how to associate authorized users with the activities of a WS-BPEL process is gaining attention. The RBAC-WS-BPEL authorization model that will be introduced in this chapter is one of the few approaches that address this problem. Another similar approach is by Konshutanski et al. [153]. They propose an authorization model for business processes based on Web services. In this approach, the authorization logic is decoupled from the application logic of the business process. Access control enforcement is based on two types of policies: access control policies and release policies. Both types of policy are expressed as logic rules specifying conditions on the credentials a user must submit to invoke business process activities. Access control policies are used to decide if a user request can be granted or not. A request is granted if it is a logical consequence of an access control policy and of the credentials submitted by the user with the request. Release policies are used when a user request is denied to determine the additional credentials that a user has to provide for the request to be granted. The enforcement process involves different components. A `Policy Evaluator` is associated with each Web services its activities are orchestrated in a business process: it makes local authorization decisions. A `Policy Orchestrator` defines an authorization business process that orchestrates the authorization processes performed by the `Policy Evaluators` of the Web services invoked to fulfill a user's request. The authorization business process is executed by a third component called `Authorization Server` that returns the result of the execution to the user. If the user request is denied, the user receives a business process that defines further actions that he has to execute in order to see this request accepted.

Another interesting proposal is BPEL4People, recently proposed by IBM and SAP. BPEL4People supports some extensions that are required by WS-BPEL to support user interactions. BPEL4People is comprised of the two following specifications:

- WS-BPEL Extension for People [5] layers features on top of WS-BPEL to describe human tasks as activities that may be incorporated as first class components in WS-BPEL process definitions.
- Web services Human Task (WS-HumanTask) [4] introduces the definition of standalone human tasks, including their properties, their behavior, and the operations used to manipulate them. Capabilities provided by WS-HumanTask may be utilized by Web service-based applications beyond WS-BPEL processes.

WS-BPEL Extension for People introduces a new basic WS-BPEL activity called `<people activity>` which uses human tasks as an implementation, and allows one to specify tasks local to a process or use tasks defined outside the process definition. The definition of standalone human tasks is given in the WS-HumanTask specification. A local task can be a) an inline task declared within the people activity, b) an inline task declared within either the scope containing the `<people activity>` or the process scope; or c) a standalone task identified using a QName. The element `<task>` is used to define an inline task within a `<people activity>`. The elements `<localtask>` and `<remotetask>` are used to specify, respectively, standalone tasks that do not offer a callable Web service interface and those that offer a callable Web service interface. The users entitled to perform a `<people activity>` are specified by a `<peopleAssignment>` element that associates with the activity a query on an organizational directory.

The WS-HumanTask specification introduces the definition of human `<tasks>`. It specifies the roles a person or a group of people resulting from a people query can play with tasks. WS-HumanTask describes how to determine who is responsible for acting on a human task in a certain generic human role. Descriptions of the operations and of an application interface to manipulate human tasks are also given. Finally, WS-HumanTask introduces a coordination protocol that supports interactions with human tasks according to a service-oriented strategy and at the same time enhances task autonomy.

8.2 Web Services Business Process Execution Language (WS-BPEL)

WS-BPEL is an XML-based language to specify business processes. The top-level element in the specification is `<process>`. It has a number of attributes, which specify the process name, the namespaces being referred to, and whether the process is an abstract process or an executable process. An executable process describes the internal implementation of the process, while an abstract process specifies the external behavior of a process. The `<partnerLinks>` element is used to identify the external Web services invoked from within the process. The `<variables>` element defines the data that flows within the process. The `<correlationSets>` element is used to bind a set of operations to a service instance. The `<faultHandlers>` element is used to handle exceptions. The `<compensationHandlers>` element is used to implement specified actions to be taken in the case of a transaction rollback. The `<eventHandlers>` are used to specify actions in response to external events. The actual business logic is represented as a group of activities, which are executed in a structured way. Activities are executed by invoking Web services. The business logic includes basic control structures: the `<sequence>` activity contains one or more activities that are performed sequentially; the `<if>` activity is used to specify conditional branching execution; the `<while>` activity supports iterative execution of an activity; the `<pick>` activity is used to trigger an activity following a specified event; the `<repeatUntil>` activity provides for repeated execution of a contained activity; the `<forEach>` activity iterates the execution of an enclosed `<scope>` activity a fixed number of times; the `<flow>` activity is used to specify one or more activities to be performed concurrently. `<links>` elements can be used within a `<flow>` activity to define explicit control dependencies between nested child activities; `<link>` specifies that the activity that includes its `<source>` element must be executed before the one that includes its `<target>` element. These activities, in turn, may contain basic activities, which are specified using one of the following elements: the `<invoke>` element, which allows the business process to invoke a one-way or request-response operation on a communication channel offered by a partner; the `<receive>` element, which allows the business process to wait in a blocking mode for a matching message to arrive, and the `<reply>` element, which allows the business process to send a message in reply to a message that was received via a `<receive>` activity. The `<scope>` activity defines a subprocess with its own variables, partner links, message exchanges, correlation sets, event handlers, fault handlers, a compensation handler, and a termination handler.

The creation of a business process instance in WS-BPEL is always implicit; activities that receive messages, that is, `<receive>` activities and `<pick>` activities, can be annotated to indicate that the occurrence of an activity results in a new instance of the business process to be created.When a message is received by such an activity, an instance of the business process is created if it does not already exist. A business process instance is terminated when one of the following conditions holds: the last activity in the process terminates; a fault occurs, and it is not handled appropriately; or a process is terminated explicitly by a terminate activity.

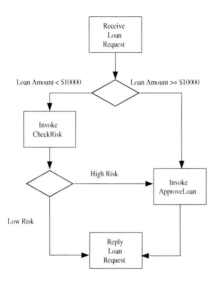

Fig. 8.1. A loan approval process specification

Example 8.1. To provide concrete examples of the proposed extensions to the WS-BPEL language, a loan approval process is introduced as a running example. Customers of the service send loan requests, including personal information and the amount being requested. Using this information, the loan service executes a simple process resulting in either a "loan approved" message or a "loan rejected" message. The decision is based on the amount requested and the risk associated with the customer. For low amounts of less than $10,000, a streamlined process is used. In the streamlined process, low-risk customers are approved automatically. For higher amounts, or medium- and high-risk customers, credit requests require further processing. For processing each request, the loan service uses two other services. In the streamlined process, used for low-amount loans, a *risk assessment* service is used to obtain a quick evaluation of the risk associated with the customer. A full *loan approval* service (possibly requiring direct involvement of a loan expert) is used to obtain assessments when the streamlined approval process is not applicable. Four main activities are involved in the process:

- **Receive Loan Request** allows a client to submit a loan request to the bank

- Invoke Check Risk invokes the operation Check Risk (provided by the *risk assessment* Web service) that computes the risk associated with the loan request
- Invoke Approve Loan invokes the operation Approve Loan (provided by the *loan approval* Web service) that states whether the loan request should be approved or rejected
- Reply Loan Request sends to the client the result of the loan request evaluation process

Figure 8.1 reports an informal specification of the process. Activities are represented by rectangular nodes while rhomboid nodes represent a conditional choice. An arc from one activity to another means that the first activity must be executed before the other.

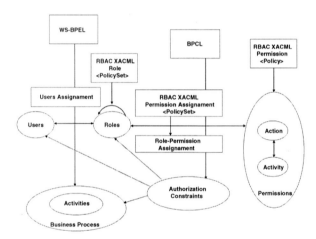

Fig. 8.2. RBAC-WS-BPEL component representation

8.3 RBAC-WS-BPEL: An Authorization Model for WS-BPEL Business Processes

A WS-BPEL process is a representation of an organizational or business process and is typically specified as a set of activities and a set of dependencies between the activities. The dependencies fall into two broad categories: those determined by the application logics of the process, such as the order of execution of the activities [226], and those determined by security requirements. WS-BPEL addresses the first category only.

This chapter deals with the second category and it focuses on developing authorization extensions to WS-BPEL. The proposed extensions include the specification of authorization information and authorization constraints. Authorization information associates activities with authorized users and enables a reference monitor to reach a decision about the legitimacy of a user request to execute an activity. Authorization constraints include separation of duty requirements, where two different users must execute two different activities, and binding of duty constraints, in which the same user is required to perform two different activities. In what follows, the main components of the RBAC-WS-BPEL model are presented (see Figure 8.2). These components support the specification of a business process and the specification and enforcement of an RBAC authorization policy for the activities composing the business process.

Roles	Attribute Conditions
Bank Director	{Employment = Bank Director, Bank = Chase}
Branch Director	{Employment = Branch Director, Bank = Chase, City = New York}
Risk Loan Manager	{Employment = Branch Director, Bank = Chase, City = New York, Branch = 2345}
Line Manager	{Employment = Manager, Bank = Chase }
Clerk	{Employment = Clerk, Bank = Chase }

(a) Roles

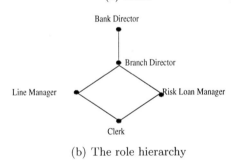

(b) The role hierarchy

Fig. 8.3. RBAC-WS-BPEL role hierarchy for the loan approval process

The model, referred to as RBAC-WS-BPEL, inherits all the components of traditional RBAC models: users, roles, permissions, role hierarchies, user-role assignment and role-permission assignment relations. Users are assigned to roles and roles are assigned to permissions. The main difference with respect to traditional RBAC models is that WS-BPEL business processes coordinate the operations of Web services provided by different organizations. Therefore, roles do not represent job functions within a single organization as in traditional RBAC models, and potential users of the business process are not the employees of an organization performing job functions identified by roles. Then, business process' users may not be known a priori and there is the need of a mechanism to identify users and assign them to roles.

In RBAC-WS-BPEL, users are identified by means of digital credentials. A credential contains a set of attributes characterizing the owner specified via (name, value) pairs. An *RBAC-WS-BPEL role* is identified by a set of conditions on users' attributes. RBAC-WS-BPEL roles are structured in a *role hierarchy* that reflects the different responsibilities associated with a business process and defines a permissions inheritance relation among the roles. A user is assigned to a role if the user's credentials match the user's attribute conditions associated with the role. The *RBAC-WS-BPEL user-role assignment relation* is represented as a set of tuples (u, r) where u represents a user and r the role to which it is assigned. A user acquires the permission to execute a business process' activity only if he is assigned to a role that has the permission to perform that activity. An *RBAC-WS-BPEL permission* represents the ability to execute an activity of a WS-BPEL business process. It is represented as a tuple $(A_i, Action)$ where A_i is the identifier of an activity in BP and *Action* identifies the type of action that can be performed on activity A_i. The association among permissions and roles is given by the *RBAC-WS-BPEL role-permissions assignment* relation.

The *RBAC-WS-BPEL authorization schema* associate with a WS-BPEL business process encompasses all the previous components. It is represented as a tuple (R, P, RA, UA) where R is a partially ordered set of roles, P is the set of permissions defined for the activities in the business process, $RA \subseteq R \times P$ is a role-permission assignment relation, and UA is the user-role assignment relation.

P_1	(Receive Loan Request,execute)
P_2	(Invoke Check Risk,execute)
P_3	(Invoke Approve Loan,execute)
P_4	(Reply Loan Request,execute)

(a) Permissions

Clerk	P_1
Clerk	P_4
Clerk	P_2
Risk Loan Manager	P_3
Branch Director	P_3
Line Manager	P_2

(b) Role-permission assignment

Fig. 8.4. RBAC-WS-BPEL permissions and role-permission assignment relation for the loan approval process

Example 8.2. Figures 8.3 and 8.4 illustrate the various components of an RBAC-WS-BPEL authorization schema for the loan approval process example. Figure 8.3 (a) illustrates the role hierarchy and defines five different roles. The most senior role is **Bank Director**, which dominates the role **Branch Director**, which in turn dominates the roles **Line Manager** and **Risk Loan Manager**; **Line Manager** and **Risk Loan Manager** dominate the role **Clerk**. Figure 8.3 (b) represents, for each role in the role hierarchy, the attribute conditions that a user has to satisfy to be assigned to the role. The set of permissions comprises the ability to execute each of the activities in the loan approval process (see Figure 8.4(a)). Figure 8.4(b) illustrates a typical permission-role assignment relation. Note that no permissions are explicitly assigned to the Bank Director role, although the role does implicitly have the rights to execute all activities in the process. Similarly, the Risk Loan Manager role has the permission to execute the Invoke Approve Loan activity.

The above authorization model is complemented by the specification of authorization constraints. In particular, RBAC-WS-BPEL allows one to specify two different types of authorization constraints: *role authorization constraints* and *user authorization constraints*. Both types of constraint are represented as a tuple $(D, (A_1, A_2), \rho)$; D is the *domain* of the constraint and is a subset of the set of roles R or of the set of users U; ρ is a relation on the set U or on the set R. An authorization constraint places some restrictions on the users and roles that can perform A_2 (the *consequent activity*) given that the user $u \in D$ or the role $r \in D$ has executed A_1 (the *antecedent activity*). Using this formalization for representing authorization constraints, $(D, (A_1, A_2), \neq)$ defines a separation of duty constraint and $(D, (A_1, A_2), =)$ defines a binding of duty constraint. Moreover, we can specify constraints that restrict the execution of two activities by users or roles, where that restriction can be expressed as a binary relation on the set of users or roles. Such relations could include "belongs-to-same-branch-as" or "is-bank-director-of".

(U, Receive Loan Request,Reply Loan Request, $=$)
(U, Invoke Check Risk,Invoke Approve Loan, $\neq$)
(R, Invoke Approve Loan,Reply Loan Request,$<$)

Fig. 8.5. RBAC-WS-BPEL authorization constraints for the loan approval process

Example 8.3. Figure 8.5 shows the authorization constraints associated with the loan approval process. $(U, ReceiveLoanRequest, ReplyLoanRequest, =)$ is a binding of duty constraint, requiring that the same user who receives the loan request communicates to the client whether the request is approved or not. $(U, InvokeCheckRisk, InvokeApproveLoan, \neq)$ is separation of duty constraints. This constraint imposes that the user who performs Invoke Check Risk Activity must be different from the user who executes Invoke Approve Loan. Finally, the last constraint is a seniority constraint that states that the role that executes Invoke Approve Loan be more senior than the role that replies to the client.

Finally, the notion of RBAC-WS-BPEL authorization specification combines all the previous notions. An *RBAC-WS-BPEL authorization specification* is a tuple (BP, AS, AC) where BP is a WS-BPEL business process, AS is the authorization schema defined for BP, and AC is the set of authorization constraints that apply to the activities in BP.

8.4 RBAC XACML: Authorization Schema

The first extension to the WS-BPEL language is the specification of the RBAC-WS-BPEL authorization schema associated with a WS-BPEL business process. This component of the language is specified using the RBAC XACML policy language [82] proposed as an alternative to the RBAC profile for XACML [12].

The authorization policy uses three different kinds of XACML policies, each represented by a `<PolicySet>` element. The set P of permissions associated with a WS-BPEL business process is represented by a `Permission` `<PolicySet>` containing a `Permission` `<Policy>` element for each permission in P. The RA role-permission assignment relation is represented by a `PermissionAssignment` `<PolicySet>` element: it includes a `<PolicySet>` subelement for each role to which the relation RA assigns a permission. Each `<PolicySet>` subelement contains a `<PolicySetIdReference>` child node for each permission assigned to the role. `<PolicySetIdReference>` refers to the `Permission` `<Policy>` element that represents the permission. Finally, a `Role` `<PolicySet>` element represents a role in the hierarchy. The `<Target>` subelement limits the applicability of the Role `<PolicySet>` to users satisfying the specified attribute conditions. The `<Target>` subelement of Role `<PolicySet>` has `<Subject>` subelements that specify the attributes' conditions that a users has to satisfy to be assigned to the role. `<PolicySetIdReference>` subelements are used to refer to the `PermissionAssignment` `<PolicySet>` element containing the set of permissions associated with the role. In addition, they are used to represent the role hierarchy, by referencing immediate junior roles.

8.5 Business Process Constraint Language

This section introduces the second extension to WS-BPEL, that is, an XML-based language for the specification of authorization constraints such as separation of duty and binding of duty. This language is called BPCL (Business Process Constraint Language). BPCL provides an XML Schema template for specifying authorization constraints. According to the proposed XML Schema, an `<AuthorizationConstraints>` element contains all the authorization constraints that apply to the activities in a WS-BPEL business process. Each constraint $C \equiv (D, (A_1, A_2), \rho)$ is represented by a `<Constraint>` element having an `Id` attribute by which it is referenced. The `<Constraint>` element has three subelements: `<Domain>`, `<Activities>`, and `<Predicate>`. The `<Domain>` element represents the domain D of the constraint C. It has two subelements,

`<Type>` and `<Subject>`. The `<Type>` data content specifies the type of the constraint C; it contains the value "role" if C is a role authorization constraint, and the value "user" if C is a user authorization constraint. The content of the `<Subject>` element is a set of roles or a set of users and depends on the content of the `<Type>` element. The `<Activities>` element specifies the two activities A_1 and A_2 to which the constraint C is applied. In particular, `<Activities>` has two child nodes, `<AntecedentActivityReference>` and `<ConsequentActivityReference>`, containing, respectively, an XLink reference to the XML element representing activities A_1 and A_2 in the WS-BPEL specification.

Finally, the `<Predicate>` element data content identifies the relation ρ in C: for example, the string "equal" identifies the relation $=$, while the string "not equal" identifies the relation $\neq$.

8.6 RBAC-WS-BPEL Authorization Specification

This section describes how the proposed extensions are incorporated into the loan approval process specification introduced in Section 8.2. WS-BPEL has been designed to be extensible. Extensions to WS-BPEL could include anything ranging from new attributes to new elements, to extended assign operations and activities, to restrictions or extensions of runtime behavior, and so on. The `<process>` element contains an `<extensions>` element having an `<extension>` child element that is used to declare namespaces of WS-BPEL extension attributes, and elements and indicate whether they carry semantics that must be understood by a WS-BPEL processor. WS-BPEL allows, also, the definition of new types of activities by placing them inside the `<extensionActivity>` element. The contents of an `<extensionActivity>` element must be a single element qualified with a namespace different from the WS-BPEL namespace. WS-BPEL extension rules specify which activities require interaction with users and the authorization information and constraints that apply to these activities. First, an `<extension>` element has been included into the process specification specifying the namespace "http://www.example.org/rbac-ws-bpel" that identifies the proposed extensions. Then, a new type of WS-BPEL activity called `<HumanActivity>` has been introduced to specify the activities that must be performed by humans: a `<HumanActivity>` contains the activity that to be performed requires interaction with a user. Finally, two new child elements have been added to the `<process>` element: the `<authorization_schema>` element and the `<authorization_constraints>` element. These elements include the references to the authorization information necessary to state which roles or users are allowed to execute the business process' activities, and the authorization constraints that apply to the activities in the process. The `<authorization_schema>` and the `<authorization_constraints>` elements have a "ref" attribute of type URI pointing, respectively, to the XML document defining the RBAC policy and the BPCL representation of the authorization constraints.

The RBAC-WS-BPEL specification shows many interesting features of the approach based on associating authorization information and authorization constraints with a business process' human activities. First, the specification of authorization information and authorization constraints in the WS-BPEL specification does not require a significant modification to the syntax of the language. It simply requires the inclusion of two new XML elements in the WS-BPEL syntax, which refer to the authorization information and the authorization constraints. Hence, the specification of a WS-BPEL business process that includes authorization information and authorization constraints is modular. Furthermore, with this approach it is easy to modify the authorization information and authorization constraints associated with the business process since only the references to them need to be modified. Second, the authorization constraint language is very expressive. It supports the specification of binding of duty constraints, separation of duty constraints and any constraint, which can be expressed as a binary relation on the set of users and roles.

8.7 RBAC-WS-BPEL Enforcement

The previous sections have presented the main components of RBAC-WS-BPEL, the access control model tailored for WS-BPEL. This section describes the algorithm to determine whether a user request to execute an activity A_i in a WS-BPEL process can be satisfied or not. When a user u sends a request to perform an activity A_i of a WS-BPEL process, the enforcement system evaluates the identity of the requester and checks the permissions he has. Further, it has to verify that the execution of the activity A_i by u does not violate any authorization constraints and does not prevent some other subsequent activities from completing because certain constraints are violated. Hence, for a given instance of a WS-BPEL process, upon receiving a request to perform an activity A_i by a user u, the enforcement system has to verify that:

- u is authorized to perform A_i;
- all the constraints in which A_i is the consequent activity are satisfied;
- the WS-BPEL process instance can complete if u performs A_i.

In what follows, an algorithm is introduced to evaluate whether a request to execute an activity by a user can be granted or not. The algorithm verifies that the WS-BPEL process instance will complete and no authorization constraints will be violated. The algorithm is performed before executing any request (u, r, i, A_k) to check whether the execution of the request prevents the WS-BPEL process instance from completing. To guarantee the completeness, before granting a request, the authorization schema associated with the

WS-BPEL process is updated with the fact that the user u under role r has executed activity A_k. Then, the algorithm computes for each activity in the WS-BPEL process the set of roles and users entitled to perform them. If one of these sets is empty, the request cannot be granted. After each request is granted, the authorization schema AS is updated with the information that the user u under role r has executed activity A_k, to ensure that the fact that a particular user and role have executed a particular activity is considered in enforcing constraints that apply to subsequent activities.

In what follows, we denote with $((A_i, A_j), \rho)$, both role and user authorization constraints. The algorithm receives as input an RBAC-WS-BPEL authorization specification (BP, AS, AC), an instance i of the WS-BPEL process BP, and a request (u, r, i, A_k) by a user u to execute activity A_k in BP under the role r. When the request (u, r, i, A_k) is received, the algorithm first adds to the authorization schema the fact that the role r of user u is executing the activity A_k. To represent this, a function IR is added: it associates with each activity A_i in BP the role that has executed A_i. This step is important to guarantee the completeness of the instance i (line 1). Then, for each pair of activities A_i and A_j, the algorithm builds $V_R(A_i, A_j)$, the set of roles that can execute A_i and A_j (in that order) given the authorization schema AS and the role authorization constraints in AC. The basic strategy to compute $V_R(A_i, A_j)$ is to initialize each $V_R(A_i)$ to the set of roles that are authorized to perform A_i (line 3) and to apply all possible role constraints defined for each pair of activities, including those derived from authorization information (lines 5/6). If for some A_i and A_j, $V_R(A_i, A_j)$ is empty, then the algorithm terminates (line 7), since no pair of authorized roles exists that complies with the role authorization constraints, and therefore no valid execution assignment exists for the instance i. Otherwise, for each task activity A_i, the algorithm re-computes the set of roles that can perform A_i (lines 10/11). The same steps (lines 12/22) are repeated to compute for each activity A_i the set $V_U(A_i)$ of users authorized to perform A_i. If the role r played by u belongs to $V_R(A_k)$, the set of roles authorized to execute the activity A_k and u belongs to $V_U(A_k)$, the set of users that are authorized to perform A_k, then the request (u, r, i, A_k) can be granted.

Algorithm 8: `Enforcement()`

Input:
(BP, AS, AC): A RBAC-WS-BPEL authorization specification
i: instance of the business process BP
(u, r, i, A_k): a request by a user u to execute activity A_k in BP under the role r

Output:
$Request\_granted$: boolean
(1) $AS:=AS \cap I_R(A_k)$;
(2)   **foreach** $A_i \in BP$
(3) $V_R(A_i):=\{r_i \in R:(r_i, P_{A_i}) \in RA \}$;
(4)   **foreach** $(A_i, A_j) \in BP$
(5)   **if** $((A_i, A_j), \rho) \in AC$
(6) $V_R(A_i, A_j):=(V_R(A_i) \times V_R(A_j) \cap \rho$;
(7)   **if** $V_R(A_i, A_j) = \emptyset$
(8) $Request\_granted:=$**false**;
(9)   **else**
(10) $V_R(A_i):=\{$set of roles in first position of $V_R(A_i, A_j)\}$;
(11) $V_R(A_j):=\{$set of roles in second position of $V_R(A_i, A_j)\}$;
(12) $AS:=AS \cap I_u(A_k)$;
(13)   **foreach** $A_i \in BP$
(14) $V_u(A_i):=\{$set of users authorized to perform $A_i \}$;
(15)   **foreach** $(A_i, A_j) \in BP$
(16)   **if** $((A_i, A_j), \rho) \in AC$
(17) $V_u(A_i, A_j):=(V_u(A_i) \times V_u(A_j) \cap \rho$;
(18)   **if** $V_u(A_i, A_j) = \emptyset$
(19) $Request\_granted:=$**false**;
(20)   **else**
(21) $V_u(A_i):=\{$set of roles in first position of $V_u(A_i, A_j)\}$;
(22) $V_u(A_j):=\{$set of roles in second position of $V_u(A_i, A_j)\}$;
(23)   **if** $(r \in V_R(A_k) \wedge u \in V_u(A_k))$
(24) $Request\_granted:=$**true**;
(25)   **return** $(Request\_granted)$;

8.8 RBAC-WS-BPEL System Architecture

This section presents an architecture that implements the enforcement process described in the previous section (see Figure 8.6). The main components are a *WS-BPEL engine*, a Web service called *RBAC-WS-BPEL Enforcement Service*, which is the core of the architecture, and three repositories, namely, the *XACML Policy Store*, the *BPCL constraints Store*, and the *History Store*. The WS-BPEL engine is responsible for scheduling and synchronizing the various activities within the business process according to the specified activity dependencies, and for invoking Web service operations associated with activities. The RBAC-WS-BPEL Enforcement Service carries out two tasks. First, it manages the execution of a business process's `<HumanActivity>` activity. Note that the Enforcement Service is able to manage the execution without requiring any extensions to legacy WS-BPEL engines. Second, it acts as a reference monitor: when a user claims a `<HumanActivity>` activity, it veri-

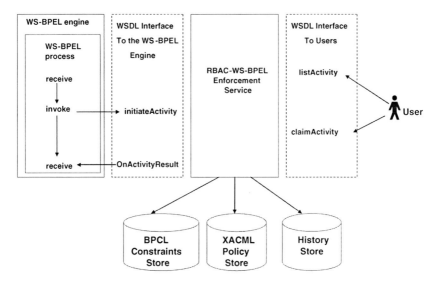

Fig. 8.6. RBAC-WS-BPEL Architecture

fies that the user is authorized to perform it according to the authorization schema and authorization constraints.

The RBAC-WS-BPEL Enforcement Service offers two WSDL interfaces: the first interface makes available the operations to start and complete the execution of a human activity. This interface provides two operations, "initiateActivity" and "onActivityResult". "initiateActivity" is a one-way operation invoked within a WS-BPEL process to start the execution of a <HumanActivity> activity. The invocation message of "initiateActivity" contains a set of information about the activity, the business process, and references to authorization schema and authorization constraints. The message received by the WS-BPEL process contains the business process variables modified by the <HumanActivity> activity.

The second interface of the RBAC-WS-BPEL Enforcement service allows users to display the activities they can claim, and to claim and execute them. This interface makes available two operations, "listActivity" and "claimActivity". The "listActivity" operation returns the list of the activities a user can claim. To claim an activity in the list, a user invokes the "claimActivity" operation. When this activity is executed, the RBAC-WS-BPEL Enforcement Service selects all possible BCPL constraints and the information in the XACML authorization schema, and runs Algorithm 1 to determine whether the user request can be granted or not. If the user is authorized, the WSDL operation providing the interface of the <HumanActivity> activity specified in the invocation message of the "initiateActivity" operation is invoked.

The XACML Policy Store contains the RBAC-WS-BPEL authorization schema associated with the business process, while the BPCL constraint Store stores the authorization constraints. The History Store is used to record information about past executions of each humanactivity, that is, the user who has performed it and whether the execution of the activity was successful or not. The history information is used to enforce authorization constraints.

8.9 Handling <HumanActivity> activity Execution and RBAC-WS-BPEL Enforcement

A prototype of the architecture which supports the execution of <HumanActivity> activities has been implemented choosing ODE as WS-BPEL engine and Oracle 10g to store for RBAC-WS-BPEL authorizations and authorization constraints. The Enforcement Service has been implemented as a JAVA Web service which has to be included to the <partnerLinks> list in the WS-BPEL process specification.

The main challenge in implementing such architecture is how to associate an interface to a <HumanActivity> activity to enable the interaction with a user and the enforcement of RBAC-WS-BPEL authorizations and authorization constraint on such activity. First, it is necessary to configure the Enforcement Service to work with a specific instance of the WS-BPEL process which requires the execution of <HumanActivity> activities. Through a configuration wizard, the WS-BPEL process administrator has to specify the name of the WS-BPEL process, the URL of the process, the variables in the process that represent the correlation set used to identify an instance of the process, and the order on which the activities are executed. Moreover, for each <HumanActivity> activity, the WS-BPEL process administrator has to specify the name of the activity, the Web service operation that is associated with the execution of the actvity, the operation portType, the template of the SOAP input message for the operation, and a jsp that is the interface for the user who has to perform the <HumanActivity> activity. The execution of a <HumanActivity> activity starts when the WS-BPEL process invokes the "initiateActivity" operation of the Enforcement Service. The process then waits to be called back by the RBAC-WS-BPEL Enforcement Service. The RBAC-WS-BPEL Enforcement Service adds the name of the activity contained in the invocation message to the list of <HumanActivity> activities that can be claimed. When a user requests the <HumanActivity> activity by invoking the "claimActivity" operation it includes in the invocation message a set of digital credentials that are encoded as SAML assertions. Then, the RBAC-WS-BPEL Enforcement Service queries the XACML Policy store to determine the roles that are authorized to perform the activity and verifies whether the user's credentials match the attribute conditions of one of these roles. If the user can be assigned to an authorized role, the RBAC-WS-BPEL Enforcement Service executes Algorithm 1 to verify that the user is authorized to perform the activity without preventing the end of the business process execution. If the user can perform the activity, the RBAC-WS-BPEL Enforcement Service removes the activity from the list of the <HumanActivity> activities that can be claimed, and then RBAC-WS-BPEL Enforcement Service instantiates a JAVA class Action. Such class retrieves the information for the <HumanActivity> activity set up by the WS-BPEL process administrator during the configuration of the RBAC-WS-BPEL Enforcement Service, and prompts the jsp interface to the user. Once the user has input the data necessary to perform the <HumanActivity> activity, the RBAC-WS-BPEL Enforcement Service populates the SOAP invocation message of the operation associated with the execution of the <HumanActivity> activity, with the data inserted by the user and then invokes the operation. If the execution of the operation completes successfully, the RBAC-WS-BPEL Enforcement Service calls back the WS-BPEL process performing passing the output message of the operation. Finally, the RBAC-WS-BPEL Enforcement Service updates the History Store recording, the name of the user who performs the activity and whether the execution was successfully or not.

9

Emerging Research Trends

The final chapter in this book covers some additional topics that, despite being very relevant for Web services and SOA, have not yet been investigated much. The chapter first discusses how Web services and the SOA approach can be leveraged on to architect and deploy security functions. The chapter then discusses issues related to privacy. Privacy techniques and tools, such as P3P, are briefly surveyed; privacy requirements specific to Web services are then discussed. The chapter is concluded by a short overview of security for the Semantic Web and a discussion on open research issues.

9.1 Security as a Service

"Security as a service" is a buzz that we increasingly hear about as a promising approach to address the increasingly complex security requirements of organizations and applications. A closer look at possible meanings of "security as a service" reveals two interpretations. The first interpretation refers to the outsourcing of security management. There are today companies advertising such services. Typical services that these companies offer are, however, limited to low-level services such as deploying and managing firewalls and antiviruses. Higher-level services, such as access control or identity management, are not typically provided. The second interpretation deals with organizing security functions as services that can be shared by several applications. While some types of security measures should still be implemented as a part of applications, for other shared, common security services it makes more sense to deploy them in a single location, especially when the environments are organized as SOAs. For example, preventing buffer overflow attacks and verifying the validity of application input data should be a responsibility of the application, as these measures are specific to the application. In contrast, the control of any access made to a certain resource is typically common to all applications using that resource, and therefore could be supported by a shared service. In what follows we elaborate on the second perspective. However, it is important

E. Bertino et al., *Security for Web Services and Service-Oriented Architectures*, DOI 10.1007/978-3-540-87742-4_9, © Springer-Verlag Berlin Heidelberg 2010

to note that understanding how to organize complex security tasks in terms of services would make it in turn possible to outsource many more of such tasks. In such a sense, the two perspectives are very much related.

9.1.1 Motivations

Different models and mechanisms to deal with identity management, authentication, access control, and privacy have emerged and evolved over time, driven by a large variety of factors, from technological advances such as biometric devices to increasing requirements for security and privacy. Operating systems provide basic mechanisms for identification, authentication, and access control, the latter mostly based on the discretionary access control model. DBMSs also support the more sophisticated RBAC mechanisms [228]. The mechanisms provided by operating systems and DBMSs are, however, not extensible; thus, whenever an application environment requires more sophisticated authentication or access controls, the application programs must include logics for such controls. Such an approach, however, leads to duplication of effort and increased cost in application development and maintenance. Because of these reasons, models and mechanisms to separate access control from the applications, such as XACML, have emerged.

At the same time, the need to drive the behavior of an access control system or an authentication system through clearly stated and machine-processable policies has fostered the development of various policy models and policy management mechanisms. The use of a policy-based approach enhances flexibility, reduces application development costs, and simplifies security management. Changes to security requirements simply entail modifying the policies, without requiring changes to the applications and the access control and authentication mechanisms. It is thus clear that an important approach to the problem of security is represented by the development of policy-based security services providing all functions for security management relevant to applications. Such an approach is particularly promising when applications are organized according to the SOA paradigm.

An important issue that has to be addressed when devising SOA-based approaches to security is how to achieve coordination among multiple security services. Security is a complex task that cannot be achieved by a single service; several services need to coordinate among each other. A possible approach to address this issue is the use of the so-called event-based model. The event-based, or notification-based, model is a commonly used pattern for inter-object communications. Examples can be found in many domains, as for example in publish/subscribe systems provided by message-oriented middleware vendors, or in system and device management domains. This notification pattern is increasingly being used in the context of Web services [204, 207]. The event-based approach is well suited for distributed environments without central control to construct component-oriented systems and to support applications that must monitor or react to changes in the environment, information interest, or in process status.

Despite its relevance, the notion of security services based on SOA and the event-based model has not been investigated, and even the issues in the development of these services need to be understood. In what follows we discuss open issues for security services by starting with a reference architectural framework. Then, to provide an example, we describe the organization and policy language of an authentication service currently under implementation [240].

9.1.2 Reference Framework for Security Services

The overall process leading to the authorization or denial of a request sent on behalf of a subject to access a protected resource can be described as a "security pipeline," that is, identification followed by authentication followed by authorization. Such a pipeline leads to the reference architectural framework shown in Figure 9.1.

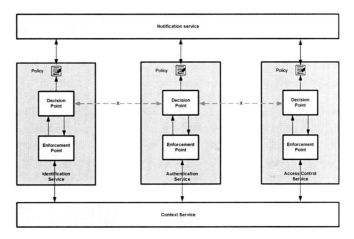

Fig. 9.1. Reference architectural framework for security as a service

First, according to SOA principles, each component of the security pipeline is a service. Moreover, by exploiting the XACML reference architecture (see Chapter 4), each security service is logically architected by distinguishing a Logical Decision Point, driven by the related policy, and one (or more) Enforcement Points. Second, in order to maintain a coherent state of the relevant security information, a notification service is included in the framework. Security services can register and subscribe to the notification service in order to be notified of relevant events. Consider a healthcare application scenario; in such a scenario an example of an *identity event* is the fact that a physician, employed by a given hospital resigns. The identity service produces such an event, which the authentication and the access control services subscribe to. Relevant events, once delivered to the proper security service, can trigger further action. It is worth noting that the same notification mechanism can be used to propagate relevant policy changes to the policy managers of the other services (for simplicity, policy managers are not shown in Figure 9.1).

As for the decision points, an important issue is to determine the situations in which a security service decision point may need to interact with another security service decision point in order to reach a security decision. A related issue is how these interactions should be architected, that is, whether they must be designed as direct interactions, through well defined protocols, or whether they can be carried out through a "mediator" service. Another issue is related to the management of shared contextual information during the execution of the security pipeline. While such contextual information could be, in principle, "propagated" through the security pipeline execution, this may lead to more complex service interfaces. Finally, a critical issue is related to the security of the event management. Confidentiality, for example is crucial in that events may often convey sensitive information, as in the case of identity management events. A solution to this issue is the adoption of an access control mechanism assuring the selective sharing of events among authorized subscribers by adopting recent access control approaches developed in the area of content distribution networks [151].

9.1.3 Authentication Service

Authentication is a fundamental security mechanism by which systems may verify identity claims of their users. It determines *who* the user is and whether his or her claim of a particular identity is true; authenticated identities are then the basis for applying other security mechanisms, such as access control.

Once the identity of a user has been verified, the system resources are made available to the user, possibly under the constraints specified by the access control policies, until the user exits the system. Such an approach may be appropriate for low-security environments or for environments in which the same strength of authentication is required for all resources. However, it is not appropriate in cases in which the same system may have resources with different requirements of authentication strengths for the subjects wishing to access them. A straightforward solution to authentication for resources with such heterogeneous requirements is based on a conservative approach, and maximizes authentication checks each time a user connects to the system. However, such a solution may result in computationally intensive authentication tasks and may also be very expensive and complex to deploy. For example, adopting one time passwords for all users of an organization, independently of the tasks they have to perform and the resources they have to access, may be very expensive; ideally, one would like to require such type of authentication only for users who need to access sensitive resources, and to use conventional passwords for the other users. If an application environment needs to apply authentication of different strengths or use different authentication mechanisms, depending on the resource to be accessed, the solution commonly applied is to implement authentication logics at the application program level. Such a solution has a lot of drawbacks, including the fact that it makes the management of authentication very difficult and error prone.

An approach to address the above issues is to organize authentication as a service able to support a variety of authentication mechanisms and to combine these mechanisms through the *authentication policies* [240]. In such an approach, authentication policies are specified through an *authentication policy language*. By using such a language, one can specify how many authentication factors are required, and of which type, for accessing specified resources, or impose constraints on the authorities by which credentials used for authentication have to be provided, thus supporting *quality-based authentication*. It is important to notice that the goals of such an authentication policy language are different from the goals of the SAML (Security Assertion Markup Language) standard [61]. SAML is a standard for encoding authentication statements; such statements typically specify that a given subject has been authenticated under a certain modality by a given entity at a given time. SAML thus does not deal with taking authentication decisions; it only deals with encoding and transmitting such decisions. The goal of the authentication policy language is to specify policies driving authentication decisions; policies expressed in this language may also take into account previous authentication decisions, taken, for example, by other sites in a distributed system, together with other information in order to reach an authentication decision.

A Reference Architecture

The reference architecture of the authentication service, referred to as the Auth-SL system, is represented in Figure 9.2. It consists of two major subsystems, the authoring subsystem and the enforcement subsystem, each corresponding to a major function in the management of policy-based authentication.

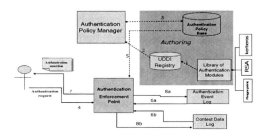

Fig. 9.2. Reference architecture for the authentication service

The *authoring subsystem* supports the specification and the management of the authentication policies. A key feature of this subsystem is that it supports the specification of which authentication mechanism to use through the specification of conditions on the features of the available mechanisms. The support of such a specification relies on the use of two components: a *library of authentication modules*, very much like a set of Pluggable Authentication Modules (PAMs); and a specialized *UDDI Registry* recording all features of the authentication modules that are relevant for the specification of the authentication policies. In addition, the registry contains attestation information used to detect unauthorized changes to the authentication module's configuration. The UDDI registry is made available only to selected parties and therefore is protected by access control policies. Each module in the library supports a specific type of authentication. Such an approach enhances extensibility in that system administrators can easily add new authentication methods by simply plugging in new modules. Such modules can then be dynamically invoked and used according to the specific authentication policies. The information required about the authentication modules in order to author authentication policies is as follows:

1. Module' authentication characteristics. These data describe the settings for the specific mechanism. For example, in password-based authentication, a characteristic would be the maximum number of tries allowed, or the minimum length of the password. For token-based authentication, a characteristic would be the authentication method (e.g., SSO, Basic-Auth credentials), the credentials (username, password, domain), X.509 client certificates, and the software used (e.g., IBM Tivoli Client RSA).
2. Implementation' data. These parameters qualify the specific implementation of a mechanism, and can refer to the storage of the secret token, the cryptographic technique used to transmit it, the audit trails, and so forth.

The authentication policies that can be expressed thus depend on the available authentication modules and on the characteristics of these modules. Such data are to be considered as part of the knowledge needed to specify adequate authentication policies. For example, if a security administrator knows that a given authentication module is weak due to implementation limits or module vulnerabilities, he or she will apply stronger authentication policies. Authored authentication policies are stored in a repository, referred to as *authentication policy base*, which provides querying capabilities to properly authorized users, such as system administrators and auditors.

The *enforcement subsystem* is in charge of processing authentication requests. It thus evaluates the applicable authentication policies and, based on these, makes authentication decisions. The evaluation is executed by the *authentication enforcement point*, which first retrieves a proper authentication policy. Policy evaluation may also take into account previous authentication events concerning the subject being authenticated. To express fine-grained constraints over past authentications, information on these authentications is collected in two different logs serving different purposes: to track user actions related to authentication and to store the conditions under which successful authentication is executed. The first log, referred to as *authentication event log*, records authentication events (events, for short) related to the subjects in the systems. An authentication event is basically an authentication executed by a subject. Such a log tracks in the chronological order all the events related to the authentication of users performed during a single working session. Once the policy is evaluated, a new event is generated and stored in the log in order to keep track of this authentication step. The second log, referred to as *context data log*, tracks specific data related to the previous authentications executed by the user in the same session. The context is crucial when a user performs several operations as part of the same session in that the information recorded by the context can be used, depending on the specific authentication policies, to avoid the execution of unnecessary authentication operations. An example is when the same type of authentication is required for two different resources accessed by a user in the same session. In such a case, once the authentication has been executed for one of the resources, it can be "reused" when the user requires access to the second resource, provided that the authentication verifies the "freshness conditions" specified in the authentication policies associated with the second resource. The output of the enforcement subsystem is an authentication assertion which can be either returned to the end user or transmitted to some other system or application.

The Authentication Policy Language

Authentication policies are the key elements to drive authentication decisions. The specification of authentication policies relies on the notion of *authentication factor*. Authentication factors define the features of a specific authentication, where by authentication we mean the execution of one authentication protocol using a single mechanism (that is, the "factor"). Authentication factors are specified in terms one or more *descriptors*. A descriptor is basically a predicate, expressing a property required by the authentication factor. An example of an authentication factor specified by two descriptors is {Mechanism = Biometrics, Feature = Fingerprint}. The first descriptor requires that the authentication be based on the use of a biometric authentication mechanism, whereas the second descriptor specifies that the feature used in the biometric authentication be the fingerprint. All the properties characterizing an authentication module are recorded in the UDDI registry, and they can be referenced in descriptors. Additional types of descriptors are related to contextual information, such as space and time, and to the issuers and verifiers of authentication tokens. Temporal descriptors are used in particular to specify "freshness conditions" concerning authentication; these conditions specify how recent an authentication action must be.

The authentication factors, as defined above, are stand-alone in that the specification of any one single factor is not related to the other factors. However, this is not adequate for the specification of complex and multifactor authentication policies. To correlate different factors and their characteristics, constraints can be specified; we refer to these constraints as *factor constraints*. Factor constraints can be simply specified as logic formulae in which the occurring variables are the factor identifiers. Consider an authentication policy requiring a subject to be identified by two credentials; an example of a factor constraint is to require that the issuers of these two credentials be different.

The previous elements, that is, authentication factors and factor constraints, are combined in the notion of authentication policy. Such a policy is composed by five elements: (i) a protected object O and a set S of operations defined on O; (ii) a list of authentication factors $[f_1, \ldots, f_k]$; (iii) an order flag; (iv) a threshold value; and (v) a set of factor constraints. As can be noticed, a policy is associated with an object and one or more operations defined on the object; this means that the authentication specified by the policy must be executed whenever one such operation is executed on the object. The specification of multiple authentication factors expresses multifactor authentication policies. The listed factors may or may not all be mandatory, as specified by the threshold value; for example, a policy may specify a list of five authentication factors, of which only three must be verified by the subject being authenticated. Additionally, the execution order of various authentication factors may or may not have relevance. If the order in which factors should be evaluated is significant, then the order flag is set to yes. The listed factors are to be evaluated accordingly. If order is set to no, the factor evaluation order is not mandated.

The specification of the ordering and the mandatory number of factors enhances the flexibility and the expressive power of the policy language. The order can be specified according to the relevance of the factors, or their sensitivity, or the cost for their verification. Thus, it can help in optimizing the usage of system resources. Similarly, the specification of the threshold enhances the flexibility of authentication by establishing the sufficient demands needed to authenticate the user.

9.2 Privacy for Web Services

Privacy is today an important concern for citizens, organizations and companies. We see an increasing number of organizations that collect data, very often concerning individuals, and use them for various purposes, ranging from scientific research, as in the case of medical data, to demographic trend analysis and marketing. Organizations may also give access to the data they own or even release such data to third parties. The number of increased data sets that are thus available poses serious threats to the privacy of individuals and organizations. To address such concerns, several privacy techniques have been developed. They range from anonymity techniques for network systems, such the Onion routing protocol [116] and the ZAP protocols [291], to privacy preserving data management techniques, such as the $k-$anonymization [247, 58], and from privacy-preserving location-based services [85] to languages for the specification and enforcement [201] of privacy policies. Some of those approaches are surveyed in what follows. It has also been recognized that comprehensive solutions to privacy require combining many different techniques, languages, and methodologies and also taking into account legal, social, and organizational issues [18].

Despite such a large body of work, privacy issues specific to Web services have not been yet investigated. A very preliminary effort is represented by the identification of privacy requirements, as part a larger set of *Web Services Architecture Requirements*, by a working group of the World Wide Web Consortium [289]. These privacy requirements are briefly surveyed in what follows, together with a discussion of additional new requirements and open research issues concerning Web service privacy.

9.2.1 P3P and the Privacy-Aware RBAC Model

Any solution to privacy should support two important functions that are complementary and very crucial: how to communicate the privacy policies of an organization to interested parties, such as the individuals whose data are being collected by the organization; and how to enforce such privacy policies within the organization.

The most well-known approach to the communication of privacy policies is the W3C's Platform for Privacy Preferences Project (P3P) [286]. P3P enables Web sites to encode their data collection and data use practices in a machine-readable XML format, known as *P3P policies*. W3C has also designed APPEL (A P3P Preference Exchange Language) [157], which allows users to specify their privacy preferences. Ideally, through the use of P3P and APPEL, a user's agent should be able to check a Website's privacy policy against the user's privacy preferences, and automatically determine when the user's private information can be disclosed. In short, P3P and APPEL are designed to enable users to play an active role in controlling their private information [34].

Each P3P policy is specified by one `POLICY` element that includes the following major elements:

- One `ENTITY` element: it identifies the legal entity making the representation of privacy practices contained in the policy.
- One `ACCESS` element: it indicates whether the site allows users to access the various kind of information collected about them.
- `DISPUTES-GROUP` element: it contains one or more `DISPUTES` elements that describe dispute resolution procedures to be followed when disputes arise about a service's privacy practices.
- Zero or more `EXTENSION` elements: they contain a Web site's self-defined extensions to the P3P specification.

- One or more **STATEMENT** elements: they describe data collection, use, and storage. A **STATEMENT** element specifies the data (e.g. user's name) and the data categories (e.g. user's demographic data) being collected by the site, as well as the purposes, recipients, and retention period of that data.

In more detail each P3P statement contains the following elements:

- One **PURPOSE** element, which describes for which purpose(s) the information will be used. It contains one or more predefined values such as current, admin, individual-analysis, and historical. A purpose value can have an optional attribute 'required', which takes one of the following values: opt-in, opt-out, and always. The value 'opt-in' means that data may be used for the purpose only when the user requests this. The value 'opt-out' means that data may be used for the purpose unless the user requests otherwise. The value 'always' means that users cannot opt-in or opt-out of this use of their data. Therefore, in terms of strength of data usage, 'always' > 'opt-out' > 'opt-in'.
- One **RECIPIENT** element, which describes with whom the collected information will be shared. It contains one or more predefined values such as ours, delivery, and public. A recipient value can have an optional attribute 'required', which is similar to that of a **PURPOSE** element.
- One **RETENTION** element, which describes for how long the collected information will be kept. It contains exactly one of the following predefined values: 'no-retention', 'stated-purpose', 'legal-requirement', 'business-practices' and 'indefinitely'.
- One or more **DATA-GROUP** elements, which specify what information will be collected and used. Each **DATA-GROUP** element contains one or more **DATA** elements. Each **DATA** element has two attributes. The mandatory attribute 'ref' identifies the data being collected. The 'optional' attribute indicates whether or not the data collection is optional. A **DATA** element may also contain a **CATEGORIES** element, which describes the kind of information this data item is, e.g., financial, demographic, health.
- Zero or one **CONSEQUENCE** element, which contains human-readable contents that can be shown to users to explain the data usage practices ramifications and why the usage is useful.

Consider the following P3P Statement:

```
<STATEMENT>
<PURPOSE> <admin required="opt-in"/ > < /PURPOSE>
<RECIPIENT> <public / > < /RECIPIENT>
<RETENTION> <indefinitely / > < /RETENTION>
<DATA-GROUP>
<DATA ref="user.home-info.postal"> < /DATA>
<DATA-GROUP>
<STATEMENT>
```

This statement specifies that the postal address will be collected only if the user consents to the collection. Once collected, the data will be kept for an indefinite length of time and may be made publicly available.

Since its proposal, P3P has received broad attention from the industry and the research community. However, its adoption by organizations raises several issues, some of which originate from the lack of a formal semantics of P3P. Such a lack may result in inconsistent P3P policies. We refer the reader to [34] for a detailed discussion on such issues.

As mentioned before, the second key component of a privacy solution is represented by mechanisms to enforce the stated privacy policies, possibly expressed according to P3P, inside the organization. An important mechanism in this respect is represented by the access control mechanisms, governing the accesses to the data by the subjects and parties inside the organization. However, as pointed by Fischer-Hubner [105], traditional security models (e.g. Bell LaPadula Model, Lattice Model, Biba Model, Clark Wilson Model, Chinese Wall Model, Role-Based Access Control (RBAC) Model, Workflow Authorization Model (WAM), Object-Oriented Security Models, etc.) are in general not appropriate for enforcing basic privacy requirements, such as purpose binding (i.e., data collected for one purpose should not used for another purpose without user consent). Therefore, a new model, known as privacy-aware role-based access control (P-RBAC) model, has been recently proposed with the goal of addressing some of the privacy requirements. According to the definition of conventional RBAC, P-RBAC is defined as a family of models meeting various demands in expressiveness and enforceability. The relationships between such models are shown in Figure 9.3.

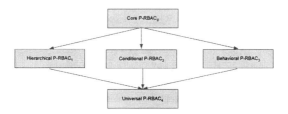

Fig. 9.3. The P-RBAC family of models

Core P-RBAC, the base model, is at the bottom, indicating that it is the minimal requirement for any system which supports P-RBAC. The bottom line of Core P-RBAC is sufficient expressiveness for public privacy policies, privacy statements and privacy notices, and privacy related acts, e.g., HIPAA [264], COPPA [80], and GLBA [265] in the US.

A preliminary definition of the Core P-RBAC model is illustrated in Figure 9.4. There are seven sets of entities, Users (U), Roles (R), Data (D), Actions (A), Purposes (Pu), Conditions (C), and Obligations(O). The user in such a model is a human being, and a role represents a job function or job

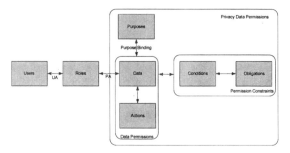

Fig. 9.4. Core P-RBAC model

title within the organization, with some associated semantics regarding the authority and responsibility conferred on a member of the role. Data means any information relating to an identified or identifiable individual. An action is an executable image of a program, which upon invocation executes some function for the user. The types of actions and data objects that P-RBAC controls depend on the type of application domain in which the access control service has to be deployed. For example, for a database management system, actions on data include SELECT or UPDATE.

The rationale for introducing Purposes, Conditions, and Obligations in Core P-RBAC comes from the OECD Guidelines on the Protection of Privacy and Transborder Flows of Personal Data [214], current privacy laws in the United States, and from public privacy policies of some well-known organizations. The OECD guidelines are a well-known set of private information protection principles, on which many other guidelines, data-protection laws, and public privacy policies are based. Purposes which are bound to actions on data in the Core P-RBAC model directly reflect the OECD Data Quality Principle, the Purpose Specification Principle, and the Use Limitation Principle. Purposes are widely used for specifying privacy rules in both acts and real public policies. HIPPA rules clearly state the purposes.

Obligations, that is, actions to be performed after an action has been executed on data objects, are necessary for some cases. For example, the OECD Accountability Principle requires that "A data controller should be accountable for complying with measures which give effect to the principles stated above." A common approach to implement this principle in an operating system or a DBMS is by logging each data access as an event. Performing a log action could be an obligation for the majority of privacy policies. For internal privacy policies, it is important that when some sensitive privacy information, such as a patient's record, is being accessed, related administrators, such as a chief doctor, be notified.

Conditions, that is, prerequisites to be met before any action can be executed, are critical for some cases. Seeking consent from a data subject (the owner of personal information) represents the essence of privacy protection and is required by the OECD Collection Limitation Principle: "There should be limits to the collection of personal data and any such data should be obtained by lawful and fair means and, where appropriate, with the knowledge or consent of the data subject." As in P3P, there are two different ways to seek consent from a data subject: "opt in" and "opt out." "Opt in" means providing the individual with the opportunity to give positive consent, that is, an individual's personal data can only be disclosed to a third party when the individual has indicated that he or she agrees to that type of disclosure; without that indication the individual's personal data should not be disclosed to third parties. "Opt out" means providing the individual with the opportunity to object to the data collection. This means that an individual may receive information such as promotional or advertising information unless or until he or she has indicated that he or she does not wish to receive such material. It may also mean that his or her personal data may be disclosed to third parties unless or until he or she has indicated his or her objection to that disclosure.

The Core P-RBAC model is thus composed by the following components and mappings among them:

- The set U of users, the set R of roles, the set D of data, the set Pu of purposes, the set A of actions, the set O of obligations, and a basic language $LC0$ to express conditions. The notation $c_j \mid LC0$ denotes a legal expression of language $LC0$.
- The set of Data Permissions $DP = \{(a, d) \mid a \in A, d \in D\}$.
- The set of Privacy-sensitive Data Permission $PDP = \{(dp, pu, o, c) \mid dp \in DP, pu \in Pu, o \in P(O), c_j \mid LC0\}$.
- User Assignment $UA \subseteq U \times R$, a many− to− many mapping user− to− role assignment relation.
- Privacy-sensitive Data Permission Assignment $PDPA \subseteq R \times PDP$ (privacy data permission assignment), a many− to− many mapping privacy-sensitive data-permission− to− role assignment relation.

The basic language $LC0$ is able to express simple conditions relevant to privacy, such as whether the owner of the data has given consent to the use of the data. The reason for the simplicity of the language is to achieve an efficient implementation. In P-RBAC, as in classical RBAC, permissions are assigned to roles, and users obtain such permissions by being assigned to roles. The distinctive feature of Core P-RBAC lies in the complex structure of privacy permissions, which reflects the highly structured ways of expressing privacy rules to represent the essence of the OECD principles and privacy acts. Therefore, aside from the data and the action to be performed on it, privacy permissions explicitly state the intended purpose along with the conditions under which the permission can be given and the obligations that are to be finally performed.

The other models in the P-RBAC family include Hierarchical P-RBAC, with functions for managing Role Hierarchy (RH), Data Hierarchy (DH), and Purpose Hierarchy (PH); Conditional P-RBAC, characterized by Attributes, Context Variables, and Boolean Expressions, thus supporting a condition language richer than *LC0*; and Behavioral P-RBAC, with support for the specification of input, output, and flow equations to define actions and to control the flow of information. We refer the reader to [201] and [202] for more details.

9.2.2 Privacy-Preserving Data Management Techniques

A first important class of techniques deals with privacy preservation when data are to be released to third parties. In this case, data, once released, are not any longer under the control of the organizations owning them. Therefore, the owners of the data are not able to control the way their data are used. The most common approach to address the privacy of released data is to modify the data by removing all information that can directly link data items to individuals; such a process is referred to as *data anonymization* [247]. It is important to note that simply removing identity information, such as names or social security numbers, from the released data may not be enough to anonymize the data. There are many examples showing that even when such information is removed from the released data, the remaining data combined with other information sources may still link the information to the individuals it refers to. To overcome this problem, approaches based on generalization techniques have been proposed, the most well-known of which is based on the notion of k-anonymity [247]. Some recent extensions to such techniques include anonymization techniques for dynamically modified data [58] and the use of clustering [59].

A second class of techniques deals specifically with privacy preservation in the context of data mining. Data mining techniques are today very effective. Thus, even though a database is sanitized by removing private information, the use of data mining techniques may allow one to recover the removed information. Several approaches have been proposed, some of which are specialized for specific data mining techniques, for example, tools for association rule mining or classification systems, while others are independent of the specific data mining techniques. In general, all approaches are based on modifying or perturbing the data in some way; for example, techniques specialized for the privacy-preserving mining of association rules modify the data so as to reduce the confidence of sensitive association rules. A problem common to most of these techniques is represented by the quality of the resulting database; if the data undergo too many modifications, they may not be any longer useful. To address this problem, techniques have been developed to estimate the errors introduced by the modifications [209]; such an estimate can be used to drive the data modification process. A different technique in this context is based on data sampling [73]. The idea is to release a subset of the data, chosen in such a way that any inference that is made from the data has a low degree of confidence. Finally, still in the area of data mining, techniques have been developed, mainly based on commutative encryption techniques, whose goal is to support distributed data mining processes on encrypted data [268]. In particular, the addressed problem deals with situations where the data to be mined is stored at multiple sites, but the sites are unable to release the data. The solutions involve algorithms that share some information to calculate correct results, where the shared information can be shown not to disclose private data.

Finally, some preliminary efforts have been reported dealing with database systems specifically tailored to support privacy policies, such as the policies that can be expressed using the P3P standard [286]. In particular, Agrawal et al. [6] have introduced the concept of Hippocratic databases, incorporating privacy protection in relational database systems. In their paper, Agrawal et al. introduce the fundamental principles underlying Hippocratic databases and then propose a reference architecture. An important feature of such an architecture is that it uses some privacy metadata, consisting of privacy policies and privacy authorizations stored in privacy tables and privacy authorization tables respectively. The privacy policy defines the intended use, the external recipients, and the retention period for each attribute of a table, while the privacy authorization defines the authorized users. The proposed architecture also adds a special attribute, "purpose," to each table, which encodes the set of purposes with which the individuals, to whom the data are referred, agree during the data collection process. The Hippocratic database performs privacy checking during query processing. Every query is submitted to the database with its intended purpose. The system first checks whether the user who issued the query is present in the set of authorized users for that purpose in the privacy authorization table. Next, the system ensures that the query accesses only the fields that are explicitly listed for the query purpose in the privacy authorization table. If the query is allowed to run, the system ensures that only records whose purpose attribute includes the query purpose are visible to the query during the execution. Agrawal et al. also discuss various technical challenges and problems in designing Hippocratic databases, such as efficiency, disclosure, retention, and safety.

9.2.3 W3C Privacy Requirements for Web Services and Research Issues

An initial effort to identify privacy issues that are specific to Web services has been undertaken by W3C, which has specified four privacy Web Service Architecture (WSA) requirements for enabling privacy protection for the consumers of Web services, possibly across multiple domains:

- The WSA must enable privacy policy statements to be expressed about Web services.
- The advertised Web service privacy policies must be expressed in P3P.
- The WSA must enable delegation and propagation of privacy policies.
- Web services must not be precluded from supporting interactions where one or more parties of the interaction are anonymous.

This above set of requirements represents a good starting point for reasoning about privacy for Web services. However, two important additional requirements should be included. The first requirement deals with auditing, that is, with a set of functions for acquiring and analyzing the record of events that may have some privacy significance. Auditing is an important component of any security solution. However, it is crucial in the context of privacy; an organization should be always able to trace the flow of data across Web services and administrative domains should a privacy breach occur, and be able to provide the individuals to whom the data are related with a full account of the use of this data. It is equally important that an organization be able to prove that it has complied with privacy promises and with other legal requirements; as such, the compliance requirement is also relevant.

Addressing the four requirements stated by W3C, and the additional requirements of auditing and compliance is a challenging task and requires comprehensive solutions. Elements of such solutions include comparing privacy policies of different Web services in order to determine whether data can flow between services; verifying Web services' internal organization and implementation to check whether they comply with the advertised privacy policies; understanding how Web services characterized by different privacy policies can interoperate; supporting dynamic changes in privacy policies and user preferences; organizing auditing functions as services and instrumenting Web services so that auditing can be efficiently supported; developing methodologies that exploit the modular architecture of SOA, to support the complex task of compliance checking; and supporting the use of anonymity techniques, such as private information retrieval and anonymous credentials, in composite Web services and workflows.

9.3 Semantic Web Security

The notion of Semantic Web represents an evolution of the World Wide Web in which Web content can be expressed not only in natural language but also in a format that can be read and used by software agents. A key goal of the Semantic Web is to provide semantic-rich descriptions of Web content in order to better support information discovery, sharing, and integration. In this respect the Semantic Web is following the same path that database technology took with the definition of first the relational model and then the semantic models. The development of such models has shown that providing a high-level description of data semantics is key to effective data usage. Several formalisms and semantic models have been proposed for the description of Web content in the Semantic Web, such as the Resource Description Framework (RDF) and the Web Ontology Language (OWL). All those formalisms and models are intended to provide a formal description of concepts, terms, and relationships within a given knowledge domain. As such they are very much similar to semantic models developed more than two decades ago in the database field.

In addition to formalisms and semantic models, the Semantic Web relies on a variety of enabling technologies, including XML and Web services. This is an important point to make, because it means that security for the Semantic Web can leverage on security techniques for XML and Web services. As such advances in Web service security, such as the ones discussed in this book, represent important steps towards the broader goal of Semantic Web security.

Additional important security issues are related to the protection of semantic information, such as those encoded in RDF and OWL, and to the problem of protection from inference. In an information protection context, the problem of inference refers to the derivation of sensitive information from non sensitive data. Such a problem is difficult to address because it entails protecting not only sensitive data, but also making sure that sensitive information cannot be disclosed from data that are not sensitive and therefore not protected. Because of the semantic-rich information and the powerful inference engines today available, inferences may pose a serious threat to information protection in the Semantic Web. Even though the problem of inference protection has been investigated in the past in the context of databases, and several foundational results have been developed (see Thuraisingham et al. [260]), to date no comprehensive approach has been reported for dealing with this problem in the context of the Semantic Web.

9.4 Concluding Remarks

Web service security represents a key requirement for today's distributed interconnected digital world and for the new Web generations, such as Web 2.0 and the Semantic Web. To date, the problem of security has been investigated very much in the context of standardization efforts; these efforts, however, have dealt mainly with adapting existing security techniques, such as encryption, for use in Web services. The standards have also focused on addressing the problem of security interoperability through the development of standard formats for security assertions, tokens, and credentials. Interoperability is certainly an important issue for Web services in that easy and flexible service composition requires that security-relevant information be seamlessly transmitted across different services.

However, several key issues have not yet been addressed, some of which have been pointed out in the previous chapters and sections. Other issues that have not been mentioned but which are crucial include revisiting security techniques in the presence of highly fragmented service systems; metrics and methodologies to assess the security provided by an application or system organized according to the SOA paradigm; understanding the impact of security and privacy on service composition; and identifying security and privacy requirements for novel collaborative environments and social networks enabled by the Web and devising solutions to address these requirements.

A

Access Control

This appendix reviews basic concepts concerning access control and then briefly describes the role-based access control (RBAC) model, a model widely deployed in commercial systems and for which a standard has also been developed. As part of the RBAC model, some relevant extensions are also surveyed, which are relevant in today's distributed systems.

The material presented in this appendix is based on a paper by Bertino and Crampton [39], to which we refer the reader for additional details.

A.1 Basic Notions

Access control is a key component in any security solution, in that it determines which subject can perform which action under which circumstances on the protected resources. Whenever a subject tries to access a resource, the access control service checks the rights of the subject against a set of *authorizations*, usually stated by some security administrator. Authorizations thus encode the *access control policies* of a given organization. Any computer system that offers any level of protection will ensure that the access control service intercepts all requests by subjects to access resources in order to ensure that all these requests are properly authorized before the subject gains access to the requested resource. Most access control policies directly or indirectly specify the set of authorized requests. An *access control model* provides a method for encoding an access control policy and states the conditions that must be satisfied for an access request to be granted. The conditions that determine whether a request is authorized may be expressed as security properties. An access control service is thus characterized by a specific access control model.

Figure A.1 illustrates a generic architecture for an access control service. The *reference monitor* intercepts each access request to the protected resource in order to decide whether it can be authorized. The reference monitor typically requires different types of information to make such a decision. It needs

E. Bertino et al., *Security for Web Services and Service-Oriented Architectures*, DOI 10.1007/978-3-540-87742-4, © Springer-Verlag Berlin Heidelberg 2010

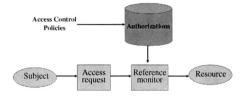

Fig. A.1. Architecture of an access control service

to know *who* is requesting access to *what*. Generally the "who" question is answered by authenticating each user of the system and associating each process, or application, that the user runs with the user's identity. Therefore whenever a process or application tries to access a protected resource, the identity used to check the process authorization is derived from the user's identity [1]. The "what" question is answered by consulting information maintained by the resource manager, for example, the operating system or the database management system (DBMS), about the protected resources. Generally, the reference monitor also needs to know *how* the subject wishes to interact with the object. The more common interactions between subjects and protected resources include read, write, and execute. The exact operational meaning of these generic interactions depends on the type of resource and other contextual information. In advanced access control models, such as the ones supporting spatial and temporal information [33], the reference monitor uses additional information, such as time, location, or the history of past accesses to the protected resources, to make access control decisions.

A.1.1 The Protection Matrix Model

A protection matrix is an abstract representation of an access control policy in that it represents the access requests authorized by the system. A protection matrix is arranged as a two-dimensional array, with each row labeled by a subject and each column labeled by a protected resource. A matrix entry in the row labeled s and column labeled r determines the authorized actions for s with respect to r. For example, assume r to be a file; then, if the matrix entry for s and r contains `read`, a request from s to read object file r is authorized. In other words, the protection matrix encodes triples of the form <subject-object-action>. The protection matrix has proved to be a powerful abstraction for the design of protection mechanisms in operating systems, DBMSs, and applications. Many access control services, such as the security reference monitor in Windows 2000, are based on the concept of the protection matrix.

---

[1] Note that in the discussion we use the term *subject* instead of *user* because very often accesses are by entities other than users. Examples of such entities are processes and applications.

A.1.2 Access Control Lists and Capability Lists

Despite its conceptual simplicity, the protection matrix can rarely be used by an actual access control service. The reason is that in a large system with many subjects and resources, the memory requirements for such a data structure would be prohibitively large. Moreover, many entries in the matrix may be empty, meaning that large amounts of memory allocated for the storage of the protection matrix would remain unused.

Different structures have thus been proposed for implementing the access control matrix, the most well known of which are the *access control list* and the *capability list*. Such structures only store the relevant matrix entries, whereas empty matrix entries are ignored. An access control list is associated with a protected resource and consists of a number of entries defining the rights assigned to each subject for that resource.

In contrast, a capability list is associated with a subject. Conceptually, a capability list is a list of permissions, each permission identifying a resource and the rights that have been assigned to the subject for that resource. In other words, each permission in a capability list for a subject specifies how that subject may interact with the resource specified in the permission.

A.1.3 Negative Authorizations

In recent years, access control models have been proposed supporting negative authorizations, that is, authorizations explicitly prohibiting certain actions. Such authorizations are particularly useful for enforcing exceptions to a more general policy. For example, suppose that one may wish to grant access to a particular set of resources to many different subjects. Clearly, the most convenient way of doing this is to create a group for those subjects and then authorize the group to access those resources. However, if there is one member s of the group g who should not be allowed access to one particular resource r, it is rather cumbersome to enforce this requirement without negative authorizations. The only option in this case is to remove s from g and then grant s access to all the resources to which members of g have access, except r. A simpler approach to address this requirement is to keep s in the group and simply prohibit access by s to r. Windows 2000 permits the inclusion of negative access control entries in access control lists. XACML, the standard for XML-based authorization policy specification and enforcement, also supports negative authorizations (see Chapter 4).

Negative authorizations, however, introduce the problem of conflicts. That is, a positive and negative authorization may exist for the same request. In the example given in the previous paragraph, s will have a positive authorization to access r from its membership of g, but also a negative authorization explicitly denying s access to r. The intention in this case is that access should be denied; however, in other cases different conflict resolution policies may be required. Therefore, access control models supporting negative authorizations

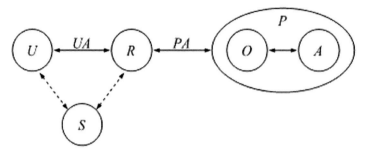

Fig. A.2. Core RBAC [228]

often provide some *policy conflict resolution mechanisms*. The most obvious and widely used mechanism is to insist that a negative authorization always takes precedence over a positive one. This is known, naturally, as the "deny-overrides" algorithm in XACML (see Chapter 4). There are other possibilities, such as "permit-overrides" and "first-applicable"; the latter assumes that authorizations are processed in a particular order and that the first relevant authorization is to be used. Windows 2000 has a hybrid approach, which groups access control entries in a particular order and implements what might be called a "deny-overrides-if-first-applicable" algorithm. This ordering of access control entries is first determined by the creator of the access control entry, with entries created by the creator of the resource (rather than those inherited from the resources container) taking precedence. Within each such group of entries, negative entries precede positive entries.

A.2 Role-Based Access Control

A crucial problem in the deployment of access control services is the administrative costs for the maintenance of access control lists or other similar access control data structures. In a system with 1,000 users, 100,000 protected resources, and ten access rights (a relatively small system by today's standards), there are $1,000 \times 100,000 = 10^9$ possible authorization triples. Role-based access control (RBAC) is a relatively recent attempt to reduce such administrative costs. It is based on the concept of a *role*, which acts an intermediary between users and permissions. The idea is that there will be far fewer roles than either users or permissions. Typically roles are associated with job descriptions, although this is not the only possibility.

The basic concepts of RBAC are illustrated in Figure A.2. The ANSI RBAC standard was released in 2004 [229], based on earlier work by Ravi Sandhu et al. [228]. RBAC includes two main components: the *core* component, which does not include role hierarchies, and the *hierarchical* component, which does.

The RBAC model is based on a set of users U, a set of permissions P, and a set of roles R. A permission is usually assumed to be a resource-action pair, where an action is synonymous with an access right. Users are associated with roles using a user-role assignment relation UA. This relation is a set of pairs of the form (u, r), meaning that user u is assigned to role R. Permissions are similarly associated with roles using a permission-role assignment relation PA. Users interact with an RBAC system by activating a *session*. Typically, the user authenticates himself to the system and chooses to act in one or more of the roles to which he is assigned.

RBAC further reduces the administration costs by introducing the idea of a *role hierarchy*, which is modeled as a directed acyclic graph in which the roles are nodes. In other words, the role hierarchy is represented as a binary relation RH on R. The transitive, reflexive closure of this relation defines a partial ordering on the set of roles. The basic idea is that a role in the hierarchy will inherit the permissions of the lower roles, without their having to be explicitly assigned to those permissions. Clearly, this significantly reduces the number of permissions that need to be assigned to more senior roles, reducing the administrative overheads in an RBAC system.

RBAC is now widely supported in commercial systems such as Oracle, Sybase, Windows 2003, and Solaris. An RBAC profile exists for XACML and it is widely used in workflow management systems. The interested reader is directed to the book by Ferraiolo et al., which provides an excellent overview of RBAC and its applications [104].

Multi-domain RBAC

The Web has made possible a large variety of collaborative applications in areas such as e-learning, healthcare, and e-government. Most of these applications require different organizations, or even different units within the same organization, to be able to establish dynamic coalitions in which users of one domain can seamlessly access resources from other domains. Approaches in which users are explicitly and directly given access to all resources they need to access across the coalition domains are not practical and do not scale. Moreover, they make authorization revocation cumbersome and error prone. Different approaches are required to keep the administration costs at a reasonable level and support a manageable authorization revocation.

One such approach has been recently proposed based on the X-GTRBAC model [45], an XML-based RBAC model supporting a large variety of temporal constraints on the use of roles by users. The key idea underlying such an approach is to associate with each role a set of preconditions for the use of roles. Each user verifying such preconditions is given permission to use the role; there is no need to grant these users explicit permission for the role, thus simplifying the management of the UA relation (see Figure A.2).

In X-GTRBAC preconditions are expressed against user credentials, which are encoded in SAML. In particular, by using the precondition language supported by X-GTRBAC, it is possible to condition the use of a role in a domain, referred to as the target domain, for the authorization of using the same role, or even another role, in another domain, referred to as the source domain. A user authorized to use a role r in the source domain can thus use a role r' in the target domain, provided that the authorization to use r is a precondition for the use of r', Assertions concerning the fact that a user can use a role r in a given domain are encoded by the source domain using SAML. In addition to accepting SAML assertions as input, X-GTRBAC also generates SAML assertions as a result of access control; therefore, whenever the X-GTRBAC instance in the target domain determines that a user can access a role, it generates a SAML assertion stating this fact. This assertion can then be used for accessing a role in another domain.

Such a type of role interoperability enhances decentralization and autonomy. Each domain can independently determine the preconditions that the users of another domain need to verify for gaining access to its local roles. Such pre-conditions can be different for users from different domains. Revoking the authorizations of remote users to use a local role is very easy, in that one only has to drop the preconditions concerning such users. Even though X-GTRBAC represents an important approach to the problem of multi-domain access control, several issues still need to be investigated, including anonymous access and delegation.

GEO-RBAC

The widespread deployment of location-based services and mobile applications, as well as the increased concern for the management and sharing of geographical information in strategic applications like environmental protection and homeland security, have resulted in a strong demand for spatially aware access control systems. These application domains impose interesting requirements on access control systems. In particular, the permissions assigned to users depend on their position in a reference space; users often belong to well-defined categories; objects to which permissions must be granted are located in that space; and access control policies must grant permissions based on object locations and user positions.

As an example, consider a mobile application for the personnel and patients of a health care organization. Individuals are given a location-aware terminal with which they can request information services provided by an application server. The organization consists of individuals who have different functional roles, e.g. nurse, doctor, and patient. We note that, depending on the organizational context, the services available to users may differ based on the functional roles of users. For example, the services available to nurses may be different from those available to doctors, not simply because of the individual preferences, but mainly because of organizational and functional reasons. Further, the availability of the services may depend on the position of the requester. For example, a nurse may be allowed to request the record of a patient only when the patient is located in the department to which she has been assigned.

To deal with the requirements listed above, an access control model with spatial capabilities is needed. Since in location-aware applications users are often grouped in distinct categories, such as *nurse* and *doctor*, RBAC represents a reasonable choice for the underlying access control framework. However, conventional RBAC does not suffice to support such applications, and needs to be extended with suitable location constraints, that is, constraints concerning the locations in which a given role can be accessed by a user. It is important to notice that locations can be physical, that is, expressed as coordinates in the reference space, or logical, that is, expressed in terms of spatial objects (such as the city of Milan or the West Valley Hospital) that have a semantics relevant to the specific application domains. When dealing with location-based applications, it is also important to take into account relevant standards for the representation of spatial objects; one such standard is by the OGC [210].

GEO-RBAC is a recently developed model that directly supports such location constraints [84]. It is based on the notion of a *spatial role*, that is, a geographically bounded organizational function. The boundary of a role is defined as a geographical feature, such as a road, a city, or a hospital, and specifies the spatial range in which the user has to be located in order to use the role. Besides being assigned a physical position, obtained from a given mobile terminal such as a GPS-based vehicle-tracking device or a cellular phone, users are also assigned a logical and device-independent position, representing the feature in which the user is located. *Logical positions* can be computed from *real positions* by using specific mapping functions, and can be represented at different granularities depending on the spatial role played by the user. If the user is located inside the spatial boundary of the role that has been selected (*activated*) during the session, the role is said to be *enabled*. To specify the type of the spatial boundary of the role and the granularity of the logical position, GEO-RBAC has introduced the concept of *spatial role schema*. Spatial roles are thus specified as instances of role schemas.

Like RBAC, GEO-RBAC encompasses a family of models:

- Core GEO-RBAC includes the basic concepts of the model, and thus the notions of spatial role, role schema, real or logical position, and activated or enabled role.
- Hierarchical GEO-RBAC extends the conventional hierarchical RBAC by introducing two distinct hierarchies, one over role schemas and one over role instances.
- Constrained GEO-RBAC supports the specification of separation of duty (SoD) constraints for spatial roles and role schemas. Since exclusive role constraints are important to support the definition and maintenance of access control policies in mobile contexts, SoD constraints are extended to account for different granularities (schema or instance level), dimensions (spatial or nonspatial), and verification times (static, dynamic at acti-

vation, dynamic at enabling). The resulting set of constraints developed for GEO-RBAC represents the first comprehensive class of constraints for spatially aware applications.

A.3 Concluding Remarks

In this appendix we have discussed the main notions and models for access control. It is important to emphasize that in addition to what has been presented here, research is very active in the area of access control, and many relevant directions are being investigated. A relevant direction is represented by access control for grid computing systems and virtualized environments. Those systems and environments are quite challenging because of the very large number of users and the distributed administration of resources. In particular, they are characterized by the fact that there is no single authority controlling all resources that may be required by a user to perform certain tasks. In such cases, the user must be able to obtain multiple authorizations from independent administrative authorities; this risks, however, conflicting authorizations.

References

1. AA. VV.: Web Services Policy 1.2 Attachment (WS-PolicyAttachment) W3C Member Submission, 25 April 2006. Online at: http://www.w3.org/Submission/WS-PolicyAttachment/
2. AA. VV.: Terminology for Policy-Based Management (IETF RFC 3198), November 2001, Online at: http://www.ietf.org/rfc/rfc3198.txt
3. Agarwal, S., Sprick, B., and Wortmann, S.: Credential based access control for semantic Web services. In *Proceedings of Semantic Web Services AAAI 2004 Spring Symposium*, Palo Alto, CA, USA, March 2004. Online at: http://www.daml.ecs.soton.ac.uk/SSS-SWS04/Papers.html.
4. Agrawal, A., et al.: Web Services Human Task (WS-HumanTask), Version 1.0., June 2007. Online at: http://www.adobe.com/devnet/livecycle/pdfs/ws_humantask_spec.pdf.
5. Agrawal, A. et al.: WS-BPEL Extension for People (BPEL4People), Version 1.0, June 2007. Online at: http://www.adobe.com/devnet/livecycle/pdfs/bpel4people_spec.pdf.
6. Agrawal, A., Kiernan, J., Srikant, R., Xu, Y.: Hippocratic databases. In *Proceedings of 28th International Conference on Very Large Data Bases*, August 20-23, 2002, Hong Kong, China. Morgan Kaufmann.
7. Ahn, G. J., Kang, M. H., Park, J. S, Sandhu, R.: Injecting RBAC to secure a Web-based workflow system. In *Proceedings of 5th ACM Workshop on Role-Based Access Control*, Berlin, Germany, July 2000, pp.1-10. Online at: http://portal.acm.org/citation.cfm?doid=344287.344295.
8. Ahn, G. J., Lam, J.: Managing privacy preferences for federated identity management. In *Proceedings of DIM '05: Workshop on Digital identity management*, pp.28-36, New York, NY, USA, 2005. ACM Press.
9. Alonso, G., Casati, F., Kuno, H., Machiraju, V.: *Web Services - Concepts, Architectures and Applications*. Springer-Verlag 2004.
10. Alves. A. et al.: Web Services Business Process Execution Language, Version 2.0, OASIS Standard, April 2007. Online at: http://docs.oasis-open.org/wsbpel/2.0/OS/wsbpel-v2.0-OS.pdf.
11. Alvestrand, H.: A Mission Statement for the IETF. (IETF RFC 3935, October 2004). Online at: http://www.ietf.org/rfc/rfc3935.txt
12. Anderson, A.: Core and Hierarchical Role Based Access Control (RBAC) Profile of XACML, Version 2.0, OASIS Standard, 2005. Online at:

http://docs.oasis-open.org/xacml/2.0/access_control-xacml-2.0-rbac-profile1-spec-os.pdf.

13. Anderson, A. Web Services Trust Language (WS-Trust). February 2005. Online at: http://download.boulder.ibm.com/ibmdl/pub/software/dw/specs/ws-trust/ws-trust.pdf.

14. Anderson, A., ed.: Web Services Profile of XACML (WS-XACML) Version 1.0. Working Draft 10 (OASIS, 10 August 2007). Online at: http://www.oasis-open.org/committees/download.php/24951/xacml-3.0-profile-webservices-spec-v1-wd-10-en.pdf

15. Anderson, R. J.: Security Engineering: A Guide to Building Dependable Distributed Systems (First edition, Wiley, ISBN: 978-0-471-38922-4, 2001). Online at: http://www.cl.cam.ac.uk/r̄ja14/Papers/

16. Anderson, R. J.: Security Engineering: A Guide to Building Dependable Distributed Systems (Second edition, Wiley, ISBN-10: 0470068523, 2008).

17. Andrieux, A., Czajkowski, K., Dan, A., T.: Web Services Agreement Specification (WS-Agreement), World Wide Web Consortium (W3C). Online at: http://www.w3. org/XML, http://www.gridforum.org/Meetings/GGF11/Documents/draft-ggf-graap-agreement.pdf.

18. Anton, A. I., Bertino, E., Li, N., Yu, T.: A roadmap for comprehensive online privacy policy management, *Communications of ACM*, 50(7):109-116, 2007.

19. Apache mod_status XSS Vulnerability Description. Online at: http://httpd.apache.org/security/vulnerabilities-oval.xml

20. Ardagna, C., Damiani, E., De Capitani di Vimercati, S., Samarati, P.: A Web Wervice architecture for enforcing access control policies. In *Proceedings of 1st International Workshop on Views on Designing Complex Architectures*, Bertinoro, Italy, September 2004, 47-62. Online at: http://dx.doi.org/10.1016/j.entcs.2004.09.044

21. Ashri, R., Denker, G., Marvin, D., Payne, T., Surridge, M.: Semantic web service interaction protocols: An ontological approach. In *Proceedings of International Semantic Web Conference (ISWC 2004)*, Hiroshima, Japan, November 2004, 304-319, Springer Verlag, LNCS 3298.

22. Ashri, R., Marvin, D., Payne, T., Surridge, M., and Taylor, S.: Towards a semantic web security infrastructure. In *Proceedings Semantic Web Services (AAAI 2004) Spring Symposium Series*, Palo Alto, CA, USA, March 2004. Online at: http://www.daml.ecs.soton.ac.uk/SSS-SWS04/Papers.html.

23. Atluri, V., Huang, W.: An authorization model for workflows. In *Proceedings of 4th European Symposium on Research in Computer Security*, Rome, Italy, September 1996, 44-64, Lecture Notes in Computer Science 1146, Springer.

24. Austin, D., Barbir, A., Ferris, C., Garg, S., eds: Web Services Architecture Requirements (W3C Working Group Note, 11 February 2004). Online at: http://www.w3.org/TR/wsa-reqs/#id2604831

25. Banerji, A., et al.: Web Services Conversation Language (WSCL) 1.0, World-Wide-Web Consortium (W3C) Note, March 2002. Online at: http://www.w3.org/TR/wscl10)

26. Benatallah, B., Casati, F., and Toumani, F.: Web service conversation modeling: A cornerstone for e-business automation. *IEEE Internet Computing*, 8(1):46-54, 2004.

27. Benatallah, B., Casati, F., Hamadi, R., Toumani, F.: Conceptual modeling of Web service conversations. In *Proceedings of 15th International Conference on*

Advanced Information Systems Engineering (CAiSE 2003), Klagenfurt, Austria, June 2003, 449-467, Springer Verlag, LNCS 2681.

28. Berardi, D., Calvanese, D., De Giacomo, G., Lenzerini, M., Mecella, M.: Automatic service composition based on behavioral descriptions. *International Journal of Cooperative Information Systems*, 14(4):333-376, 2005.

29. Berners-Lee, T.: Universal Resource Identifiers in WWW A Unifying Syntax for the Expression of Names and Addresses of Objects on the Network as used in the World-Wide Web (IETF RFC 1630, June 1994). Online at: http://www.w3.org/Addressing/rfc1630.txt

30. Berners-Lee, T.: Axioms of Web Architecture - Mandatory Extensions. 2000/02/01. Online at: http://www.w3.org/DesignIssues/Mandatory.html

31. Berners-Lee, T., Connolly, D.: Web Architecture: Extensible Languages. 10 Feb 1998. Online at: http://www.w3.org/DesignIssues/Extensible.html

32. Berners-Lee, T., Fielding, R., Irvine, U. C., Masinter L.: Uniform Resource Identifiers (URI): Generic Syntax (IETF RFC 2396, August 1998). Online at: http://www.ietf.org/rfc/rfc2396.txt

33. Bertino, E., Bonatti, P., Ferrari, E.: TRBAC: A temporal role-based access control model. *ACM Transactions on Information and System Security*, 4(3):191-233, 2001.

34. Bertino, E., Byun, J. W., Li, N.: Privacy-preserving database systems. *Foundations of Security Analysis and Design III, FOSAD 2004/2005*, Tutorial Lectures. Lecture Notes in Computer Science 3655, Springer, 2005.

35. Bertino, E, Carminati, B, Ferrari, E.: Merkle tree authentication in UDDI registries. *International Journal on Web Service Research*, 1(2): 37-57, 2004.

36. Bertino, E., Carminati, B, Ferrari, E., Thuraisingham, B., Gupta, A.: Selective and authentic third-party distribution of XML documents. *IEEE Transacations on Knowledge and Data Engineering*, 16(10): 1263-1278, 2004.

37. Bertino, E., Ferrari, E., Squicciarini, A. C.: Trust negotiations: concepts, systems and languages. *IEEE Computing in Science Engineering*, 6(4): 27-34, 2004.

38. Bertino, E., Ferrari, E., Squicciarini A. C.: Trust-χ: A peer-to-peer framework for trust establishment. *IEEE Transactions on Knowledge and Data Engineering*, 16(7):827-842, 2004.

39. Bertino, E., Crampton, J.: Security for Distributed Systems: Foundations of Access Control. In *Information Assurance: Survivability and Security in Networked Systems*, Tipper, D., Krishnamurthy, P., Qian, Y., and Joshi, J., eds. Morgan Kaufmann Publishers, January 2008.

40. Bertino, E., Martino, L., Paloscia, I., Squicciarini, A. C.: Ws-AC A fine grained access control system for Web services. *World Wide Web*, 9(2):143-171, 2006.

41. Bertino, E., Martino, L., Paci, F., and Squicciarini, A. C.: An adaptive access control model for Web services. *International Journal of Web Services Research (JWSR)*, 3(3):27-60, 2006.

42. Bertino, E., Sandhu, R.: Database security - concepts, approaches and challenges. *IEEE Transactions on Dependable and Secure Computing*, 2(1):2-19, 2005.

43. Bertino, E., Atluri, V., Ferrari, E.: The specification and enforcement of authorization constraints in workflow management systems. *ACM Transactions on Information and System Security*, 2(1):65-104, 1999.

44. Bhargav-Spantzel, A., Squicciarini, A., Bertino, E.: Integrating federated digital identity management and trust negotiation issues and solutions. *Security & Privacy Magazine, IEEE*, 5(2):55-64, 2007.

45. Bhatti, R., Bertino, E., Ghafoor, A., Joshi, J.: X-GTRBAC: an XML-based policy specification framework and architeture for enterprise-wide access control. *ACM Transactions on Information and System Security* 8(2):187-227, 2005.

46. V. Biron, P., Malhotra, A.: XML Schema Part 2: Datatypes, W3C Recommendation, October 2004. Online at: http://www.w3.org/TR/xmlschema-2.

47. Bishop, M.: *Computer Security Art and Science*, Addison-Wesley, 2003.

48. Booth, D., et al., eds.: Web Services Architecture. (W3C Working Group Note, 11 February 2004). Online at: http://www.w3.org/TR/2004/NOTE-ws-arch-20040211.

49. Booth, D. et al. eds: Web Services Architecture. (W3C Working Group Note 11 February 2004). Online at: http://www.w3.org/TR/2004/NOTE-ws-arch-20040211/#wsstechno

50. Botha, R. A. , Eloff, J. H. P.: Separation of duties for access control enforcement in workflow environments. *IBM Systems Journal*, 40(3):666-682, 2001.

51. Boyer, J.: Canonical XML Version 1.0 (W3C Recommendation 15 March 2001), Online at: http://www.w3.org/TR/xml-c14n

52. Bormans, J., Hill, K., eds.: MPEG-21 Overview v.5 (ISO/IEC JTC1/SC29/WG11/N5231, October 2002), Online at: http://www.chiariglione.org/mpeg/standards/mpeg-21/mpeg-21.htm

53. Bray, T., Hollander, D., Layman, A., Tobin, R., eds.: Namespaces in XML 1.0 (Second Edition) (W3C Recommendation, 16 August 2006). Online at: http://www.w3.org/TR/REC-xml-names/

54. Bray, T., Paoli, J., Sperberg-McQueen, C. M., Maler, E., Yergeau, F.: XML Specification. (W3C Recommendation, August 2006). Online at: http://www.w3.org/TR/REC-xml/

55. Buecker, A., et al.: Understanding SOA Security Design and Implementation (IBM Redbooks SG24-7310-00, published 13 February 2007, last updated 20 February 2007).

56. BUGTRAQ. http://www.securityfocus.com/archive/1

57. Bugzilla. http://www.bugzilla.org/

58. Byun, J.W., Sohn, Y., Bertino, E., Li, N.: Secure anonmyzation for incremental datasets. In *Proceedings of Secure Data Management*, 2006.

59. Byun, J. W., Kamra, A., Bertino, E., Li, N.: Efficient k-anonymization using clustering techniques. In *Proceedings 12th International Conference on Database Systems for Advanced Applications, DASFAA 2007*, 2007.

60. Camenisch, J., Herreweghen, E. V.:Design and implementation of the idemix anonymous credential system. In *Proceedings of CCS '02: 9th ACM Conference on Computer and Communications Security*, pages 21–30, New York, NY, USA, 2002. ACM Press.

61. Cantor, S.: Assertions and Protocols for the OASIS Security Assertion Markup Language (SAML) V2.0. OASIS Standard, March 2005. Online at: http://docs.oasis-open.org/security/saml/v2.0/.

62. Cantor S., Kemp, J., Philpott, R., Maler, E., eds.: Assertions and Protocol for the OASIS Security Assertion Markup Language (SAML) V2.0. (OASIS Standard, 15 March 2005). Online at: http://docs.oasis-open.org/security/saml/v2.0/saml-core-2.0-os.pdf

63. CAPEC Common Attack Pattern Enumeration and Classification. Online at: http://capec.mitre.org/

64. Carminati, B., Ferrari, E., Bertino, E.: Securing XML data in third-party distribution systems. In *Proceedings of Conference on Information and Knowledge Management (CIKM)*, 2005.

65. Casati, F., Castano, S., Fugini, M.: Managing workflow authorization constraints through active database technology, *Information Systems Frontiers*, 3(3):319-338, 2001.

66. Charanjit, S., and Yung, M.:. Paytree: amortized signature for flexible micropayments. In *Proceedings of the 2nd USENIX Workshop on Electronic Commerce*, 1996.

67. Christensen, E., Curbera, F., Meredith, G., & Weerawarana, S.: Web Services Description Language (WSDL) Version 1.1 (W3C Note). Online at: http://www.w3.org/TR/2001/NOTE-wsdl-20010315.

68. Clark, J.: The Design of RELAX NG. Online at: http://www.thaiopensource.com/relaxng/design.html

69. Clark, J.: TREX Tree Regular Expressions for XML. Online at: http://www.thaiopensource.com/trex/

70. Clark, J.: XSL Transforms (XSLT) Version 1.0. (W3C Recommendation, November 1999). Online at: http://www.w3.org/TR/1999/REC-xslt-19991116.html

71. Clark, J., DeRose, S.: XML Path Language (XPath) Version 1.0, W3C Recommendation, November 1999. Online at: http://www.w3.org/TR/1999/REC-xpath-19991116

72. Clement, L., Hately, A., von Riegen, C., Rogers, T., eds.: UDDI Version 3.0.2 UDDI Spec Technical Committee Draft (OASIS). Online at: http://www.uddi.org/pubs/uddi_v3.htm

73. Clifton, C.: Using sample size to limit exposure to data mining. *Journal of Computer Security*, 8(4), 2000.

74. Common Vulnerabilities and Exposures (CVE). Online at: http://www.cve.mitre.org/about/

75. Common Vulnerabilities and Exposures Terminology. Online at: http://cve.mitre.org/ about/terminology.html

76. Common Weakness Enumeration. Online at: http://cwe.mitre.org/

77. Common Weakness Enumeration Vulnerability Type Distributions in CVE. Online at: http://cwe.mitre.org/documents/vuln-trends/index.html

78. Community Development of Java Technology Specification. JSR-000105 XML Digital Signature APIs (Final Release). Online at: http://jcp.org/aboutJava/communityprocess/final/jsr105/index.html

79. Community Development of Java Technology Specification. JSR-000106 XML Digital Encryption APIs (Close of Public Review, 11 January 2006) Online at: http://jcp.org/aboutJava/communityprocess/pr/jsr106/index.html

80. COPPA: Children's Online Privacy Protection Act of 1998, October 1988. Online at: www.cdt.org/legislation/105th/privacy/coppa.html.

81. Crampton, J.: A reference monitor for workflow systems with constrained task execution. In *Proceedings of the 10th ACM Symposium on Access Control Models and Technologies*, Stockholm, Sweden, June 2005, 38-47. Online at: http://portal.acm.org/citation.cfm?doid=1063979.1063986

82. Crampton, J.: XACML and role-based access control, Presentation at *DIMACS Workshop on Security of Web Services and e-Commerce*, DIMACS Center, CoRE Building, Rutgers University, Piscataway, NJ, May 2005.

83. Czajkowski, K., et al.: From Open Grid Services Infrastructure to WS-Resource Framework: Refactoring and Evolution. IBM White paper, May 2004. Online at: http://www.ibm.com/developerworks/webservices/library/specification/ws-resource/gr-ogsitowsrf.html.

84. Damiani, M. L., Bertino, E., Catania, B., Perlasca, P.: GEO-RBAC: A spatially aware RBAC. *ACM Transactions on Information and System Security* 10(1):1-42, 2007.

85. Damiani, K.L., Silvestri, C., Bertino, E.: Hierarchical domains for decentralized administration of spatially-aware RBAC systems. In *Proceedings of the Third International Conference on Availability, Reliability and Security, ARES 2008*, March 4-7, 2008, Technical University of Catalonia, Barcelona , Spain, IEEE Computer Society 2008.

86. Davidson, A., Fuchs, M., Hedin, M., et al.: Schema for Object-Oriented XML 2.0 (W3C, July 1999). Online at: http://www.w3.org/TR/NOTE-SOX

87. Davis, M., Durst, M.: Unicode Normalization Forms Revision 18.0 (Unicode Technical Report #15, 1999-11-11). Online at: http://www.unicode.org/unicode/reports/tr15/tr15-18.html

88. De Capitani di Vimercati, S., Samarati, P.: Access control: policies, models and mechanisms. In Foundations of Security Analysis and Design - Tutorial Lectures, R. Focardi and F. Guerrieri, Eds. (2001). Springer Verlag 20-30 LNCS 2171.

89. de Lahitte, H.: WS-I BSP 1.0 Sample Application. Hernan de Lahitte's blog. Online at: http://weblogs.asp.net/hernandl/archive/2005/ 05/21/wsibspsampleapp.aspx.

90. Della-Libera, G., Gudgin, M., et al.: Web Services Security Policy Language (WS-SecurityPolicy). Version 1.1, July 2005

91. Denker, G., Finin, T., Kagal, L., Paolucci, M., Sycara, K.: Security for DAML Web services: annotation and matchmaking. In *Proceedings of 2nd International Semantic Web Conference (ISWC 2003)*, Sanibel Island, FL, USA, October 2003, 335-350, Springer Verlag, LNCS 2870.

92. Devanbu, P., Gertz, M., Martel, C., and Stubblebine, S. G.: Authentic Third-party Data Publication. In *Proceedings of the 14th Annual IFIP WG 11.3 Working Conference on Database Security*, Schoorl, The Netherlands, August 2000.

93. Dierks, T., Rescorla, E.: The Transport Layer Security (TLS) Protocol Version 1.1 (IETF RFC 4346, April 2006). Online at: http://tools.ietf.org/html/rfc4346

94. Dovier, A., Piazza, C., Policriti, A.: An efficient algorithm for computing bisimulation equivalence. *Theoretical Computer Science*, 311(1-3):221-256, 2004.

95. Dun & Bradstreet Data Universal Numbering System. Online at: http://www.dnb.com/us/duns_update/index.html

96. Eastlake, D., Reagle, J., eds.: XML Encryption Syntax and Processing. W3C Recommendation, 10 December 2002. Online at http://www.w3.org/TR/xmlenc-core/

97. Eastlake, D., Reagle, J., Solo, D., eds: XML-Signature Syntax and Processing W3C Recommendation, 12 February 2002. Online at: http://www.w3.org/TR/xmldsig-core/

98. Emig, C., Abeck, S., Biermann, J., Brandt, F., Klarl, H.: An access control metamodel for Web service-oriented architecture. In *Proceedings of the 2nd International Conference on Systems and Networks Communications (CSNC 2007)*, Cap Esterel, French Riviera, France, August 2007.

99. Enterprise Vulnerability Description Language v0.1 OASIS Draft (OASIS, February 2005). Online at: http://www.evdl.net/latest/doc/

100. Finnish IT Center for Science.   The Haka Federation.   Online at: http://www.csc.fi/english/institutions/haka.

101. Federal Trade Commission. Children's online privacy protection act of 1998. Online at: http://www.cdt.org/legislation/105th/privacy/coppa.html.

102. Federal Trade Commission: FTC Announces Settlement with Bankrupt Website, Toysmart.com, Regarding Alleged Privacy Policy Violations, 21 July 2000. Online at: www.ftc.gov/opa/2000/07/toysmart2.htm.

103. Feng, X., Hao, H., Jun, X., Li, X.: Context-aware role-based access control model for Web services. In *Proceedings of GCC 2004 International Workshops, IGKG, SGT, GISS, AAC-GEVO, and VVS*, Wuhan, China, October 2004, 430-436.

104. Ferraiolo, D., Chandramouli, R., Kuhn, R.: *Role-Based Access Control*, Second edition. Artech House, 2003.

105. Fischer-Hubner, S.: IT-security and privacy: design and use of privacy-enhancing security mechanisms. In *IT-Security and Privacy: Design and Use of Privacy-Enhancing Security Mechanisms*, Lecture Notes in Computer Science, Vol. 1958/2001.

106. Ford, W. et al..: XML Key Management Specification (XKMS) (W3C Note, 30 March 2001). Online at: http://www.w3.org/TR/xkms/

107. Forouzan, B.: *Cryptography & Network Security*. McGraw-Hill, 2007.

108. Foster, I., et al.: Modeling Stateful Resources with Web Services. IBM White paper, May 2004. Online at: http://www.ibm.com/developerworks/library/ws-resource/ws-modelingresources.pdf

109. Foster, I., Kesselman, C., Nick, J., Tuecke, S., : The Physiology of the Grid: An Open Grid Services Architecture for Distributed Systems Integration, Globus Project, 2002. Online at: http://www.globus.org/research/papers/ogsa.pdf.

110. Freier, A. O., Karlton, P., Kocher, P. C.: The SSL Protocol Version 3.0. Internet Draft, November 18, 1996. Online at: http://wp.netscape.com/eng/ssl3/draft302.txt

111. Gamma, E., Helm, R., Johnson, R., & Vlissides, J.: Design Patterns: Elements of Reusable Object-Oriented Software. (Addison-Wesley, 1995).

112. Goldfarb, C.H.: Design Considerations for Integrated Text Processing Systems. (IBM Cambridge Scientific Center Technical Report No. 320-2094 May 1973). Online at: http://www.sgmlsource.com/history/G320-2094/G320-2094.htm

113. Goldreich, O.: Secure Multi-party Computation. Working Draft, Version 1.4, 2002.

114. Goldfarb, C. H.: The SGML History Niche. Online at: http://www.sgmlsource.com/history/index.htm

115. Gollmann, D.: *Computer Security*. John Wiley & Sons, 2006.

116. Goldschlag, D. M., Reed, M. G, Syverson, P. F. : Onion routing. *Communications of ACM*, 42(2): 39-41, 2004.

117. Goodrich, M. T., Shin, M., Tamassia, R., Winsborough, W. H..:: Authenticated dictionaries for fresh attribute credentials. In *Proceedsings of iTrust Conference*, 2003.

118. Graham, S., et al.: Building Web Services with Java. 2nd edn, Sams Publishing, 2005.
119. Graham, S., Karmarkar, A., Mischkinsky, J., Robinson, I., Sedukhin, I: Web Services Resource Framework v 1.2, OASIS Standard, 1 April 2006. Online at: http://docs.oasis-open.org/wsrf/wsrf-ws_resource-1.2-spec-os.pdf.
120. Gudgin, M., et al.: SOAP Version 1.2 Part 1: Messaging Framework (Second Edition) (W3C Recommendation, 27 April 2007). Online at: http://www.w3.org/TR/2007/REC-soap12-part1-20070427/
121. Gudgin, M., et al.: SOAP Version 1.2 Part 2: Adjuncts (Second Edition) (W3C Recommendation, 27 April 2007). Online at: http://www.w3.org/TR/2007/REC-soap12-part2-20070427/
122. Gudgin, M., Mendelsohn, N., Nottingham, M., Ruellan, H., eds: W3C XML-Binary Optimized Packaging (W3C Recommendation, 25 January 2005). Online at: http://www.w3.org/TR/2005/REC-xop10-20050125/
123. Gudgin, M., Mendelsohn, N., Nottingham, M., Ruellan, H., eds: W3C SOAP Message Transmission Optimization Mechanism (W3C Recommendation, 25 January 2005). Online at: http://www.w3.org/TR/2005/REC-soap12-mtom-20050125/
124. The Gridshib Project. Online at: http://gridshib.globus.org/.
125. Hallam-Baker, P., Mysore, S. H., eds.: XML Key Management Specification (XKMS 2.0) Version 2.0 (W3C Recommendation, 28 June 2005). Online at: http://www.w3.org/TR/2005/REC-xkms2-20050628/.
126. Hansen, M., Schwartz, A., Cooper, A.: Privacy and identity management. IEEE Security and Privacy, 6(2):38-45, March/April 2008.
127. HIPAA: Health Insurance Portability and Accountability Act of 1996. Online at: http://www.hep-c-alert.org/links/hipaa.html, 1996.
128. Hess, A., Holt, J., Jacobson, J., Seamons, K.: Content-triggered trust negotiation. *ACM Transactions on Information and System Security*, 7(3):428–456, 2004.
129. Higgins Trust Framework, 2006. Online at: http://www.eclipse.org/higgins/.
130. Hirsch, F., Just, M., eds.: XML Key Management (XKMS) 2.0 Requirements. (W3C Note, 05 May 2003). Online at: http://www.w3.org/TR/xkms2-req
131. Hirsch, F., Philpott, R., Maler E., eds.: Security and Privacy Considerations for the OASIS Security Assertion Markup Language (SAML) V2.0 (OASIS Standard, 15 March 2005). Online at: http://docs.oasis-open.org/security/saml/v2.0/saml-sec-consider-2.0-os.pdf
132. Hodges, J., et al.: Glossary for the OASIS security assertion markup language (SAML) v.2.0. OASIS standard, 2005. Online at: http://www.oasis-open.org/committees/security/#documents.
133. Hogg, J., et al.: Web Service Security: Scenarios, Patterns, and Implementation Guidance for Web Services Enhancements (WSE) 3. 0, Microsoft Press, 2006.
134. Hommel W., Reiser, H.: Federated identity management: shortcomings of existing standards. In *Proceedings of IM '05: 9th IFIP/IEEE International Symposium on Integrated Network Management*, 2005.
135. Housley, R.: Internet X.509 Public Key Infrastructure Certificate and CRL Profile (rfc 2459), 1999. Online at: http://www.ietf.org/rfc/rfc2459.txt
136. IBM WebSphere® MQ V6 Fundamentals. 2005. Online at: http://www.redbooks.ibm.com/redbooks/SG247128/wwhelp/wwhimpl/js/html/wwhelp.htm

137. In Common Federation. Online at: http://www.incommonfederation.org/.
138. Internet2. Shibboleth. Online at: http://shibboleth.internet2.edu.
139. Introduction to UDDI: Important Features and Functional Concepts (OASIS, October 2004). Online at: http://uddi.org/pubs/uddi-tech-wp.pdf
140. ISO 10181-3 Access Control Framework. 1996
141. ISO 3166 International Standard for Country Codes. Online at: http://www.iso.org/iso/en/prods-services/iso3166ma/index.html
142. Iyer, B., Mehrotra, S., Mykletun, E., Tsudik, G., Wu, Y.: A framework for efficient storage security in RDBMS. In *Proceedings of 9th International Conference on Extending Database Technology (EDBT 2004)*, Heraklion, Crete, Greece, March 14-18, 2004, Proceedings. Lecture Notes in Computer Science 2992 Springer 2004
143. Iwasa, K., ed.: Web Services Reliable Messaging TC WS-Reliability 1.1 (OASIS Standard, 15 November 2004). Online at: http://docs.oasis-open.org/wsrm/ws-reliability/v1.1/wsrm-ws_reliability-1.1-spec-os.pdf
144. JSR-000105 XML Digital Signature APIs (Final Release). Online at: http://jcp.org/aboutJava/communityprocess/final/jsr105/
145. JSR-000106 XML Digital Encryption APIs (Close of Public Review, 11 January 2006). Online at: http://jcp.org/aboutJava/communityprocess/pr/jsr106/
146. Kagal, L., Denker, G., Finin, T., Paolucci, M., Srinivasan, N., Sycara, K.: Authorization and privacy for semantic Web services. *IEEE Intelligent Systems*, 19(4):50-56, 2004.
147. Kaliski, B.: PKCS #7: Cryptographic Message Syntax Standard Version 1.5. (IETF RFC 2315, March 1998). Online at: http://www.ietf.org/rfc/rfc2315.txt
148. Karmarkar, A., Gudgin, M., Lafon, Y., eds.: W3C Resource Representation SOAP Header Block (W3C Recommendation 25 January 2005). Online at: http://www.w3.org/TR/2005/REC-soap12-rep-20050125/
149. Kissel, R. ed.: Glossary of Key Information Security Terms NIST IR 7298, April 25 2006. Online at: http://csrc.nist.gov/publications/nistir/NISTIR-7298_Glossary_Key_Infor_Security_Terms.pdf
150. Knorr, K., Stormer, H.: Modeling and analyzing separation of duties in workflow environments. In *Proceedings of IFIP TC11 16th Annual Working Conference on Information Security: Trusted Information: The New Decade Challenge*, June 2001, 199-212.
151. Koglin, Y., Yao, D., Bertino, E.: Efficient and secure content processing and distribution by cooperative intermediaries. *IEEE Transactions on Parallel and Distributed Systems*, 19(5):615-626, 2008.
152. Kohl, U., Lotspiech J., Kaplan M. A.: Safeguarding digital library contents and users protecting documents rather than channels. (D-Lib Magazine, September 1997). Online at: http://www.dlib.org/dlib/september97/ibm/09lotspiech.html
153. Koshutanski, H. and Massacci, F.: Interactive credential negotiation for stateful business processes. In *Proceedings of 3rd International Conference on Trust Management (iTrust 2005)*, Rocquencourt, France, May 2005, 256-272, Springer Verlag, LNCS 3477.
154. Kostutanski, H., Massacci, F.: An access control framework for business processes for Web services. In *Proceedings of ACM Workshop on XML Security*, George W. Johnson Center at George Mason University, Fairfax, VA, USA, October 2003, 15-24.

155. Kumar, P.: *J2EE Security for Servlets, EJBs, and Web Services*. (Prentice Hall Press, 2003).

156. Kundu, A., Bertino, E.: Structural signatures for tree data structures. *CERIAS Technical Report*, 2008.

157. Langheinrich, M.: A P3P preference exchange language 1.0 (APPEL1.0). W3C Working Draft, April 2002.

158. Lassesen, K., Bandiera, L.: Oval 5.x Services Oriented Architecture: Interpreter Services Proposal (Patchlink Corporation, 1997-2005). Online at: http://oval.mitre.org/oval/documents/docs-06/soa.pdf

159. Lee, A. J., Winslett, M., Basney, J., and Welch V.: The Traust authorization service. *ACM Trans. Inf. Syst. Secur.*, 11(1), 2008.

160. Lee, D., Chu, Wesley W.: Comparative analysis of six XML schema languages. In *ACM SIGMOD Record*, 29(3):76-87, 2000.

161. Adam J. Lee and Marianne Winslett, "Towards Standards-Compliant Trust Negotiation for Web Services," in Proceedings of the Joint iTrust and PST Conferences on Privacy, Trust Management, and Security (IFIPTM 2008), June 2008

162. Leymann, F.: Web services flow language (WSFL 1.0), IBM Software Group, 2001. Online at: http://www-306.ibm.com/software/solutions/webservices/pdf/WSFL.pdf.

163. Li, F., Hadjieleftheriou, M., Kollios, G., Reyzin, L.: Dynamic authenticated index structures for outsourced databases. In *Proceedings of SIGMOD Conference*, 2006.

164. Li, F., Yi, K., Hadjieleftheriou, M., Kollios, G.: Proof-infused streams: enabling authentication of sliding window queries on streams. In *Proceedings of VLDB Conference*, 2007.

165. Li, J., Li, N., Winsborough, W. H.: Automated trust negotiation using cryptographic credentials. In *Proceedings of ACM Conference on Computer and Communications Security*, pages 46-57. ACM, 2005.

166. Liberty Alliance Project. Online at: http://www.projectliberty.org.

167. Liberty ID-WSF implementation guidelines. Online at: https://www.projectliberty.org/specs/liberty-idwsf-overview v1.1.pdf.

168. Liberty trust model guidelines. Online at: https://www.projectliberty.org/specs/liberty-trust-models-guidelines v1.0.pdf.

169. Lipner, S., Howard, M.: The Trustworthy Computing Security Development Lifecycle (Microsoft Corporation, March 2005). Online at: http://msdn.microsoft.com/en-us/library/ms995349.aspx

170. Lockhart, H., et al.: Web Services Federation Language (WS-Federation), Version 1.1. December 2006. Online at: http://download.boulder.ibm.com/ibmdl/pub/software/dw/specs/ws-fed/

171. Mahmoud, Q. H.: Securing Web Services and the Java WSDP 1.5 XWS-Security Framework. March 2005. Online at: http://java.sun.com/developer/technicalArticles/WebServices/security/index.html

172. Martel, C., Nuckolls, G., Devanbu, P., Gertz, M., Kwong, A., Stubblebine, S.: A general model for authenticated data structures. *Algorithmica*, 39(1):21-41, 2004.

173. Martin, D., et al.: OWL-S: Semantic Markup for Web Services. Online at: http://www.daml.org/services/owl-s/1.1/overview/.

174. McIntosh M., Gudgin, M., Scott Morrison K., Barbir, A., eds.: Basic Security Profile Version 1.0 Final Material (WS-I, 2007-03-30). Online at: http://www.ws-i.org/Profiles/BasicSecurityProfile-1.0.html

175. Mecella, Bertino, E., Ouzzani, M., Paci, F.: Access control enforcement for conversation-based web services. In *Proceedings of 15th International World Wide Web Conference (WWW 2006)*, Edinburgh, Scotland, UK, May 2006, 257-266.

176. Meier, J. D., Mackman, A., Vasireddy, S., Dunner, M., Escamilla, R., Murukan, A.: Improving Web Application Security Threats and Countermeasures (Microsoft Corporation, 2003). Online at: http://msdn.microsoft.com/en-us/library/ms994921.aspx

177. Meier, J. D., Mackman, A., Wastell, B.: Threat Modeling Web Applications (Microsoft Corporation, May 2005). Online at: http://msdn2.microsoft.com/en-us/library/ms978516.aspx

178. Mell, P., Scarfone, K., Romanosky, S: A Complete Guide to the Common Vulnerability Scoring System Version 2.0. Online at: http://www.first.org/cvss/cvss-guide.html

179. Merkle, R. C.: A certified digital signature. In *Proceedings of Advances in Cryptology (CRYPTO)*, 1989.

180. Merrels, J.. Sxip Identity. DIX: Digital Identity Exchange Protocol, March 2006. Internet Draft.

181. Metro Web Service Stack Overview Implementation Version: 1.2 FCS. Online at: https://metro.dev.java.net/discover/

182. Microsoft Message Queuing MSMQ 3.0 Feature List. March 28, 2003. Online at: http://www.microsoft.com/windowsserver2003/technologies/msmq/whatsnew.mspx

183. Microsoft Security Bulletin. Online at: http://www.microsoft.com/technet/security/current.aspx

184. Microsoft Security Response Center Security Bulletin Severity Rating System (Revised, November 2002). Online at: http://www.microsoft.com/technet/security/bulletin/rating.mspx

185. Microsoft .NET Framework Developer's Guide What's New in the .NET Framework Version 2.0. Online at: http://msdn2.microsoft.com/en-us/library/t357fb32.aspx.

186. Minimum Security Requirements for Federal Information and Information Systems. (Federal Information Processing Standards Publication FIPS PUB 200, March 2006). Online at: http://csrc.nist.gov/publications/fips/fips200/FIPS-200-final-march.pdf

187. Mitra, N., Lafon, I.: SOAP Version 1.2 Part 0: Primer (Second Edition) (W3C Recommendation, 27 April 2007). Online at: http://www.w3.org/TR/2007/REC-soap12-part0-20070427/

188. Moses, T.: Extensible Access Control Markup Language (XACML), Version 2.0 (OASIS Standard, 2005). Online at: http://docs.oasis-open.org/xacml/2.0/access_control-xacml-2.0-core-spec-os.pdf.

189. Motahari Nezhad, H. R., Benatallah, B., and Saint Paul, R.: Protocol discovery from imperfect service interaction data. In *Proceedings of VLDB 2006 Ph.D. Workshop*, Seoul, Korea, September 2006, CEUR-WS (ISSN 1613-0073), vol. 170. Online at: http://sunsite.informatik.rwth-aachen.de/Publications/CEUR-WS//Vol-170/.

190. Mozilla Foundation Security Advisories. Online at: http://www.mozilla.org/security/announce/
191. Mozilla Known Vulnerabilities in Mozilla Products. Online at: http://www.mozilla.org/projects/security/known-vulnerabilities.html
192. Mozilla Security Center. Online at: http://www.mozilla.org/security/
193. Moving Picture Experts Group home page. Online at: http://www.chiariglione.org/mpeg/
194. Nadalin, A., Goodner, M., Gudgin, M., Barbir, A., Granqvist, H., eds.: WS-SecureConversation 1.3 (OASIS Standard, 1 March 2007). Online at: http://docs.oasis-open.org/ws-sx/ws-secureconversation/200512/ws-secureconversation-1.3-os.html
195. Nadalin, A., Goodner, M., Gudgin, M., Barbir, A., Granqvist, H., eds.: WS-SecurityPolicy 1.2 OASIS Standard (OASIS, 1 July 2007). Online at: http://docs.oasis-open.org/ws-sx/ws-securitypolicy/200702/ws-securitypolicy-1.2-spec-os.html
196. Nadalin, A., Goodner, M., Gudgin, M., Barbir, A., Granqvist, H., eds.: WS-Trust 1.3 OASIS Standard (OASIS, 19 March 2007). Online at: http://docs.oasis-open.org/ws-sx/ws-trust/200512/ws-trust-1.3-os.html
197. Nadalin, A., Kaler, C., Hallam-Baker, P., Monzillo, R., eds.: Web Services Security: SOAP Message Security 1.0 (WS-Security, 2004) (OASIS Standard, March 2004). Online at: http://docs.oasis-open.org/wss/2004/01/oasis-200401-wss-soap-message-security-1.0.pdf
198. Naor, M., and Nissim, K.: Certificate Revocation and Certificate Update. In *Proceedings of the 7th USENIX Security Symposium*, 1998.
199. National Information Assurance Glossary. Committee on National Security Systems, May 2003, revised June 2006. Online at: http://www.cnss.gov/Assets/pdf/cnssi_4009.pdf
200. National Vulnerability Database Version 2.0. National Institute of Standards and Technology (NIST). Online at: http://nvd.nist.gov/
201. Ni, Q., Bertino, E., Lobo, J., Trombetta, A.: Privacy-aware role based access control. In *Proceedings of SACMAT 2007: 12th ACM Symposium on Access Control Models and Technologies*, edited by Lotz, V., and Thuraisingham, B., Sophia Antipolis, France, June 2007 (ACM, New York 2007), 41-50.
202. Ni, Q., Bertino, E., Lin, D., Lobo, J.: Conditional privacy-aware role based access control. In *Proceedings of ESORICS 2007: 12th European Symposium On Research In Computer Security*, edited by Biskup, J., and Lopez, J., Dresden, Germany, September 2007 (Springer, Berlin Heidelberg New York 2007).
203. Ni, Q., Bertino, E., Lobo, J.: An obligation model bridging access control policies and privacy policies. In *Proceedings of SACMAT 2008: 13th ACM Symposium on Access Control Models and Technologies*, edited by Ray, I., and Li, N., Estes Park, CO, USA, June 2008 (ACM, New York 2008), 133-142.
204. Niblett, P., Graham, S.: Events and service-oriented architecture: The OASIS Web Services Notification specifications. *IBM System Journal* Vol. 44, No. 4, 2005.
205. North American Industry Classification System (NAICS). Online at: http://www.census.gov/epcd/www/naics.html
206. Nuutila, E., Soisalon-Soininen, E.: On finding the strongly connected components in a directed graph. *Information Processing Letters*, 49(1):9-14,1994.
207. OASIS. Web Services Base Notification 1.3 (WS-BaseNotification) OASIS Standard, 1 October 2006.

208. O'Neill, M.: *Web Services Security*. (McGraw-Hill/Osborne 2003).
209. Oliveira, S. R. M., and Zaiane, O. R.: Privacy preserving frequent itemset mining. In *Proceedings of IEEE ICDM Workshop on Privacy, Security and Data Mining*, 2002.
210. Open GIS Consortium: Open GIS Simple Features Specification for SQL. Revision 1.1, 1999.
211. Open Vulnerability and Assessment Language. Online at: http://oval.mitre.org/
212. Oracle Inc. BPEL Tutorial 6: Working with the TaskManager service, 2006. Online at: http://www.oracle.com/technology/products/ias/bpel/pdf/orabpel-Tutorial6-TaskManagerServiceTutorial.pdf.
213. Orchard, N.: Extensibility, XML Vocabularies, and XML Schema. Online at: http://www.xml.com/pub/a/2004/10/27/extend.html
214. Organisation for Economic Co-operation and Development. OECD guidelines on the protection of privacy and transborder flows of personal data of 1980. Online at http://www.oecd.org/.
215. OWASP Top 10 Methodology. Online at: http://www.owasp.org/index.php/Top_10_2007-Methodology
216. Paci, F., Bertino, E., and Crampton, J.: An access control framework for WS-BPEL. *International Journal of Web services Research*,5(3):20-43, 2008.
217. Parastatidis, S., Rischbeck, T., Watson, P., Webber, J.: A Grid Application Framework Based on Web Services Specifications and Practices, Technical Report, North East Regional e-Science Centre, University of Newcastle.
218. Paurobally, S., Jennings, N. R.: Protocol engineering for Web services conversations. *International Journal of Engineering Applications of Artificial Intelligence*,18(2):237-254, 2005.
219. Pieprzyk, J., Hardjono, T., Seberry, J.: *Fundamentals of Computer Security*. Springer, 2003.
220. Poha, V. V.: *Internet Security Dictionary*. Springer, 2002.
221. Powers, C., Schunter, M., eds.: The Enterprise Privacy Authorization Language (EPAL 1.2) IBM Research Report. Online at: http://www.zurich.ibm.com/security/enterprise-privacy/epal/Specification/ index.html
222. Ragouzis, N., Hughes, J., Philpott, R., Maler, E., eds.: Security Assertion Markup Language (SAML) 2.0 Technical Overview Working Draft 03 (OASIS, 20 February 2005). Online at http://www.oasis-open.org/committees/download.php/20645/sstc-saml-tech-overview-2%200-draft-10.pdf
223. RELAX NG home page. Online at http://relaxng.org/
224. Roman, D., Keller, U., Lausen, H., de Bruijn, J., Lara, R., Stollberg, M., Polleres, A., Feier, C., Bussler, C., Fensel, D.,: Web service modeling ontology, *Applied Ontology*, 1(1): 77-106, 2005.
225. Ross, R., Katzke, S., Johnson, A., Swanson, M., Stoneburner, G., Rogers, G., Lee, A.: Recommended Security Controls for Federal Information Systems (NIST Special Publication 800-53, February 2005). Online at: http://csrc.nist.gov/publications/nistpubs/800-53/SP800-53.pdf
226. Rusinkiewicz, M., Sheth, A. P.: Specification and execution of transactional workflows. In *Modern Database Systems: The Object Model, Interoperability, and Beyond*, 592-620, Addison-Wesley, 1995.

227. Samar, V.: Single Sign-on using cookies for Web Applications. In *WETICE '99: Proceedings of the 8th Workshop on Enabling Technologies on Infrastructure for Collaborative Enterprises*, pages 158-163, Washington, DC, USA, 1999. IEEE Computer Society.

228. Sandhu, R., Coyne, E., Feinstein, H., Youman, C.: Role-based access control models. *IEEE Computer*, 29(2):38-47, 1996.

229. Sandhu, R., Ferraiolo, D., Kuhn, R.: American National Standard for Information Technoloby Role Based Access Control, ANSI INCITS 359-2004, February 3, 2004.

230. SANS Critical Vulnerability Analysis Scale Ratings. Online at: http://www.sans.org/newsletters/cva/?portal=49d3578c03d98ed5f5934311fd3 38282#atrisk

231. Seamons, K. E., Winslett, M., and Yu, T.: Limiting the disclosure of access control policies during automated trust negotiation. In *Proceedings of Network and Distributed System Security Symposium*, San Diego, CA, USA, February 2001, Internet Society (ISBN 1-891562-10-X). Online at: http://www.isoc.org/isoc/conferences/ndss/01/2001/INDEX.HTM.

232. Seamons, K. E., Winslett, M., and Yu, T., Smith, B., Child, E., Jacobson, J., Mills H., and Lina Yu, L.: Requirements for policy languages for trust negotiation. In *Proceedings of 3rd International Workshop on Policies for Distributed Systems and Networks*, 68-79, 2002.

233. Schneier B.: Attack trees: Modeling security threats. *Dr. Dobb's Journal*, December 1999

234. Schneier B.: Secrets & Lies: Digital Security in a Networked World. Wiley, January 2004.

235. Security in a Web Services World: A Proposed Architecture and Roadmap A joint security white paper from IBM Corporation and Microsoft Corporation, April 7, 2002, Version 1.0. Online at: http://download. boulder.ibm.com/ibmdl/pub/software/dw/library/ws-secmap.pdf

236. SecurityFocus Vulnerability Database. Online at: http://www.securityfocus. com/about

237. Sirer, E. G., Wang, K.: An access control language for Web services. In *Proceedings of 7th ACM Symposium on Access Control Models and Technologies (SACMAT 2002)*, Monterey, CA, USA, June 2002, 23-30, ACM Press.

238. Skogsrud, H., Benatallah, B., Casati, F.: Trust-serv: Model-driven lifecycle management of trust negotiation policies for Web services. In *Proceedings of 13th International World Wide Web Conference (WWW 2004)*, New York, NY, USA, May 2004, 53-62, ACM Press.

239. Squicciarini, A. C., Bertino, E., Ferrari, E., Paci, F., Thuraisingham, B.: PP-Trust-X: a system for privacy preserving trust negotiations. *ACM Transactions on Information Systems and Security*, 827-842, July 2007.

240. Squicciarini, A. C., Czeskis, A., Bhargav-Spantzel, A., Bertino, E.: Auth-SL - a system for the specification and enforcement of quality-based authentication policies. In *Proceedings of 9th International Conference on Information and Communication Security (ICICS 2007)*, Zhengzhou, China, December 12-15, 2007, Lecture Notes in Computer Science 4861 Springer 2008.

241. Srivatsa, M., Iyengar, A., Mikalsenz, T., Rouvellouz, I., Yin, J.: An Access Control System for Web Service Compositions. In *Proceedings of IEEE International Conference on Web Services (ICWS 2007)*, Marriott Salt Lake City Downtown, Salt Lake City, Utah, USA, July 2007.

242. Stallings, W.: *Cryptography and Network Security* (4th Edition), Prentice Hall, 2005.
243. Standards for Security Categorization of Federal Information and Information Systems. (Federal Information Processing Standards Publication FIPS PUB 199, December 2003). Online at: http://csrc.nist.gov/publications/fips/fips199/FIPS-PUB-199-final.pdf
244. Steel, C., Nagappan, R., Lai, R.: *Core Security Patterns: Best Practices and Strategies for J2EE, Web Services, and Identity Management.* Prentice Hall Professional Technical Reference, 2005.
245. Stirling, C.: Modal and temporal logics for processes. In *Proceedings Logics for Concurrency: Structure versus Automata (8th Banff Higher Order Workshop)*, F. Moller and G. M. Birtwistle, eds., LNCS vol. 1043 (1996), Springer Verlag.
246. Sun Java System Message Queue 4.1 Technical Overview (Sun Microsystems Inc., 2007). Online at: http://docs.sun.com/app/docs/doc/819-7759/6n9mco7el?a=view
247. Sweeney, L.: Achieving k-anonymity privacy protection using generalization and suppression. *International Journal on Uncertainty, Fuzziness and Knowledge-based Systems*, 10(5):571-588, 2002.
248. Swidersky, F., Snyder W.: Threat Modeling. Microsoft Press, 2004.
249. Sycara, K., Berardi, D., Bussler, C., Cabral, L., Cimpian, E., Domingue, J., Moran, M., Mecella, M., Paolucci, M., Stollberg, M., Zaremba, M.: Semantic Web services tutorial. In *Proceedings of 2nd European Semantic Web Conference (ESWC 2005)*, Heraklion, Greece, May 2005.
250. The Information Security Automation Program and The Security Content Automation Protocol (National Institute of Standards and Technology (NIST)). Online at: http://nvd.nist.gov/scap.cfm
251. The Swiss Education & Research Network. Switchaai Authentication and Authorization Infrastructure (AAI). Online at: http://www.switch.ch/aai/.
252. Tarjan, R. E.: Depth-first search and linear graph algorithms. *SIAM Journal on Computing*, 1(2):146-160, 1972.
253. Thatte, S.: XLANG Web Services for Business Process Design. Microsoft Corporation, 2001. Online at: http://www.gotdotnet.com/team/xml_wsspecs/xlang-c/default.htm.
254. The Open Source Vulnerability Database. Online at: http://osvdb.org/
255. The Open Web Application Security Project (OWASP). Online at: http://www.owasp.org/index.php/Main_Page
256. The Web Services Interoperability Organization. http://www.ws-i.org/
257. Thompson, H. S., Beech, D., Maloney, M., Mendelsohn, N.: XML Schema Part 1: Structures (W3C Recommendation, October 2004). Online at: http://www.w3.org/TR/xmlschema-1/
258. Thompson, H. S., Beech, D., Maloney, M., Mendelsohn, N.: XML Schema Part 1: Structures (W3C Recommendation, October 2004). Online at: http://www.w3.org/TR/xmlschema-1/
259. Thuraisingham, B. M.: *Database and Applications Security Integrating Information Security and Data Management.* Auerbach Pubblications, 2005.
260. Thuraisingham, M. B., Ford, W., Collins, M., O'Keeffe, J.: Design and implementation of a database inference controller. *Data & Knowledge Engineering* 11(3): 271-289, 1993.
261. UK Oxford University. Shibgrid. Online at: http://www.oesc.ox.ac.uk/activities/projects/index.xml?ID=ShibGrid.

262. United Nations Standard Products and Services Code System (UNSPSC).
263. University of Manchester. Shibboleth Enabled Bridge to Access the National Grid. Online at: http://www.mc.manchester.ac.uk/research/shebangs.
264. United States Department of Health: Health Insurance Portability and Accountability Act of 1996. Online at http://www.hhs.gov/ocr/hipaa/.
265. United States Senate Committee on Banking, Housing, and Urban Affairs. Information regarding the Gramm-Leach-Biley act of 1999. Online at http://banking.senate.gov/conf/.
266. US-CERT Vulnerability Notes Database. Online at: http://www.kb.cert.org/vuls/
267. US-CERT Vulnerability Notes Database - Field Descriptions. Online at: http://www.kb.cert.org/vuls/html/fieldhelp#metric
268. Vaidya, J., and Clifton, C.: Privacy-preserving association rule mining in vertically partitioned data. In *Proceedings of the Eighth ACM SIGKDD International Conference on Knowledge Discovery and Data Mining*, July 23-26, 2002, Edmonton, Alberta.
269. van der Stock A., Williams J.: OWASP Top 10. The Ten Most Critical Web Application Security Vulnerabilities, 2007 UPDATE. Online at: http://www.owasp.org/images/e/e8/OWASP_Top_10_2007.pdf
270. Wainer, J., Barthelmess, P. and Kumar, A.:W-RBAC − A workflow security model incorporating controlled overriding of constraints. *International Journal of Cooperative Information Systems*,12(4):455-486, 2003.
271. Wang, Q., Yu, T, Li, N., Lobo, J., Bertino, E., Irwin, K., Byun, J. W.: On the correctness criteria of fine-grained access control in relational databases. In *Proceedings of VLDB 2007: 33rd International Conference on Very Large Data Bases*, Vienna, Austria, September 2007, 555-566.
272. Wayman, J.: Biometrics in identity management Systems,*IEEE Security and Privacy*, 6(2):30-37, March/April, 2008.
273. Web Application Security Consortium. Online at: http://www.webappsec.org/
274. Web Application Security Consortium. Threat Classification. Online at: http://www.webappsec.org/projects/threat/v1/WASC-TC-v1_0.pdf
275. Web Services Enhancements 3.0 (Web service specifications supported by WSE), Microsoft. Online at: http://msdn.microsoft.com/en-us/ library/aa529362.aspx
276. Web Services Policy Assertions Language (WS-PolicyAssertions) Version 1.0, December 18, 2002. Online at: http://download.boulder.ibm.com/ ibmdl/pub/software/dw/specs/ws-polas/ws-polas.pdf
277. Web Services Secure Conversation Language (WS-SecureConversation) February 2005. Online at: http://download.boulder.ibm.com/ibmdl/pub/ software/dw/specs/ws-secon/ws-secureconversation.pdf
278. Web Services Security Kerberos Token Profile 1.1 (OASIS Standard Specification, 1 February 2006). Online at: http://www.oasis-open.org/committees/download.php/16788/wss-v1.1-spec-os-KerberosTokenProfile.pdf
279. Web Services Security X.509 Certificate Token Profile (OASIS, January 2004). Online at: http://docs.oasis-open.org/wss/2004/01/oasis-200401-wss-x509-token-profile-1.0.pdf
280. Web Services Security XrML-Based Rights Expression Token Profile (Working Draft 03, 30 January 2003). Online at: http://www.oasis-open.org/committees/wss/documents/WSS-XrML-03-changes.pdf

281. Wikipedia: Data Universal Numbering System. Online at: http://en.wikipedia.org/wiki/D-U-N-S

282. Windows CardSpace. Online at: http://cardspace.netfx3.com/.

283. Winsborough W. H., Li, N.: Safety in automated trust negotiation. *ACM Transactions on Information System Security*, 9(3):352-390, 2006.

284. Winslett, M., Yu, T., Seamons, K. E.: Supporting structured credentials and sensitive policies through interoperable strategies for automated trust negotiation. *ACM Transactions on Information System Security*, 6(1):1-42, 2003.

285. Wonohoesodo, R., Tari, Z.: A Role based access control for Web services. In *Proceedings of IEEE International Conference on Services Computing (SCC 2004)*, Shangai, China, September 2004, 49-56, IEEE Computer Society. Online at: http://www.w3.org/TR/2006/REC-ws-addr-core-20060509/.

286. W3C. Platform for Privacy Preferences (P3P). http://www.w3.org/P3P/

287. Woodruff, D., and Staddon, J.: Private inference control. In *CCS '04: Proceedings of the 11th ACM conference on Computer and communications security*, pages 188-197, New York, NY, USA, 2004. ACM Press.

288. Wordnet. Princeton University. Available at http://wordnet.princeton.edu/

289. WS-Privacy. Online at: http://www.serviceoriented.org/ws-privacy.html

290. Yang, Y., Papadias, D., Papadopoulos, S., Kalnis, P.: Authenticated join processing in outsourced databases. To appear in *Proceedings of the ACM Conference on the Management of Data (SIGMOD)*, Providence, RI, USA, June 29th - July 2, 2009.

291. Wu, X., Bertino, E.: An analysis study on zone-based anonymous communication in mobile ad hoc networks. *IEEE Transactions on Secure and Dependable Computing*, in print.

292. Wysopal, C., Dustin, E., Nelson, L., Zovi, D. D.: *The Art of Software Security Testing*. Addison-Wesley, 2006.

293. XrML 2.0 Technical Overview Version 1.0 (Contentguard, March 8, 2002). Online at: http://www.xrml.org/Reference/XrMLTechnicalOverviewV1.pdf

Index

Breinigsville, PA USA
08 April 2010
235661BV00006B/9/P